NEW FOUNDATIONS FOR KNOWLEDGE IN EDUCATIONAL ADMINISTRATION, POLICY, AND POLITICS

Science and Sensationalism

NEW FOUNDATIONS FOR KNOWLEDGE IN EDUCATIONAL ADMINISTRATION, POLICY, AND POLITICS

Science and Sensationalism

Edited by

Douglas E. Mitchell
University of California, Riverside

LEA LAWRENCE ERLBAUM ASSOCIATES, PUBLISHERS
2006   Mahwah, New Jersey   London

Copyright © 2006 by Lawrence Erlbaum Associates, Inc.

All rights reserved. No part of this book may be reproduced in any form,
by photostat, microform, retrieval system, or any other means, without prior written permission of the publisher.

Lawrence Erlbaum Associates, Inc., Publishers
10 Industrial Avenue
Mahwah, New Jersey 07430
www.erlbaum.com

Cover design by Tomai Maridou

Cover photo by Steve Walag

CIP information for this book can be obtained by contacting the Library
of Congress

ISBN 0-8058-5432-0 (cloth : alk. paper)
ISBN 0-8058-5433-9 (pbk. : alk. paper)

Books published by Lawrence Erlbaum Associates are printed on acid-
free paper, and their bindings are chosen for strength and durability.

Printed in the United States of America
10   9   8   7   6   5   4   3   2   1

*To Tedi, who for half a century now
has been my partner and friend
in all things wise and wonderful.*

Contents

0897432

Preface

In 2003 a grant from the Bank of America provided the resources to support a small invitational conference at the University of California, Riverside. The focus of the conference was on the theoretical and practical foundations of knowledge in educational administration, policy, and politics. The starting point for our reflection was a recognition that the promise of a truly scientific basis for knowledge development in these fields, a promise that dominated scholarly and professional inquiry a half-century ago, has remained elusive. The results have been modest and, more importantly, the very idea of reliable general knowledge has become increasingly controversial.

The contributors to this volume, who were the participants in that invitational conference, were asked to prepare papers on the theme, "Whatever happened to the promised science of educational administration, policy, and politics?" The 3-day conference devoted to discussing these papers stimulated both a sense of excitement about the potential for reconstructing the foundations of knowledge, and a sense of great urgency that clear expression be given to a convincing basis for arbitrating and legitimating knowledge claims in these fields so central to effective schools. All of the conference contributors endorsed the core idea that knowledge claims are now unacceptably cacophonous, divergent, and contradictory, so much so that the role of the university as an institution for producing and disseminating knowledge has been seriously undermined, and the ability of either training programs or policy studies to provide reliable professional guidance is in jeopardy.

The problem, we agreed, is fundamentally an intellectual one—we need to rethink the foundations of knowledge, not just expand inquiry targets or elaborate the methods of data collection, analysis, and interpretation. The whole relationship between academic knowledge and political power needs to be recast. A half-century ago we had a naive optimism that knowledge, born of the application of social science methods to the interpretation of schooling, would empower professional educators to liberate the next generation of students from the scourges of ignorance, poverty, prejudice, and political subjugation. As the 20th century came to an end, however, we could see more and more clearly that the relationship between knowledge and power has all too often been reversed—that those in positions of political privilege and power can and often do control the definition of useful knowledge and thus contain and direct inquiry in ways that perpetuate disadvantage and enhance subjugation rather than ending it. Moreover, the university—the institution historically charged with winnowing knowledge claims and teaching each new generation how to understand and think about social goals and how they might be realized—has lost much of its credibility. Critics on one side charge the university with being a handmaiden to established interests, whereas those on the other side see university scholars as preoccupied with esoteric and irrelevant ideas while real social needs go unmet.

The tension between knowledge as factual truth and knowledge as the empowerment of moral action is now recognized as a central issue in the discovery of new foundations for educational administration, policy, and politics knowledge. This tension surfaces again and again throughout this volume. On the one hand, we all have recognized that knowledge is inherently theoretical; that Sergeant Friday's "Just the facts, Ma'am" will never be sufficient to guide serious professional action. The advice of early social science advocates to set aside questions of morals and values and concentrate on the reliability of observable evidence, made it impossible to know how scientific inquiry can inform professional practice. None of the chapters presents a completely satisfying resolution to this basic tension. Some of us would join the burgeoning movement to urge more explicit moral commitments among university scholars. Some see a way forward by shifting the emphasis in knowledge claims away from verified relationships among variables and on to the development of narratives that offer a coherent accounting of the dynamics of institutional stability and change. Some wish that we would specify more narrowly the applicability of scientific findings so that they are not used to guide actions for which they are not relevant. Finally, we argue for close attention to epistemological philosophy, and call for both scholars and professionals to recognize that the primary function of human knowledge is to orient us to a field of action, to reconstitute our taken-for-granted presuppositions, and to tell us how to think about action alternatives rather than prescribe what to do.

In short, the coherence of this collection of chapters does not spring from any general agreement about how to resolve fundamental issues. Quite to the contrary, the chapters tackle a diverse set of issues and offer quite different perspectives on the fundamental questions of how knowledge is produced and how it can become reliable and professionally useful. What makes this volume coherent is the agreement that there has been a shaking of the foundations—that we must rebuild our understanding of inquiry and knowledge development if we are ever to understand schools and how to lead them.

ACKNOWLEDGMENTS

In addition to thanking the contributors to this volume for their ingenuity, dedication, and patience, there are several others whose contributions have been vital to the development of this book. Special thanks to the Bank of America, whose support made our 2003 conference possible. Thanks also to Michael Batie for his dedicated staff work. He managed the conference, kept communication channels open, reproduced draft papers, recorded the deliberations, and handled financial details. Heartfelt thanks also to our Lawrence Erlbaum Associates editor, Naomi Silverman, and the extramural reviewers she engaged to evaluate our proposal and manuscript. Their repeated expressions of confidence in the importance of this work sustained our efforts and their penetrating critiques helped much to improve our thinking and our expression. The students of my year-long Inquiry and Research Methods course at the University of California, Riverside also deserve special recognition. Most of the key ideas in this book were tried out on them over the last 3 years and I learned much from them about what makes sense and what does not. Finally, a special thank-you to my wife, Tedi, who tracked down references, read chapter drafts, and provided helpful feedback on focus and clarity of expression.

Douglas E. Mitchell
University of California, Riverside
August 2005

Introduction: Dreary Ideas and Exhausted Patience

Douglas E. Mitchell
University of California, Riverside

Forty years ago, publication of the National Society for the Study of Education's seminal volume, *Behavioral Science and Educational Administration,* edited by Daniel E. Griffiths (1964), marked a dramatic sea change in the framing of public policy and the organization of administration and leadership departments within the Education Schools of America's major universities. Research-based policy proposals sprouted like spring flowers in May sunshine. Scholarly standards and job opportunities for university scholars and policy consultants shifted toward the social science disciplines, with a promise that rigorous scientific knowledge would make it possible to meter attainment, prescribe programs and policies, and, eventually, hold professional educators accountable for school performance. Despite mountains of evidence apparently supporting new policies, the appointment of scores of highly trained new faculty and policy consultants, and millions of dollars spent on high-quality research projects, the promised knowledge base is proving inadequate. Moreover, critical theorists and postmodernists are challenging the social science knowledge paradigm itself. Meanwhile, Congress tries to legislate scientific standards and define school improvement methodologies. It is time to step back for a moment and take stock of this generation-long search for reliable knowledge and efficacious policy guidance to see why it has foundered and how it might become more fertile. This book, rooted in groundbreaking work begun at a University of California, Riverside conference in November of 2003, frames this stock-taking process by probing the intellectual foundations of scholarly inquiry into educational administration, policy, and politics.

The question of whether, and if so how, social science theories and methods contribute to an understanding of educational administration, policy, and politics has never been more contested than it is today. Critics on the right (see, e.g., Kaufman, 2002) proclaim that science is not adequately respected and is frequently deformed in the pursuit of political goals. With equal sharpness, those on the left (see, e.g., Lugg, 2003) proclaim that contemporary education scholarship involves an uncritical embrace of a social science that is utterly incapable of recognizing, much less adequately interpreting, critical truths regarding the human condition.

Though debate over the meaning and utility of the social sciences has reached into the core of scholarship devoted to educational administration, policy, and politics in the last few years, it is not particularly novel in the larger scholarly arena. Charges that the universities had lost either their capacity for disinterested, objective inquiry or their commitment to using scholarship in service to the human community were prominent in the early decades of the 20th century. In the warm afterglow of the Allied victory in World War II, the American universities basked in a brief period of national pride about how "Yankee ingenuity" had won the war. But by the mid-1950s new concerns were being raised. Right-wing critics, like Senator Joseph McCarthy, challenged the loyalty of university scholars while Peter Bryant's (1958) novel *Red Alert* (the novel on which the movie *Dr. Strangelove: Or How I Learned to Stop Worrying and Love the Bomb* was based) charged the scientific community with hubris and disdainful disregard for human life. Soon the debate raged within the social science mainstream; senior sociologists (most notably Talcott Parsons) were charged with theoretical and methodological flaws that led inevitably to political conservatism. By the end of the 1960s, political pressure to ensure that scientific research was suitably harnessed to public interests had become a matter of formal governmental policy. Social science evaluation of federal programs, mandated by John F. Kennedy, began to receive millions of dollars from federal program funds. The National Science Foundation was required to develop its Research Addressed to National Needs program as a condition of funding renewal, and the National Institute of Education funded a landmark study of social science utilization by state legislatures (for a summary of this history, see Mitchell, 1981).

Also, during the 1960s, interest in the proper uses of social science research became a central issue in leadership and administration programs in schools of education. Publication of Daniel Griffiths' *Behavioral Science and Educational Administration* in 1964 was the most visible turning point in educational scholarship and the training of public school leaders. A dramatic shift from professional wisdom to scientific analysis transformed the prepa-

ration of administrators and policy scholars and gave rise to a new Ed
School elite—steeped in the social sciences and dedicated to the use of social scientific methods to study and improve school policy and administration. In less than four decades, however, important voices have begun to argue that this revolution has exhausted its capacity to define policy issues,
inspire scholarship, or guide professional training. The training of educators has moved significantly toward a renewed emphasis on professional
practice knowledge (accompanied by increased authority for this training
bestowed on local school systems). The federal Congress, believing that the
universities are failing to honor rigorous standards of scientific inquiry, has
tried to legislate scientific standards. Postmodern and critical theorists are
proclaiming the failure of both the social science methods advocated by
Griffiths and the leadership of an elite corps of scholars who followed his
advice. Professional educators are not only resistant to the call for a social-
science-based practice; they are routinely massaging their data to defend
themselves against what they perceive to be illegitimate political pressures.
Moreover, the social science scholars whose status was enhanced by the
Griffiths revolution are increasingly proclaiming educational programs and
policies to be either unstable and tenuous (Cuban & Usdan, 2003), ineffec-
tive (House, 1998), or not even implemented with sufficient integrity to test
them for effectiveness (Ramirez, 1991).

Recognizing the timeliness of reviewing the whole movement toward in-
corporating the social sciences into the training of scholars, educators, and
policymakers, the Graduate School of Education at the University of California, Riverside convened an invitational conference of leading scholars to
reexamine the question of whether there really is a scientific basis for evaluating and improving educational administration, politics, and policy. The
purpose was to tackle the question of epistemology directly—to ask anew
what rules of scholarly conduct should guide research and practice in our
field, and how those rules of inquiry should guide the training of scholars
and education professionals. This book has resulted from a thorough editing of the papers presented at that conference, placing them in a common
intellectual framework for rebuilding confidence in social science inquiry
and the legitimacy of the university as an arbiter of scientific knowledge
claims.

The book is divided into four parts. Part I addresses historically and theoretically fundamental questions regarding the relationship between universities and the government in their roles as agencies for stimulating the
production of useful knowledge and for arbitrating competing claims to
knowledge by individuals and groups whose interpretations lead to divergent or contradictory characterizations of the status and dynamics of educational administration, policy, and politics. Chapters 1 and 2 tackle these
questions historically. In chapter 1 Margaret Nash reviews the vicissitudes of

the working relationship between the universities and government. She concludes this review by highlighting the emergence of the politically motivated "think tank" approach to knowledge production and dissemination, noting with concern that these think tanks approach knowledge production as if it were primarily a tool or weapon of political debate and thus tend to self-consciously develop knowledge claims in service to identifiable political ideologies.

In chapter 2, Flora Ida Ortiz and I probe the intellectual history of changing knowledge frameworks used to analyze educational administration, policy, and politics. This chapter highlights the important contributions of Daniel Griffiths and the other participants in a close-knit group of university scholars who succeeded in launching what came to be known as the theory movement in educational administration. This movement redirected university training programs and restructured the research agendas of a whole generation of education scholars.

Chapters 3 and 4 approach questions of knowledge generation and assessment by educational scholars from a more theoretical perspective. In chapter 3, Brian Rowan examines the research and analysis strategies advocated by the theory movement, proclaims himself a member of that movement, and insists that it still represents the best way to develop meaningful interpretations of how and why school systems work as they do and what might be done to improve them. In chapter 4, Paul Green uses the apparent conflict between "opportunity" and "results" as the targets of the equal protection clause of the 14th amendment to the Constitution as a case study in the nature of judicial analysis. He shows that legal knowledge is constructed through carefully analyzing networks of concepts whose meanings influence judicial interpretations as they become crystal clear and coherently interdependent. From this perspective, advancing legal knowledge consists in: (a) identifying apparent gaps and contradictions in the use of core legal concepts and (b) discovering how these limitations can be overcome through formal analysis of conceptual meanings and knitting them together into a coherent interpretive system.

Part II examines the status of knowledge claims in the fields of educational administration and administrative policy. In chapter 5, Ronald Heck undertakes a review of current scholarship in this field to document the extent to which knowledge claims are characterized by divergent theoretical frameworks and competing claims to the proper interpretation of core issues. He sees scholarship in matters of administration and policy as standing at a "crossroads" intersection, requiring some basic decisions about how to validate knowledge and apply it to school practices. Gail Furman's contribution, chapter 6, spotlights the problem of linking knowledge about school administration to the fundamentally moral purposes of education. She challenges the emphasis on technical knowledge that dominates research in this field, arguing that technical efficiency and effectiveness cannot possibly add up to managerial wisdom unless they are explicitly linked to the basic moral purposes of education. Without moral validation, knowledge claims are as likely to be distracting and destructive as they are to provide guidance for professional policy and practice.

The foundations of knowledge in educational politics and public policy are tackled by the two chapters in Part III. In chapter 7, Kenneth Wong examines the mainstream approach to political scholarship by showing how scholarship in this field links empirical evidence to theoretical frameworks that interpret its meaning and significance. He illustrates this process through a detailed review of contemporary strategies for restructuring school governance in the nation's largest cities. His analysis shows that this strategy for developing reliable knowledge can both inform our understanding of the historical processes through which we are living and empower us to imagine alternative political strategies and processes that could lead to more desirable outcomes. In chapter 8, Dorothy Shipps takes a very different tack on the problem of political knowledge development and interpretation. She casts the problem of political knowledge in terms of a grand "narrative" that tells the story of how and why school systems work the way they do. She identifies competing narratives that raise fundamentally different questions and lead to very different conceptions of what might result from alternative policy commitments. She argues that political knowledge lies not so much in documenting the details of specific programs or policies as in interpreting the grand schemas that are used by policymakers, professional educators, and attentive publics to identify the purposes of schooling and specify a set of presuppositions about how institutions and individuals serve to realize or frustrate those purposes. The presuppositions embedded in these competing narratives serve to focus attention, shape robust expectations about which specific actions can be relied on to realize those purposes, and mobilize commitment to those purposes and supporting strategic actions.

Finally, Part IV consists of two chapters that approach the question of scholarly epistemology directly. Chapter 9 examines the epistemological blind alleys that have resulted from trying to use Platonic idealism and Aristotelian essentialism to resolve the question of how reliable and meaningful knowledge can be distilled from sense experiences. The analysis developed in this chapter shows how Platonic idealism separates knowledge from data, making it impossible to test the adequacy of various claims to knowledge, with the result that knowledge cannot be separated from political ideology. At the same time, the analysis in this chapter shows that the Aristotelian effort to establish objective truth requires a suppression of fundamentally human processes of knowing and validating knowledge claims. The chapter concludes with an exploration of the phenomenological alternative to idealism and essentialism, showing how this approach to knowledge construction and testing promises to bring facts and values together in a reliable and meaningful way.

Utilizing the epistemological framework developed in chapter 9, chapter 10 argues that a phenomenological approach to both knowledge development and the interpretation of professional practices can restructure our understanding of the knowledge claims made throughout the earlier chapters. The aim of this concluding chapter is to show how the entire collection of chapters in this volume can be integrated into a common framework for identifying reliable, coherent knowledge and confident professional practices. This summary analysis shows how reliance on Platonic and Aristotelian epistemologies has created irreconcilable approaches to the evaluation of knowledge claims and indicates how and why the intellectual status of social science research is so deeply contested. The chapter ends by offering a reinterpretation of the proper role of the university as the institution in a free society responsible for arbitrating claims to knowledge and teaching education professionals how to critically appraise the legitimacy of policy and program mandates that purport to represent research-based guidelines for technically effective and morally appropriate educational strategies.

REFERENCES

Bryant, P. (1958). *Red alert.* New York: Ace Books.

Cuban, L., & Usdan, M. D. (2003). *Powerful reforms with shallow roots: Improving America's urban schools.* New York: Teachers College Press.

House, E. R. (1998). *Schools for sale: Why free market policies won't improve America's schools, and what will.* New York: Teachers College Press.

Kauffman, J. M. (2002). *Education deform: Bright people sometimes say stupid things about education.* Lanham, MD: Scarecrow Press.

Lugg, C. A. (2003). Sissies, faggots, lezzies, and dykes: Gender, sexual orientation, and a new politics of education? *Educational Administration Quarterly, 39*(1), 95–134.

National Society for the Study of Education, Committee on Behavioral Science and Educational Administration, & Griffiths, D. E. (1964). *Behavioral science and educational administration.* Chicago: NSSE; distributed by the University of Chicago Press.

Ramirez, J. D., et al. (1991). *Longitudinal study of structured english immersion strategy, early-exit and late-exit transitional bilingual education programs for language-minority children. Final Report. Volumes 1 and 2.* San Mateo, CA: Aguirre International.

Part I

ATTACKS AND REBUTTALS: THE CONTROVERSIAL STATUS OF SOCIAL SCIENCE KNOWLEDGE

If anyone doubts the contested and uncertain status of the social sciences in public education, reading the first four chapters of this volume will surely provide convincing evidence that knowledge claims are contested and the status of the university as an institution to evaluate and arbitrate competing knowledge claims has been weakened to the point that policymakers, civic leaders, education professionals, and the general public are turning to more overtly political agencies for support. The uncertain status of scientific knowledge can be seen in the roller-coaster history of the relationship between university scholarship and American public policy—a history poignantly developed by Margaret Nash in chapter 1. The tension is equally clear in the rise and fall of respect for social science knowledge in the training of school administrators—a history sketched out in chapter 2. After less than four decades as a dominant theme in administrative training, the whole idea of a scientific basis for school improvement needs to be reconsidered. Indeed, just as university scholars have become agonized about how best to define the appropriate methods and theories to be used in interpreting school programs and organizations, the federal government has lost patience and begun to legislate politically approved standards.

In chapter 3, Brian Rowan develops a detailed and elegant defense of the social science legacy of the theory movement in educational scholarship. He argues that it not only produced substantial advances in scholarly knowledge, but also directed the attention of both policymakers and education professionals to the consequences of this knowledge. Rowan argues that criticisms of theoretically grounded empirical research are overblown, that they are the result of having unrealistic and inappropriate expectations of scholarly work. He not only defends the vitality of the sort of science embraced by Daniel Griffiths and other leaders of the theory movement, but also argues that this approach to developing and arbitrating claims to knowledge will sustain educational scholarship in the years to come.

A quite different view of the status of educational scholarship is presented by Paul Green in chapter 4. Focusing his attention on how legal knowledge is generated and reviewed, Green argues that postmodern and critical theorists are leading university scholars to new and vitally important insights into schools that cannot be generated using the kind of social science theories and methods advocated by empirical social scientists utilizing the methods defended by Brian Rowan in chapter 3. Using the hotly debated issue of educational equity as a case study, Green illustrates the most important distinction between legal knowledge claims and those made in the fields of history, political science, sociology, and anthropology that are represented in the other chapters of this volume. He shows us the importance of conceptual clarity and coherence in framing legal knowledge claims. In demonstrating that legal knowledge is grounded in explicit and detailed conceptualization of issues, Green is also showing why weak theory development is so often the Achilles' heel of knowledge claims in other fields of education scholarship.

Taken together, these first four chapters demonstrate that the question of what counts, or should count, as scholarly knowledge in the fields of educational administration, policy, and politics not only involves complex intellectual issues, but also requires reexamination of the institutional status of the university and the working relationship between research scholars, public policymakers, education professionals, and the public at large.

Chapter 1

The Relationship Between Academic Social Scientists and Educational Policymakers: A Brief Historical Overview

Margaret A. Nash
University of California, Riverside

One of the basic premises of this book is that there was a time when federal and state policymakers actively sought out the insights and opinions of academic social scientists. University scholars were valued for their research, and their research was seen as directly relevant to policy. Today, many policymakers see universities as irrelevant, at best. The authors of the chapters in this book are addressing the question of how to once again be taken seriously by policymakers. How did we get from there to here, and how do we find our way back? But is there reason to bemoan an idealized past in which the research produced by academic social scientists mattered to educational policymakers, or was there no Golden Age? Is the question, "How do we find our way back?" or is it, "How do we make ourselves newly relevant?"

In this chapter I trace the history of the relationship between academic social scientists and policymakers, beginning with the Progressive Era. I argue that changing conceptions of knowledge, and in particular beliefs about the objectivity (or lack thereof) of scientific research, have had a direct impact on this relationship. In a period when many people believed that scientific methods yielded objectively true results, universities were seen as a source of unbiased information useful to policymakers. Yet as early as the 1920s, doubts were cast regarding claims to objectivity. By the 1980s, challenges to this ideal came from multiple directions. There have been three major results of these challenges. First, a growing cultural mistrust of science and of the so-called experts who produce scientific knowledge strained the once optimistic relationship. Whereas in an earlier era, average citizens may have trusted in the knowledge of social scientists, by the 1980s much of that trust had been eroded, leaving academic social scientists in a position of needing to defend their work. Second, as social science became seen as politicized rather than as objective, it became more expedient for policymakers to seek scientific backing from more overtly ideological sources. Universities, supposedly neutral but suspected of being too liberal by conservatives and of being too controlled by a military-industrial complex by liberals, no longer dominated in the production of the social science research used by policymakers. This in turn led to the third major result of the challenges to the ideal of objective research: the growth in privately funded research institutions ("think tanks") that tied social science research to ideological positions. The consequence, then, is that academic social scientists have become increasingly marginal to the world of policymakers. This is especially true in schools of education, which have never been held in high regard.

FROM THE PROGRESSIVE ERA TO THE GREAT SOCIETY

Government has long made use of scientific methods of data collection. Researchers and policymakers have collected statistics on schools and schooling since the early 19th century. The first state superintendent for schools, the redoubtable Horace Mann, collected statistics on the condition of school buildings, enrollment and attendance of students, length of terms, and textbooks used in Massachusetts in the 1830s; other states followed suit. The federal government began collecting statistics on education shortly after the Civil War, under the auspices of the Department of Education (soon renamed the Bureau of Education). The federal data collection agency on education worked with states and local school districts to standardize data, acting somewhat like the National Center for Education Statistics, founded a century later in 1965. In addition to collecting data, the late 19th-century federal Bureau of Education also identified promising practices in hopes that other schools or districts would replicate them, a mission still central to the recently created Institute of Education Sciences.[1] Although some of these functions have remained constant, little else is the same. One of the many differences is that, in the 19th century, data collection and identification of exemplary programs primarily were done in-house, by federal government workers. In the 20th century, such work was more likely to be con-

[1]The IES was established in November 2002, replacing the Office of Educational Research and Improvement.

tracted out, and often the contracts went to university researchers (Justiz & Bjork, 1988; Vinovskis, 1999).

The link between university and government was forged most strongly, or expressed most clearly, during the Progressive Era—the decades immediately before and after the turn of the 20th century. That university researchers should provide governments, especially state governments, with relevant information and expertise related to questions of policy, was epitomized by what became known as the Wisconsin Idea. According to Charles Van Hise, President of the University of Wisconsin from 1903 to 1918, the Wisconsin Idea was that the boundaries of the university campus were the boundaries of the state. This meant that faculty should apply the knowledge accrued through study and research to the real problems faced by local communities and the state. Some of those problems were scientific, technical, and agricultural (e.g., better designed machinery, drought- or pest-resistant crops, soil erosion), and could be addressed through extension courses for farmers and mechanics. Other problems were economic and social, such as labor issues, urban planning for fast-growing cities, poverty, crime, and disease prevention. University faculty could serve their communities as disinterested scholars—that is, detached scholars who were interested only in the truth, without political agendas of their own—and who could provide objective information for the legislators who then could make informed decisions on important matters. The practice of direct scholarly aid to state governments became known as the Wisconsin Idea (McCarthy, 1912).

Van Hise and other reformers of American universities looked to Germany for models. What Van Hise saw there was a system in which university scholars were key participants in the administration of the government. "Almost every prominent German and Austrian professor," wrote Van Hise, "is an official adviser to the government." He saw the beginnings of this system in the United States, citing, for example, the professors who served on tax commissions, or who figured the valuation of railroads (Van Hise, 1904, pp. 194–205). Within a short time, Lloyd Short, a University of Missouri scholar, turned the equation around, arguing that "the duties of public officers" are "technical or professional, highly specialized," requiring advanced training. Thus, universities should not only advise, but "should be a recruiting ground for the public service" (Van Hise, 1933, p. 19). Van Hise sought to keep the center of power in the university; by providing advice to government officials and by training public officers, they would fulfill their duty "to control the destinies of the nation" (Van Hise, 1904, p. 194).

In the Progressive Era, the notion that university-trained researchers might control the destiny of the nation did not have the same heavy-handed ring that it does today. This was, after all, the era of scientific management and social efficiency—the beliefs that every job could be broken down to its component parts, and each part should be handled by someone trained specifically to do only that. In manufacturing, this took the form of Taylorism and the creation of the assembly line, in which each worker did only one job, over and over, epitomized in Henry Ford's revolutionary approach to auto production. In business, this led to the growth of multilevel functionally differentiated jobs within corporations, such as directors of sales and directors of marketing; in clerical fields, there were people who only typed, others who only filed, and still others who took dictation. In city government, this took the form of citizens electing a mayor who then appointed city managers specially trained to run various functions of city life. In short, this was an era of specialization.

The new penchant for specialization figured prominently in the creation of universities in the first place. They were not like the earlier liberal arts colleges, in which each student studied essentially the same set of subjects and emerged a well-rounded, educated person capable of entering any number of possible professions. By the late 19th and early 20th centuries, such general study had its detractors. Reformers created universities in order to move beyond the college's mission of teaching students the body of already existing knowledge. At universities, knowledge would not merely be transmitted from one generation to another; it would be created. Furthermore, the creators of this new knowledge would need to specialize in one particular field, whether it be physics, mathematics, or the newly emerging social sciences. Graduate students, under the direction of highly specialized faculty, would conduct experiments, carry out studies, investigate issues, and add to the existing body of knowledge.

Not only did the new universities create and maintain specialized fields, but social scientists also organized themselves into professional societies. Modeling themselves after the 1865 American Social Science Association, the earliest of such societies, the American Economic Association, was formed in 1885 (Silva & Slaughter, 1984). Its purpose was the expert investigation into the "special problems" of American industrialization, and the shaping of state policies toward the "best utilization of [national] resources" ("Constitution of the Society for the Study of National Economy" [1885], cited in Silva & Slaughter, pp. 79–80). Other scholars founded the American Political Science Association in 1903, and the American Sociology Society in 1905 (Silva & Slaughter).

Leaders of these new professional societies were quite explicit about their role in shaping policy and solving social ills. Lawrence Lowell, President of Harvard and leader of the American Political Science Association during the Progressive Era, used the fall of the Roman Empire as an example of the imperative of educated academic experts in government. The generation of the Founding Fathers made frequent allusions to the Roman Empire, and promoted the forging of a strong republic based on the morality of its citizens; in the 1780s and 1790s, much public discourse centered on the relationship between poor morals and the fall of Rome (see, e.g., Winterer, 2002). Lowell, however, firmly ensconced in the very different milieu of the Progressive Era, wrote that the fall of Rome had nothing to do with morals; instead, it was due to "the lack of experts in public service." "Government by a succession of amateurs, without expert assistance," he wrote, "proved itself hopelessly incapable of maintaining an orderly administration" (Lowell, 1913, p. 481). Government was too important an undertaking to be left to the untrained.

Government run by experts had another advantage besides efficiency. The model of specially trained officials was more democratic, many argued, than a government run by those who could simply buy their way into office; in fact, continuing this argument, the country had nearly been ruined by just such a system of patronage. The so-called Gilded Age was a period known for rampant corruption in politics. Idealistic reformers of the Progressive Era wanted to clean up the political system, end patronage, and return government to the people. Instead of government being run by those with the most money, or those who paid for the most votes, it would be run by trained specialists. Government could become a profession into which any ambitious person with proper preparation could enter (Levine, 1986).

Yet the views of Progressive Era scholars were not always met with a warm welcome. As the newly forming specialized fields emerged, and academics began speaking and writing about their areas of expertise, their conclusions sometimes met with strenuous objection. Some scholars were fired from their positions for holding unacceptable views. Richard T. Ely, an economist at the University of Wisconsin-Madison, was accused in 1894 of being vocally pro-union and prostrike, and of teaching socialism in his classes, and was nearly dismissed. Although the Board of Regents issued a statement that has been regarded as one of the earliest and strongest defenses of academic freedom, Ely himself softened the public expression of his opinions (Schlabach, 1998). Other academics were not so fortunate as to have the Board's backing. Another economist whose views were found to be controversial, John R. Commons, was dismissed from Indiana University in 1895, and later had funding withdrawn for his position at Syracuse University; sociologist Edward A. Ross was dismissed from Stanford University (Hofstadter & Metzger, 1955). As a result of these and many other dismissals, based not on the quality of scholarship or teaching but on reaching contentious conclusions, faculty in research universities joined together to form the American Association of University Professors (AAUP) to establish procedures for determining whether discipline or dismissal cases involved issues of academic freedom. The AAUP argued that academic freedom "is essential in promoting inquiry and advancing knowledge, providing general instruction to students, and developing experts for the various

branches of public service" (Hansen, 1998, p. 4). Thus, even as reformers
saw the crucial need for academic social scientists and those scientists
wanted to help solve social problems, academics experienced a tension between expressing the conclusions to which their work led them and expressing conclusions that did not embroil them in controversy. As we will
see, the need to preserve the autonomy of academic research resurfaced in
subsequent decades.

The crisis caused by World War I was an early time in which the federal
government explicitly reached out to academic experts, and a time in
which academics offered their service to the war effort. As historian Carol
Gruber (1975) noted, university leaders assumed, based on the Progressive
Era service ideal, that higher education had a special contribution to make.
This seemed all the more true because this was a more technological war
than any previous wars had been (Gruber). Mechanical and electrical engineering departments at some universities offered their expertise to the
Navy, and other institutions offered their laboratories and equipment to
the federal government (Gruber). A meeting of 150 representatives of
higher education resulted in a resolution to offer "every resource at their
command, to offer to the Nation their full strength without reservation"
(Kolbe, 1919, p. 27). The Intercollegiate Intelligence Bureau provided
names and specialties of academic experts to various government agencies.
The Bureau was voluntary and short-lived, and few faculty participated, although likely this was simply due to the small-scale nature of the enterprise,
rather than refusal on the parts of faculty (Levine, 1986).

Social scientists as well as natural scientists contributed in highly visible
ways to the war effort. President Wilson convened another key group of academics, called The Inquiry, to supply background knowledge on diplomatic issues. It was The Inquiry group—historians and classicists, among
others—that redrew the boundary lines of modern Europe following World
War I. Wilson's entourage to the Paris Peace Conference included 35 of
these scholars (Levine, 1986). For the newly professionalizing fields within
social science, these visible roles also enhanced their status within academe
and with the general public. Charles Beard (1917) wrote that the fields of
political science, economics, and sociology were proving themselves to be
essential to solving world problems, and John Dewey (1918) wrote that new
approaches to social problems, as foregrounded in the war, would revolu-
tionize social science. For some academics, contributing to the war effort
had the added benefit of being good public relations. Harvard's Albert
Bushnell Hart noted that the war was a time for institutions of higher education "to show that they are worth while" (Gruber, 1975, pp. 105–106).

Yet the social scientists who attempted to prove their worth inadvertently
contributed to growing public skepticism. A group of historians took on the
task, in cooperation with the U.S. Bureau of Education, of writing high

school curricula that would help build support for the war. Their curricula portrayed the Germans in simplistic and consistently negative ways, even using medieval history to justify the current war (Gruber, 1975; Thompson, 1918). This backfired following the war, as the obvious lack of objective scholarship was publicized and pilloried. Articles published in the popular magazine *American Mercury* in 1927, for example, criticized academics who had "prostituted themselves" by "offering their intellectual gifts upon the altar of the nation" (Gruber, p. 1). Furthermore, by 1927 the work done by the scholars of The Inquiry group at Versailles was being castigated as "imbecile schemes," and as evidence of academicians' "debauch in the arms of Uncle Sam" (Grattan, 1927, cited in Gruber, p. 2). Thus, a wariness existed early on regarding the uses to which social science research could be put, and a caution arose regarding claims to objectivity within social science research.

Between the end of World War I and the end of World War II, the involvement of social scientists in policymaking fell, rose, and fell again. The influence of social scientists in presidential administrations tapered off a bit in the post-Progressive Era, although President Hoover did bring scores of college professors and college graduates to Washington. Besides employing some academics in the Commerce Department, he also invited their participation in the conferences he sponsored on a wide range of issues (Levine, 1986). Hoover also established a Committee on Social Trends, which was the first federally sanctioned (if not funded—Hoover arranged for the Rockefeller Foundation to fund the project) sociological study of American life. Begun in 1929 and published in 1933, the Committee's report was an astounding 1,600 pages of data and analysis of social changes that had taken place between 1900 and 1930. Chaired by leading academicians, the project involved several hundred social scientists (Lacey & Furner, 1993; President's Research Committee on Social Trends & Mitchell, 1934). Despite the scope of this project, Hoover's administration did not look to social scientists for much help in the creation of policy overall.

Franklin D. Roosevelt established strong links with social scientists, and an argument could be made that his administration was the heyday of social scientific influence. In the Depression Era, Roosevelt enlisted the aid of social scientists (sometimes referred to as his Brain Trust) hoping to find solutions to the enormous social problems facing the country. According to one estimate, about 680 social scientists worked in Washington in 1931; by 1937, as New Deal programs were developed, the number of social scientists grew to 2,150 (Binderman & Crawford, 1968). During World War II, the federal government turned to both natural and social scientists in the goal of defending the United States.

Whether the Cold War years represented a boon or a bust for social scientists is open to interpretation. According to one appraisal, after the crises of the Depression and the War passed, the perception of the need for social scientists fell. Research in medicine and in the natural sciences was seen as far more immediately relevant (Greenberg, 1968; Vinovskis, 1999; Wood, 1993). Not only was this type of research favored, but social science research was more liable to be slapped with labels of "procommunism" or "antidemocracy." Although anticommunist sentiment had been widespread ever since the Russian Revolution, it waned during World War II when the Soviet Union was an ally of the United States, but had a strong resurgence following the war in the face of aggressive Soviet expansion and the extension of communism into China. One well-known manifestation of the fear of a communist takeover in the United States was the political witch hunts directed by Senator Joseph McCarthy of Wisconsin, which had a sobering, but not paralyzing, effect on academics in the social sciences and humanities (Lazarsfeld & Thielens, 1958; Schrecker, 1986). In just 5 years, from 1945 to 1950, over 200 cases involving violations of academic freedom had been sent for investigation to the AAUP (MacIver, 1955). By 1950, 26 states had passed legislation requiring teachers and professors to sign loyalty oaths, and in 14 states, educators had to pledge that they were not members of any subversive organization or were not going to teach their students to overthrow the government (Ravitch, 1983). Applicants for fellowships for government grants also had to sign loyalty oaths, and claims regarding what patriotism entailed squashed some research agendas as "[w]hole areas of inquiry now became . . . un-American" (MacIver, p. 43). In the face of all this, one could certainly argue that the Cold War years were not good years for the relationship between academic social scientists and policymakers.

However, another interpretation holds that these years were good ones for social scientists. Strategic lapses during the war convinced many, including officials in military and intelligence agencies, of a dire need for certain types of expertise. The federal government encouraged the creation of area studies, such as the Russian Institute at Columbia, founded in 1946, and the Russian Research Center at Harvard in 1947. Social scientists helped in other ways, as well. The State Department put together a coterie of psychologists, anthropologists, historians, economists, and radio experts to help in the goal of more effective message transmissions over the Voice of America and by other means (Larson, 2000).

THE KENNEDY-JOHNSON YEARS AND BEYOND

If the Roosevelt administration was not the zenith of social science influence in presidential policymaking, then the Kennedy and Johnson years surely were. After the election and before his inauguration, Kennedy formed policy task forces; 53% of the members of these task forces were academics from institutions of higher education (Wood, 1993). In 1961, the Juvenile Delinquency and Youth Offense Control Act raised the central concerns of poverty. Juvenile delinquency, according to the architects of this bill, could not be solved without dealing with the underlying problem of poverty. Following Kennedy's assassination, Johnson formed more policy task forces, and appointed more people with doctorates in cabinet and subcabinet positions, than any other president. Daniel Patrick Moynihan referred to this era as a period of the "professionalization of reform," as "experts turned advocates" during the War on Poverty (Moynihan, 1969).

The War on Poverty not only relied on the work of social scientists, but also included an explicit focus on education. Many social scientists saw education as a key weapon in the War on Poverty. Benjamin Bloom, for instance, argued that intelligence was not fixed, and that the first 5 years of life were critical for cognitive development. If minority children were not succeeding in school, it was because the home environment in which they spent their early and most formative years was lacking. These poor children, then, needed educational experiences that would "compensate" for their inferior home cultures and their inadequate parents (Bloom, 1964; Bloom, Davis, Hess, & Silverman, 1965).

Two major changes reflect this idea of education as key to the fight against poverty: Head Start and the 1965 Elementary and Secondary Education Act (ESEA). Head Start began in 1964 when President Johnson and Sargent Shriver organized a planning committee that included university professors of psychology along with pediatricians and social workers. The director of the Office of Child Development, the agency that would administer Head Start, was Edward Zigler, professor of psychology and later director of the Child Study Center at Yale. Building on the ideas of Bloom, J. McVicker Hunt, and others, Head Start was designed to improve children's cognitive functioning while also improving the parenting skills of impoverished parents; some Head Start proponents also hoped that the program would empower disenfranchised poor minorities (Hunt, 1961; Kagan, 2002). Meanwhile, the ESEA dramatically increased the role of the federal government in education. Designed to help disadvantaged and poor children, the ESEA funded a range of programs and initiatives including cultural enrichment, library innovations, parental involvement activities, nutrition programs, and medical services. With an increase in budget from $7 million in 1963 to $70 million in 1966, the ESEA greatly amplified federal involvement in research on education. Some of the funding was used to establish university-based research and development centers, regional educational laboratories, and the Educational Resources Information Center (ERIC). The impetus behind this act was the issues raised by social scientists, who linked education to many of the social problems of the day (Anderson & Anderson, 1988; Lagemann, 2000; Timpane, 1988; Wood, 1993).

The 1960s saw a confidence in the role of social scientists to solve social problems that paralleled the Progressive Era's confidence in scientific management. Historian Elaine Tyler May (1988, pp. 26–28) called the decades following World War II the "era of the expert," and David Halberstam (1969, p. 43) spoke of the experts who moved from the halls of academe to wield considerable power in foreign policy in this period as the "thinker-doers." Harold Lasswell and Daniel Lerner, editors of a volume on what was called "policy sciences," wrote that such experts would solve "the new human problems" raised by modern society, and would even "improve the practice of democracy" (cited in Nathan, 2000, p. 15; Lerner, 1959, p. 14). In 1967, Pulitzer prize winner Theodore H. White referred to the social scientists involved in federal policymaking as a "new priesthood of action-intellectuals," a "brotherhood of scholars" who had become "the most provocative and propelling influence on all American government and politics"; they would redesign our cities, reorganize our schools, guide foreign policy, and manage our economic system (White, 1967, cited in Wood, 1993, p. 33).

This renewed respect for academic scholars was reflected in federal funding of university research. Before 1957, funding for research made up less than 5% of the federal budget; by 1966, it accounted for 15%. Not all of this funding went to universities, but much of it did. Between 1958 and 1964, the proportion of federal money for academic research doubled, from representing 0.1 to 0.2% of the gross national product (or from $468 million to $1,275 million). By 1962, a full 75% of the money universities spent on research came from the federal government. At universities with large federal contracts for research, as much as half of the university's entire budget came from the federal government. The bulk of that funding, however, went to medical, biological and physical sciences, and to engineering. Only 2% of the federal research budget went to the social sciences (Barber, 1966; Geiger, 1993).

However, the Johnson years also saw a change in attitude toward social scientists. The escalation of the war in Vietnam had much to do with these changes, primarily because the cost of the war depleted the federal budget and left little money for the domestic policies recommended by the social scientists. In addition, grassroots activists and student groups led a charge that the group of experts offering advice was an elite group, and not truly representative of the broader public. The media portrayed the possibility of Orwellian control and brainwashing (Weiss, 1978). This fear was exacerbated by the publicity surrounding Project Camelot, a project funded by the U.S. Army that conducted social scientific research in Latin American and other countries in order to aid the U.S. government in "counterinsurgency," or in "predicting and influencing social change" in volatile regions. When the project became known, diplomatic protests against espionage resulted. Chilean diplomat Jorge Montes accused the United States of using "a covert form of espionage, which they try to present in terms of scientific research" (Larson, 2000, pp. 153–154; Montes, 1967, pp. 121–126; National Research Council, Advisory Committee on Government Programs in the Behavioral Sciences, 1968; Simpson, 1998). In the minds of many on the American left, including some antiwar students, academic researchers became linked with the Army and with suspect policies, including the use of behavioral research in order to effect broad political and social control.

Other critics opined that too much power, or at least too much money, was in the wrong hands. The same Theodore White who sang the praises of the "priesthood of action-intellectuals" also worried whether this band of scholars knew enough to determine appropriate policy. The studies and surveys these academics produce are road maps, said White, and the designers of them should remember that they are map makers, not tour directors (White, 1967, pp. 85–86). In short, social scientists should not overextend their reach.

Furthermore, some argued, much social science was useless, as it was conducted on irrelevant topics. Senator William Proxmire of Wisconsin publicly ridiculed some of these studies in his annual Golden Fleece awards, which he began issuing in 1975, pointedly arguing that taxpayer dollars should not be used for such nonsense. Awards for misuse of funds that first year included one for a study of why people fall in love, and another for a 7-year study to determine under what conditions rats, monkeys, and humans bite and clench their jaws.[2] The Golden Fleece awards went to all sorts of government-funded projects and did not target only social scientists, but the awards did contribute to a public mistrust of, if not disdain for, academic research that seemed worthless at best.

By the 1970s, social scientists were experiencing criticism not only from external sources, but from within their own ranks as well. A backlash against the programs of the New Frontier and the Great Society was reflected in attacks on the effectiveness of the programs and on the academic research behind the reforms. Blue ribbon commissions examined the use and methodologies of social science in the previous decade and found them wanting; most of the panel members were themselves social scientists. The following list of titles illustrates the tenor of the times: Irving Louis Horowitz's (1971) collection of essays *The Use and Abuse of Social Science*, the *New York Times* article "Knowledge Dethroned" (Nisbet, 1975), the scholarly symposium "Social Science: The Public Disenchantment" (1976), and the National Acad-

---

[2]A complete list of Golden Fleece awards can be found online at http://www.taxpayer.net/awards/goldenfleece/1975-1980.htm (see, e.g., Atkinson, 1999; Larsen, 1992).

emy of Sciences' (1978) volume of essays *Knowledge and Policy: The Uncertain Connection* (Wood, 1993). If there had been a honeymoon, it now was over.

The condemnations took several forms. One repeated criticism was that social scientists tried too hard to adopt the methodologies of the natural sciences, a stance that was doomed to failure given the changeability of human behavior; unlike research in the physical sciences, "constant or stable phenomena can rarely be relied on" as bases for understanding change or predicting results when it comes to human actions (Kamarck, 1983, p. 18; Thurow, 1983, p. 8). Perhaps because of trying too hard to be something they are not, social scientists, according to some critics, did not understand their own methodologies or the possibilities and limitations of their fields. Charles E. Lindblom and David K. Cohen wrote of the possibility that "social scientists (ourselves included) hold a fundamentally wrong conception of social science," and that "ordinary knowledge and casual analysis . . . are often sufficient or better than" social science (Lindblom & Cohen, 1979, pp. 6, 10).

Some of the academic critique was of the underlying assumptions made by previous social scientists. Whereas the earlier group believed that social problems could be cured through intervention, the new group believed that some social problems were incurable because they stemmed from genetic, not environmental, differences. For this group, intelligence was fixed and static, as could be measured in IQ tests, and that therefore compensatory education was useless. Changing the environment of children in poverty could not change the fact that they were genetically inferior (Ginsburg, 1972; Jensen, 1969). For many of these academics, the role of social science should be to measure the results of policy, not to try to formulate it.

As the premises of the Great Society programs were challenged, even the programs that at first had seemed the most successful now were being questioned, and the questioning grew louder as social scientific studies inveighed against them. The Nixon administration, which disliked the community action aspect of Head Start, directed a study that concluded that early education made little difference and had no lasting cognitive effect on children. The release of this study, referred to as the Westinghouse study, set off a flurry of new critiques. One set of social scientists pointed out what they saw as flaws in the methodology of the Westinghouse study, and publicly called the study "sloppy." At the same time, another set of social scientists claimed that the critics of the Westinghouse study were just "stubborn ideologues," not scientists calmly evaluating data (Moynihan, 1973, pp. 150–151, 211; Semple, 1969, p. 44; Westinghouse Learning Corporation & Ohio University, 1970, p. 1).

For many people outside of academe, these challenges eroded the credibility of the social sciences. If social scientists themselves could not agree on which policies work and which do not, and if they could not agree on appropriate methodology to determine whether a policy works, then there was no clear link between reliable knowledge and responsible policy (Wood, 1993). In addition, social science research was tainted by the brush of the Tuskegee study. In 1972 the *New York Times* reported the story of a study on syphilis in which African American men, told they were being treated for "bad blood," instead went untreated so that researchers could study the long-term effects of syphilis (Heller, 1972). Although this experiment was conducted by medical researchers associated with the U.S. Public Health Services, and not by social scientists, it nonetheless raised serious doubts about both ethical standards and racism in scientific research, and about governmental abuse of disenfranchised groups (Heller, 1972; Jones, 1993). Embodying the public's mistrust of scientific work was the book *Betrayers of the Truth* (Broad & Wade, 1982), which argued that fraud in science was common and accused scientists of misconduct (Davis, 1999). The same year that the Tuskegee story broke, one analyst concluded that the "greatest dilemma confronting legislators today lies in a conflict between the need for information and the inability or unwillingness to trust those who possess it" (Adrian, 1972, cited in Mitchell, 1981, p. 7).

None of this resulted in a complete exclusion of social science from federal policymaking, however. The idea that substantive knowledge should be a part of policy decisions, and that much of the requisite knowledge could be found in universities, seemed solidly accepted. Also, the Planning-Programming-Budgeting System (PPBS) analysis, first introduced in Johnson's administration, was firmly rooted and was used in successive administrations, both Democratic and Republican, under different names.[3] This system required specially trained policy analysts, especially in quantitative fields such as economics; policy experts in history and sociology were less in demand. To meet the need for experts in these quantitative areas, new programs, and sometimes new schools, were established in scores of universities; by the late 1970s, there were over 200 such policy schools, most offering master's degrees (Wood, 1993).

The spate of new academic programs did not in any way stop the internal attacks, which continued in the 1980s and 1990s. Some critics complained that academic experts had lost all sight of any Progressive Era ideal of the "disinterested scholar." Instead, they were the handmaidens of industry

---

[3]Wood (1993) suggested that the budgeting and planning systems in subsequent administrations were very similar processes. Nixon abolished PPBS, and both Nixon and Carter set up new systems. Nathan agrees that the new systems had "similarly inflated expectations" as the PPBS, and that it left a legacy of "the growth in the size and stature of the planning staffs in federal agencies." Nixon's system was MBO (management by objectives), and Carter's was ZBB (zero-based budgeting). Both systems required frequent performance reports, necessitating the employment of social scientists in evaluating programs (Jardini, 2000; Nathan, 2000; Wood).

and government, designing studies to prove the importance of maintaining the status quo of an unjust system. This criticism is epitomized by one critique published in 1984, entitled *Serving Power*. In this volume Silver and Slaughter argued that social science supported "vested political economic interests" by writing reports and designing studies that purported to prove the superiority of capitalism and that supported an apparent oligarchy (Silva & Slaughter, p. 5). Another line of criticism argued that objectivity was impossible and should not be a goal; instead, researchers ought to be overt about their political viewpoint, which surely shaped their research, rather than be "disguised vehicles of oppression," or pretend to an unattainable objectivity (Searle, 1990, p. 34). Still other critics believed that the approach taken by social scientists was "too narrow, the programs too specifically focused, and the assessment of their impact too simplistic" (Wood, 1993, p. 166). What was needed instead was big picture analysis, policy frameworks based on political theory, and not just a hodgepodge of programs (DeHaven-Smith, 1988).

These criticisms helped spur the growth of an alternative site of social science research: independent private research institutions, commonly known as "think tanks." The first criticism, a leftist critique that said that social science researchers were in the pockets of government and industry, fueled the belief on the parts of many on the ideological right that universities were too liberal. On the heels of student antiwar protests in the late 1960s and early 1970s, these critiques confirmed for many that academics tended to be liberal, and therefore their work was unlikely to support Republican policies. The first and second criticisms both spoke to the impossibility of neutrality, and a preference for naming the political viewpoints that shape one's perspectives. The desire for big picture analysis and holistic program planning also required a particular ideological framework in order to be coherent. Therefore, policymakers needed places where research could be done from particular standpoints, where particular kinds of research could be conducted, and where coherently integrated policies could be articulated. A growth in "knowledge-producing and [knowledge]-brokering institutions" followed. By the late 1980s, there were as many as 1,200 think tanks in the United States (Lacey & Furner, 1993, pp. 52–53).

The growth of think tanks may have been aided in part by a push factor from academic institutions. Providing information that will help shape policymaking is not always a comfortable fit with the requirements and expectations of academe. What is of most use to policymakers is not what is of most prestige to academics. Policymakers want concise statements of problems and solutions, and they want those bullet-point memos timed to meet the demands of legislative sessions (State Legislative Leaders Foundation, 1995). Academic work, on the other hand, is rewarded for its richness and complexity, and its appearance in top-tier professional journals. Think tanks, which proliferated after 1970, became a more hospitable home for many social scientists, because career advancement in the think tanks was not tied only to publishing in academic journals. For a variety of reasons, then, the glory days for scientific management based on academic expertise had dimmed by the 1980s.

WITHIN SCHOOLS OF EDUCATION

But what of social scientists within schools of education? Their story overlaps this overview of social science in the universities in general, but also has unique characteristics. Schools of education generally have had to fight for acceptance within colleges and universities. Formal training for teachers first was conducted primarily in academies and seminaries, and then in "normal" schools, most of which had either closed or evolved into state teachers colleges by the 1940s; finally, formal training for teachers largely took place in state colleges and universities (Clifford & Guthrie, 1988). Older universities established departments of education, largely to compete for students. None of these departments or colleges had the same cachet as did other fields within the universities. This may have been because of the elite status of pure over applied research, or because of the association of teaching with "women's work," or because of the association of teaching institutions with vocational training, or a combination of these (Astin, 1988). Nonetheless, schools of education seldom were highly regarded. Columbia University, for instance, treated its teaching college in the same way it, and other prestigious institutions, treated the idea of education for women: by banishing it to the sidelines (Lagemann, 2000). Just as Columbia educated women only through its separate "coordinate" college, Barnard, so too it educated teachers only through the separate Teachers College.[4]

Early scientific research on education was led primarily by the field of psychology in the late 19th and early 20th centuries. An early practitioner was Edward L. Thorndike, known as the "father of the measurement movement," who, according to Ellen Lagemann, "helped establish statistics . . . as a vital new method of education research" (Lagemann, 2000, p. 65). Yet the statistical analysis promoted by Thorndike and others was limited. Although these researchers wanted to collect data and quantify most aspects

_____

[4]Several universities in the Progressive Era established separate colleges for women, called "coordinate" colleges, rather than admit women. For example, Harvard established Radcliffe, Brown established Pembroke, and Columbia established Barnard (Solomon, 1985).

of schooling and learning, they were less likely to theorize about the results. Instead, long after other social scientists had moved on to theoretical constructs, the educational psychologists clung to "social bookkeeping, the censuslike description of social data," until at least the 1940s (Lagemann, p. 87). This lack of theory and analysis added to already existing credibility problems for schools of education.

Another early practitioner was Lewis M. Terman, who brought the testing movement to the front and center of education issues in the first few decades of the 20th century. As large school systems looked for means to more efficiently sort students into educational tracks, testing became more widely used. By the mid-1920s, educational psychologists staffed research bureaus in dozens of large cities, and nearly one fifth of all U.S. high school students took such tests, along with scores of students at younger grades.[5] Interestingly, as a further example of the low regard with which schools of education have generally been held, once Terman won recognition for his work in testing, he moved from a position in Stanford's School of Education to its Department of Psychology (Lagemann, 2000).

Between the World Wars, professors of education may have gained a bit of status. The field was burgeoning, there were a plethora of new doctorates in specialized fields within education, and application of principles of scientific management to the curriculum planted education specialists in firm ground.[6] Many urban school districts opted to apply Taylor's model of management, based on a factory system of maximum efficiency. Despite criticism, Taylorism held sway. A prime mid-20th-century proponent of this was Daniel E. Griffiths. Taylorism and Griffiths are discussed in detail in chapters 2 and 8 of this volume. Shortly after World War II the federal government expanded its involvement in research on education through the Cooperative Research Act of 1954, which funded small research grants. Appropriations were small, especially compared to research programs in science, defense, health, and space, but it did fund research within schools of education (Timpane, 1988).

Whatever gains there may have been were largely lost when the Soviet Union successfully launched Sputnik in 1957. Already critics had been warning that schools had gotten too "soft," and had lost all academic rigor. With Sputnik, those warnings seemed doubtlessly true. The Russians seemed to have a clear advantage, and books like *What Ivan Knows That*

---

[5]Terman himself recommended caution in broadly interpreting data from IQ tests, warning that any conclusions regarding race differences, for instance, could not be made based on these tests. Nonetheless, many people did draw such conclusions. Information on Terman, Robert Yerkes, and the testing movement is widely available (Gould, 1981).

[6]According to Lagemann (2000), by 1930, more doctorates were given in education than in any field other than chemistry. By 1940, 14.3% of all doctorates given in the United States were in education (Clifford & Guthrie, 1988).

Johnny Doesn't (Trace, 1961) drove home the point that Russian children were studying advanced math and science while American children were taking classes in "life adjustment education" (Urban & Wagoner, 2000). The professional educators had forfeited their right to determine the best educational practices, including curriculum; they were people who had "only the most fleeting glimpse of the great world of science and learning" (Bestor, 1952, p. 114, 1953).[7]

Curriculum content, many pundits now declared, should be determined by specialists in particular disciplines, not by professional educators. Critic after critic publicly assailed faculty in schools of education. Everyone seemed to agree with Francis Keppell, dean of Harvard's Graduate School of Education from 1948 to 1962 and U.S. Commissioner of Education from 1962 to 1966, that "education is too important to be left solely to the educators" (Lagemann, 2000, p. 161). Renewed attention to education during these post-Sputnik years reflected this disparagement of schools of education. Although it was a period of high visibility for social scientists working on issues of education, scholars within schools of education were underrepresented in federal grants. By 1963, noneducationists were the majority of applicants for grants from the Cooperative Research Program of the federal Office of Education, and the Research and Development centers that were established that same year were designed to be separate from schools of education (Lagemann). Determined to improve American schools, the federal government poured money into the design of new curricula, especially in math, science, and languages. This funding, however, went to the National Science Foundation (NSF), not to faculty in schools of education.[8]

These curricular innovations were abysmal failures. The changes represented an imposition of content, form, and values that many parents, community and religious groups, and teachers did not accept. Parents schooled in basic arithmetic could not help their children with their homework in the "new math." Some religious groups objected to what seemed to them to be lessons in moral relativism in the MACOS (Man: A Course Of Study) curriculum. Teachers could not help but feel alienated from curricula that reflected little recognition of the reality of classrooms. The failure of these reforms reinforced many people's negative attitudes toward academics as out-of-touch

---

[7]Notice that Bestor's (1952, 1953) critiques preceded the launching of Sputnik.

[8]As one example of the NSF's intent to keep science out of the hands of teachers, the NSF produced films for classroom use. The NSF did so at least in part to circumvent the teachers they viewed as incompetent, or to take science education out of the hands of teachers and put it into the hands of "the experts who prepare the instructional films." One science curriculum project member was worried about the "funny results" that might occur if the films did not take up the whole class period, and teachers would lead discussion (Rudolph, 2002). For a general account of the NDEA, see Urban and Wagoner (2000, pp. 295–298).

ivory tower dwellers filled with "scientific hubris."[9] The devaluing of academic science, however, did not result in an inverse amount of respect for faculty in schools of education. The general public probably did not make a distinction, lumping all academics into the same heap of arrogance. Within many academic institutions and among some policymakers, the schools of education still had the inferior status that had led to the funding of the academic disciplines over the schools of education in the first place.

Perhaps the most well-known piece of scholarly work on education in this period is *Equality of Educational Opportunity*, published in 1966 and commonly referred to as the Coleman Report. This study, required by the Civil Rights Act of 1964, was designed to collect data on educational opportunities for various groups of people. Not only did it document differential availability of high-quality buildings, laboratories, libraries, resources, and low teacher-student ratios, it also attempted to document different educational outcomes for students. A huge undertaking, the report was both praised and criticized, and Coleman has written about the ways his research was misused and misread. Nonetheless, the report surely was a highly visible piece of social science research in education, and Coleman's work moved educational research in the direction of assessing outcomes as well as resources.

The Coleman Report highlights two aspects of the story of social science and education. First, when the National Center for Educational Statistics, which was charged with ensuring that the legislatively mandated report was done, hired Coleman to lead the work, it fit the prevailing tendency to hire social scientists outside schools of education; Coleman was a sociologist who never held a position within a school of education (Coleman, 1966; Grant, 1973; Lagemann, 2000). Second, many policymakers interpreted the Coleman Report as concluding that schools made little difference in student achievement; the more important variables were socioeconomic status and peer influence. Money spent on improving schools, on better training of teachers, or on designing new programs for poor children, then, would be wasted (Coleman; Jencks, 1972; Mosteller & Moynihan, 1972). The entry of discipline-based social scientists—sociologists, political scientists, economists, and others—into schools of education came, then, at a particularly low point for schools of education generally.

MOVING TOWARD SOLUTIONS

If academic researchers within schools of education want policymakers to see them as important resources, history suggests several tactics they might

---

[9]Thanks to Doug Mitchell (personal communication, January 12, 2004) for this formulation; for more on the failure of these curricula, see Rudolph (2002) and Urban and Wagoner (2000).

employ. One strategy is to alter the ways that social scientists present themselves and their work to the broader public. Historian Mary Furner (1975) wrote about a schism among economists in the late 19th century, and her point about the tension within professions is no less true today. "Tenuous at best," Furner wrote, "the scholar's claim to authority weakens dangerously when battles within the scholarly community become public. If experts disagree, then who can claim the sanction of science?" (p. 7). If the general public is to see social scientists as having authoritative knowledge, then the scientists need to present a clear sense of a coherent and agreed-on body of knowledge. But obviously social scientists do not all agree—not about methods, not about research questions, not about conclusions, and not about the values underlying all of these. For professional societies, then, a tension arises between presenting a coherent picture to the outside world in order to be acknowledged as having authoritative knowledge, and yet allowing for rational difference and for academic freedom.

If the general public wants a coherent sense of who the experts are and what they conclude, this preference is even more true of policymakers. It is one thing for academics to agree that multiple positions are possible; presenting the multiplicity of viewpoints to policymakers who want clear and succinct answers is another matter altogether. According to Matthew Miller (2003), senior fellow at the Center for American Progress, the "pluralistic and complex" view of social problems put forth by academic researchers is not useful in a political and media culture that demands "sound bites" and clear answers.

In a related vein, a second tactic is to bridge the disjuncture between what policymakers want and the type of work that is rewarded by academic institutions. If academic success is judged by publications in professional journals, then researchers who want to climb the academic ladder will not rise to the top if they put their research into language and forms that will be most easily used by policymakers. Think tanks, on the other hand, were designed to produce and promote studies to shape policy. Edwin J. Feulner, President of the Heritage Foundation, said that a plan for shaping policy cannot be "hiring nine academics for the summer to do the definitive work on this or that. It has to be, 'What's your Web site going to look like, how are you going to get the right message out to the right editorial writers, and the person who is doing the booking on Fox News, CNN, or Jim Lehrer?' " (cited in Miller, 2003, p. 13). As Robert Wood said, "the academy had shot itself in the foot" already in the 1980s by not reckoning policy work as worthy of recognition (1993, p. 165). Academic work may be quite relevant to policymakers, but it is not presented in ways that are useful. Increasingly, then, policymakers may prefer to turn to think tanks rather than to universities.

A third strategy is for social scientists to reduce the tension between the concepts of expertise and common knowledge. A group of experts is, by definition, an elite group, and historically, we seem to both want an elite and simultaneously mistrust it. As Richard Hofstadter (1963) convincingly argued, mainstream American culture has a long-standing history of ambivalence toward intellectuals. Votes in state and national elections may be based on many qualities besides the candidates' educational attainment or apparent intellectual aptitude, including leadership and charisma. Most citizens want to know, though, that behind any elected figurehead, there are trained experts waiting in the wings to proffer advice. Yet there is a long tradition of disdain for "eggheads" or "bluestockings," full of book learning but lacking in basic common sense. If social scientists want to portray their knowledge and expertise as essential for the general good, they need to walk a fine line. Their expertise needs to be couched in utilitarian language, made accessible to all. But if their knowledge seems too pedestrian, then their claim to special insight might be diminished.

Similarly, there exists a tension between a notion of a democracy in which all citizens contribute equally, and a democratic notion of meritocracy, in which those most able are the ones who govern. This tension has expressed itself in nearly every era. I leave aside here the question of whether there has ever been a democracy in which all voices are given equal weight, or whether a meritocracy is possible in a class-based system; my point here is about ideals and rhetoric. In the Progressive Era, the Era of Scientific Management, both views were present. For instance, in 1909 a college president felt it justifiable to comment with satisfaction on the "growing understanding of the real value of the expert" in American society (Levine, 1986, p. 33). Yet nearly simultaneously, Woodrow Wilson (himself a social scientist and former college president) claimed to fear "a government of experts." Wilson said in 1912:

> God forbid that in a democratic country we should resign the task and give the government over to experts. What are we for if we are to be scientifically taken care of by a small number of gentlemen who are the only men who understand the job? Because if we don't understand the job, then we are not a free people. (Hofstadter, 1963, pp. 209–210)

A general mistrust of experts and instead a preference for common sense is evident today in California's historic recall of an elected governor. Over 100 citizens threw their hats in the ring to run for governor in the fall of 2003, some of them defiantly asserting their lack of expertise as their strongest qualification for the position. Said one such candidate, a largely unknown small business owner, "The state is in a fiscal meltdown and we need a common sense candidate to go up to Sacramento and straighten this mess out" (Renz, 2003, p. A22). This candidate did not win, of course, but the comment speaks to a general disparagement of so-called expertise, and a respect for the efficacy of simple common sense. Moreover, the winner, Arnold Schwarzenegger, presented himself as the candidate of determined action, not of extraordinary expertise.

How, then, are social scientists to define themselves and the knowledge they produce? They are both experts with special knowledge and also common citizens who are called on to participate with their equals. To claim special privilege for their voice due to their expertise can smack of intellectual elitism. Couching that expert knowledge in terms of a meritocracy—that anyone is permitted to ascend the ivory tower if they are willing to work hard enough—still runs the risk of discounting the intelligence and common sense of the average person. This is especially difficult when even social scientists publicly claim, as Lindblom and Cohen did in 1979, that "ordinary knowledge and casual analysis" are superior to social science, and that researchers waste money and time studying whatever they most enjoy with no regard to its social utility (pp. 10, 87).

The field of education might be particularly vulnerable to this type of criticism. Even when a majority of citizens might accept the need for social science research in economics, demographics, or land use patterns as the foundation for policymaking in arenas of health care, urban planning, and commercial development, these same citizens might not accept the need for research into education. Arguments abound over the extent to which teaching is a science at all, or whether it is an art for which someone either has a talent or not. In addition, educational systems promulgate values; indeed, the so-called culture wars over what moral position will hold sway in public schools has dominated most local and national discussions regarding educational reform. The issue of local control also keeps the focus on the teachers, administration, curricula, and buildings of one's own children, rather than fostering a broad view of providing the best education for all children. To the extent that people view teaching as an art, education primarily as a means of inculcating morals into future citizens, and educational policy as only a local concern, then scientific studies seem of little use in training teachers, designing curricula, or determining the best broad-scope or long-range planning. The familiar mantra, heard in political, educational, and parental circles, that "parents know what is best for their children," is one answer to the long-standing tension between expert knowledge and common sense. Social scientists need to present their work as providing useful information that will improve schools without stepping over the boundaries of parental rights, and that will build on, rather than dismiss, the insights that parents bring. Ideally, the expert knowledge of social scientists can augment the common sense of parents and other concerned citizens.

Finally, the long-standing disrespect for schools of education in this country contributes to the difficulty that social scientists who are housed in schools of education have had being taken seriously. From the earliest normal schools that trained teachers (and others) in the 19th century, to departments, schools, and colleges of education in universities today, the intellectual activity associated with education is disparaged. Policymakers looking for insight are unlikely to turn to any education schools but those in the most prestigious institutions, and perhaps not even then, as long as education faculty are considered lesser beings than faculty in arts and sciences. The proliferation of think tanks has worsened this situation, because policymakers have many options other than schools of education.

It is not clear that there ever were halcyon days for social science researchers in schools of education. Perhaps believing that there were gives us hope that those days might come again. To the extent that policymakers have turned to institutions of higher learning for their expertise, they have tended to do so in times of national crisis, and less so in times of peace or economic prosperity. Even then, however, it was not necessarily to schools of education that policymakers looked. If education faculty want to be relied on more, history suggests that they need to develop and communicate clear rationales for their research methodologies, find ways to alter the academic reward system so that policy-related work is respected, grapple with the tension of expertise within democracy, and continue the project of elevating the status of schools of education.

Some of these changes, such as clarifying how and why particular research is conducted, or wrestling with the meaning of expertise, cause no misgivings. However, finding ways to make academic research fit the needs of policymakers does raise concerns. What might schools of education become if they try to fit their work into the shape called for by policymakers? Sound bites might be easy to use, but do they reflect the best thinking, the careful consideration, and the thoughtful analysis that we hope universities are capable of producing? If universities do not do this type of work, where will it be done? What are the costs to the broader culture if the value of intellectual investigation is further diminished? Accommodating the needs of policymakers may be a good short-term strategy, but it is not clear that it is a good long-term strategy. Ideally, academics can use more accessible language while also cultivating a regard for nuanced thinking among both the general public and policymakers. We must find ways to bridge the best of several worlds, honoring the unique contributions of academic research, the social commitments of the body politic, and the pragmatic agendas of policymakers.

REFERENCES

Anderson, L. W., & Anderson, J. C. (1988). The impact of research on American education. In M. J. Justiz & L. G. Bjork (Eds.), *Higher education research and public policy* (pp. 283–304). New York: American Council on Education and Macmillan.

Astin, A. W. (1988). The decline in public faith in educational research. In M. J. Justiz & L. G. Bjork (Eds.), *Higher education research and public policy* (pp. 147–156). New York: American Council on Education and Macmillan.

Atkinson, R. (1999). The golden fleece, science education and U.S. science policy. *Proceedings of the American Philosophical Society, 143*(3), 407–417.

Barber, R. J. (1966). *The politics of research.* Washington, DC: Public Affairs Press.

Beard, C. (1917). Political science in the crucible. *New Republic, 13*(Suppl.), 3–4.

Bestor, A. E., Jr. (1952). Aimlessness in education. *Scientific Monthly, 75,* 114.

Bestor, A. E., Jr. (1953). *Educational wastelands: The retreat from learning in our public schools.* Urbana: University of Illinois Press.

Binderman, A. D., & Crawford, E. (1968). *The political economics of social research: The case of sociology.* Washington, DC: Bureau of Social Science Research.

Bloom, B. (1964). *Stability and change in human characteristics.* New York: Wiley.

Bloom, B. S., Davis, A., Hess, R. D., & Silverman, S. B. (1965). *Compensatory education for cultural deprivation. [A report] based on working papers contributed by participants in the Research Conference on Education and Cultural Deprivation.* New York: Holt, Rinehart and Winston.

Broad, W., & Wade, N. (1982). *Betrayers of the truth.* New York: Simon & Schuster.

Clifford, G. J., & Guthrie, J. W. (1988). *Ed school: A brief for professional education.* Chicago: University of Chicago Press.

Coleman, J. S. (1966). *Equality of educational opportunity.* Washington, DC: U.S. Office of Education, National Center for Education Statistics.

Davis, M. (1999). *Ethics and the university.* London: Routledge.

DeHaven-Smith, L. (1988). *Philosophical critiques of policy analysis: Lindblom, Habermas, and the Great Society.* Gainesville: University of Florida Press.

Dewey, J. (1918, April 6). A new social science. *New Republic, 14,* 292–294.

Elementary and Secondary Education Act. (1965). *Focus on pace projects to advance creativity in education: Title III: Supplementary center and services.* U.S. Department of Health, Education, and Welfare/Office of Education.

Furner, M. O. (1975). *Advocacy and objectivity: A crisis in the professionalization of American social science, 1865–1905.* Lexington: University Press of Kentucky.

Geiger, R. L. (1993). *Research and relevant knowledge: American research universities since World War II.* New York: Oxford University Press.

Ginsburg, H. (1972). *The myth of the deprived child; poor children's intellect and education.* Englewood Cliffs, NJ: Prentice Hall.

Gould, S. J. (1981). *The mismeasure of man.* New York: Norton.

Grant, G. (1973). Shaping social policy: The politics of the Coleman report. *Teachers College Record, 75,* 17–54.

Grattan, C. H. (1927, August). The historians cut loose. *American Mercury, 11,* 427–430.

Greenberg, D. S. (1968). *The politics of pure science.* New York: New American Library.

Gruber, C. S. (1975). *Mars and Minerva: World War I and the uses of the higher learning in America.* Baton Rouge: Louisiana State University Press.

Halberstam, D. (1969). *The best and the brightest.* New York: Ballantine Books.

Hansen, W. L. (1998). Introduction. In W. L. Hansen (Ed.), *Academic freedom on trial: 100 years of sifting and winnowing at the University of Wisconsin-Madison* (pp. 1–16). Madison: University of Wisconsin Press.

Heller, J. (1972, July 26). Syphilis victims in the U.S. study went untreated for 40 years. *The New York Times,* pp. 1, 8.

Hofstadter, R. (1963). *Anti-intellectualism in American life.* New York: Knopf.

Hofstadter, R., & Metzger, W. P. (1955). *The development of academic freedom in the United States.* New York: Columbia University Press.

Horowitz, I. L. (1971). *The use and abuse of social science.* New Brunswick, NJ: Transaction Books.

Hunt, J. M. (1961). *Intelligence and experience.* New York: Ronald Press.

Jardini, D. R. (2000). Out of the blue yonder: The transfer of systems thinking from the Pentagon to the Great Society, 1961–1965. In A. C. Hughes & T. P. Hughes (Eds.), *Systems, experts, and computers: The systems approach in management and engineering, World War II and after* (pp. 311–357). Cambridge, MA: MIT Press.

Jencks, C. (1972). *Inequality: A reassessment of the effect of family and schooling in America.* New York: Basic Books.

Jensen, A. (1969). How much can we boost IQ and scholastic achievement? *Harvard Educational Review, 39,* 1–2.

Jones, J. H. (1993). *Bad blood: The Tuskegee syphilis experiment* (rev. ed.). New York: Free Press.

Justiz, M. J., & Bjork, L. G. (1988). Academic science and public policy. In M. J. Justiz & L. G. Bjork (Eds.), *Higher education research and public policy* (pp. 1–15). New York: American Council on Education and Macmillan.

Kagan, J. (2002). Empowerment and education: Civil rights, expert-advocates, and parent politics in Head Start, 1964–1980. *Teachers College Record, 104,* 518–519.

Kamarck, A. M. (1983). *Economics and the real world.* Philadelphia: University of Pennsylvania Press.

Kolbe, P. R. (1919). *The colleges in war time and after: A contemporary account of the effect of the war upon higher education in America.* New York: Appleton.

Lacey, M. J., & Furner, M. O. (1993). Social investigation, social knowledge, and the state: An introduction. In M. J. Lacey & M. O. Furner (Eds.), *The state and social investigation in Britain and the United States* (pp. 3–62). Cambridge, England and New York: Woodrow Wilson Center Press and Cambridge University Press.

Lagemann, E. C. (2000). *An elusive science: The troubling history of education research.* Chicago: University of Chicago Press.

Larsen, O. N. (1992). *Milestones and millstones: Social science at the National Science Foundation, 1945–1991.* New Brunswick, NJ: Transaction.

Larson, D. W. (2000). The Cold War and the university. *Diplomatic History, 24,* 151–152.

Lazarsfeld, P. F., & Thielens, W., Jr. (1958). *The academic mind: Social scientists in a time of crisis.* Glencoe, IL: Free Press.

Lerner, D. (1959). Social science: Whence and whither? In D. Lerner (Ed.), *The human meaning of the social sciences* (pp. 13–39). Gloucester, MA: Smith.

Levine, D. O. (1986). *The American college and the culture of aspiration, 1915–1940.* Ithaca, NY: Cornell University Press.

Lindblom, C. E., & Cohen, D. K. (1979). *Usable knowledge: Social science and social problem solving.* New Haven, CT: Yale University Press.

Lowell, A. L. (1913). Expert administrators in popular government. *American Political Science Review, 7,* 481.

Lynn, L. E., Jr. (1978). *Knowledge and policy: The uncertain connection.* Washington, DC: National Academy of Sciences.

MacIver, R. M. (1955). *Academic freedom in our time.* New York: Columbia University Press.

May, E. T. (1988). *Homeward bound: American families in the Cold War era.* New York: Basic Books.

McCarthy, C. (1912). *The Wisconsin idea.* New York: Macmillan.

Miller, M. (2003). A challenge for liberal foundations. *Chronicle of Philanthropy, 15,* 13.

Mitchell, D. E. (1981). *Shaping legislative decisions: Education policy and the social sciences.* Lexington, MA: Lexington Books.

Montes, J. (1967). A communist commentary on Camelot. In I. L. Horowitz (Ed.), *The rise and fall of Project Camelot: Studies in the relationship between social science and practical politics* (pp. 232–236). Cambridge, MA: MIT Press.

Mosteller, F., & Moynihan, D. P. (1972). *On equality of educational opportunity.* New York: Vintage Books.

Moynihan, D. P. (1969). *Maximum feasible misunderstanding.* New York: Free Press.

Moynihan, D. P. (1973). *The politics of a guaranteed income: The Nixon administration and the family assistance plan.* New York: Random House.

Nathan, R. P. (2000). *Social science in government: The role of policy researchers* (rev. ed.). Albany, NY: Rockefeller Institute Press.

National Research Council, Advisory Committee on Government Programs in the Behavioral Sciences. (1968). *The behavioral sciences and the federal government.* Washington, DC: Author.

Nisbet, R. (1975, September 28). Knowledge dethroned; Only a few years ago, scientists, scholars and intellectuals had suddenly become the New Aristocracy. What happened? *New York Times,* p. 239–242.

President's Research Committee on Social Trends, & Mitchell, W. C. (1934). *Recent social trends in the United States: Report of the President's Research Committee on Social Trends.* London and New York: Whittlesey House and McGraw-Hill.

Ravitch, D. (1983). *The troubled crusade: American education, 1945–1980.* New York: Basic Books.

Renz, R. R. (2003, September 23). Faces of the recall. *The Los Angeles Times,* p. A22.

Rudolph, J. L. (2002). From world war to Woods Hole: The use of wartime research models for curriculum reform. *Teachers College Record, 104,* 212–241.

Schlabach, T. F. (1998). An aristocrat on trial: The case of Richard T. Ely. In W. L. Hansen (Ed.), *Academic freedom on trial: 100 years of sifting and winnowing at the University of Wisconsin-Madison* (pp. 37–57). Madison: University of Wisconsin Press.

Schrecker, E. (1986). *No ivory tower: McCarthyism and the universities.* New York: Oxford University Press.

Searle, J. (1990, December 6). The storm over the university. *The New York Review of Books, 37,* 34.

Semple, R., Jr. (1969, April 27). White House advisers stand by report critical of head start. *The New York Times,* p. 44.

Silva, E. T., & Slaughter, S. (1984). *Serving power: The making of the academic social science expert.* Westport, CT: Greenwood Press.

Simpson, C. (1998). *Universities and empire: Money and politics in the social sciences during the Cold War.* New York: New Press.

Social science: The public disenchantment. (1976). *The American Scholar, 45,* 335–359.

Solomon, B. M. (1985). *In the company of educated women: A history of women and higher education in America.* New Haven, CT: Yale University Press.

State Legislative Leaders Foundation. (1995). *State legislative leaders: Keys to effective legislation for children and families.* Centerville, MA: Author.

Thompson, J. W. (1918). The deeper roots of Pan-Germanism. *Historical Outlook, 9,* 360–366.

Thurow, L. C. (1983). *Dangerous currents: The state of economics.* New York: Random House.

Timpane, P. M. (1988). Federal progress in educational research. In M. J. Justiz & L. G. Bjork (Eds.), *Higher education research and public policy* (pp. 17–31). New York: American Council on Education and Macmillan.

Trace, A. S. (1961). *What Ivan knows that Johnny doesn't.* New York: Random House.

Urban, W. J., & Wagoner, J. L. (2000). *American education: A history* (2nd ed.). Boston: McGraw-Hill.

Van Hise, C. R. (1904). Inaugural address. *Science, 20,* 194–205.

Van Hise, C. R. (1933). *Higher education and the state.* Columbia: University of Missouri.

Vinovskis, M. (1999). *History and educational policymaking.* New Haven, CT: Yale University Press.

Weiss, C. H. (1978). Improving the linkage between social research and public policy. In L. E. Lynn, Jr. (Ed.), *Knowledge and policy: The uncertain connection* (pp. 23–81). Washington, DC: National Academy of Sciences.

Westinghouse Learning Corporation, & Ohio University. (1970, August). The Kirschner re-
    port. *Head Start Newsletter, 5,* 1.
White, T. H. (1967, June 23). The action intellectuals. *Life, 62,* pp. 44–74.
Winterer, C. (2002). *The culture of classicism: Ancient Greece and Rome in American intellectual life,
    1780–1910.* Baltimore: Johns Hopkins University Press.
Wood, R. C. (1993). *Whatever possessed the president? Academic experts and presidential policy,
    1960–1988.* Amherst: University of Massachusetts Press.

Chapter 2

The Evolution of Educational Administration Knowledge

Douglas E. Mitchell
Flora Ida Ortiz
University of California, Riverside

This chapter traces the evolution of educational administration theory, research, and practice. The focus is on four historically distinct stages in the evolution of scholarly inquiry in this field and on the changing conceptions of knowledge used to organize scholarship during each stage. Special attention is given to the emergence and impact of what has come to be known as the theory movement, with its emphasis on rigorous methodical inquiry into administrative behavior, leadership, and decision making. The life and work of Daniel E. Griffiths, a key figure in the emergence and popularization of the theory movement, is given particular emphasis. This review is important to the overall theme of this book because it reveals when and how the currently troubled state of knowledge in the field of educational administration took form, establishing a "paradigm" (Kuhn, 1962) aligning educational administration scholarship with the functionalist tradition in sociology (which Mitchell, in chap. 9 of this volume, identifies with an Aristotelian epistemological perspective). Widespread calls for reconsideration of the intellectual foundations of scholarship in this field spring directly from the perceived inadequacies in the theory movement's research and development agenda for public education. Coming to grips with the arguments developed in the remainder of this volume will be greatly facilitated by an adequate understanding of the evolution of educational administration and policy scholarship delineated here.

To anticipate the detailed argument presented later, the theory movement came to prominence in the third of four distinct stages in administrative scholarship. As the four stages are outlined, the nature of the fourth stage's challenge to the conception of knowledge inherent in the theory movement as it was understood and promoted by Daniel Griffiths and his colleagues becomes evident and the nature of the intellectual crisis that this volume has been designed to address becomes clear.

A PRÉCIS OF THE KNOWLEDGE PROBLEM

Before turning to delineation of the four distinct historical stages in the evolution of administrative theory, let us sketch out the key elements in our analysis, showing how critical conceptions of knowledge and truth evolved alongside scholarly methods and emphases. Central dimensions in the evolution of administrative theory are captured in the five questions shown in the leftmost column of Table 2.1. These five questions have persisted since the beginnings of formal scholarly and professional reflection on administrative problems and practices and they continue to inform research and scholarly inquiry in the field. They include:

1. What do we need to know about in order to manage and lead public schools?
2. How do educational leaders and managers influence, control, direct, or supervise the work of practicing professional educators?
3. What is the theory of educational productivity used to determine whether school programs and practices are effective?
4. What is the cultural, practical, and professional meaning of administrative work?
5. What abiding concepts from each stage in the evolution of administrative theory have continued to frame the interpretation of educational administration problems and practices?

As our description of the historical unfolding of administrative scholarship shows, these five questions have received distinctively different answers during each of the historical periods. During the first stage (which we dub the Scientific Management Era), the question of what we need to know was answered through detailed task analysis and can be summarized as: We need to know what task structures and techniques are the most efficient and effective means of achieving desired educational outcomes. The managerial control question was answered as: Work organization and execution is a matter of managerial prerogative and responsibility; good workers do as they are directed, using techniques specified by supervisors. The third question (how to conceptualize educational productivity) was answered by the affirmation that educational work is, above all, practical work made more

TABLE 2.1
How the Definition and Construction of Administrative Knowledge Evolved Over a Century of Professional and Scholarly Inquiry

Dimension	Stage 1: Scientific Management	Stage 2: Executive Leadership	Stage 3: Theory Movement	Stage 4: Institutional Productivity
1. What do we need to know about to make schools effective?	Task structure and techniques	Worker motivation and leadership decision making	Organizational and environmental factors influencing work effectiveness	Social power relationships and their effect on perception and action
2. How is work directed and controlled?	Management prerogative	Working conditions and supervision of antonomous workers	Multivariate systems operations	Interested sociopolitical influence over perception and purpose
3. What is the theoretical perspective on productivity?	Practical action objectively managed	Coordination of motivated workers	Application of process or product knowledge	Constructed meaning with moral purpose
4. What is the cultural and practical meaning of administration?	Analyzed tasks empower effective supervision of good workers	Sensitive leadership and proper conditions inspire high performance	Realistic theory enables leaders to guide complex actions	Cultural interpretation exposes abuse and inspires commitment
5. What abiding concepts still frame educational administration?	Education is task structured and managed	Leadership involves decision making and worker motivation	Schools are complex organizations influenced by a broad range of social, demographic, and structural variables	Education is a political institution where power is directed to morally important purposes

31

efficient through close supervision. Fundamentally, administration was culturally defined as reliance on task analysis to guide the supervision of compliant workers whose duties were morally defined as subordination to managerial control. The abiding legacy of this period is that education is a task-structured enterprise, made effective through proper understanding of these tasks and aggressive supervision of their execution. This view remains central to contemporary views of educational leadership as policymakers and professionals continue to believe that "what works" is defined, above all, by proper utilization of educators' technical skills.

During the second historical epoch (which we call the Executive Leadership period), the focus on essential knowledge shifted from the tasks to the decision-making and worker-motivation activities of administrators. The central problems of administration seemed to be less a matter of what tasks needed to be performed than how to motivate and coordinate workers in the execution of tasks that were seen as relatively straightforward in character. Work was thus seen as controlled less by managerial prerogatives and more by the manipulation of working conditions and the coordination of resources and support services. Indeed, high productivity in the school came to be seen as depending primarily on the proper division of labor, followed by the stimulation and coordination of work efforts. The cultural meaning of effective administration moved away from the strong supervisory management and toward the idea of leadership, with its emphasis on sensitivity to worker needs and interests and on the capacity to inspire the efforts that result in high performance. And it is this shift from management of task performance to motivational leadership and creative decision making that remains the primary legacy of this second scholarly period.

By the third historical period (the era intellectually dominated by what came to be known as the theory movement), attention returned to the complex structuring of educational tasks. Now, however, administration scholars emphasized that these tasks were embedded in a web of complex social and organizational forces whose understanding and analysis are essential to the development of proper techniques of task execution and coordination. During this period, control over work performance moved away from direct supervision and coordination as the focus shifted to multivariate system operations. School operations came to be seen as a matter of programs rather than tasks. Curriculum differentiation, staff specialization, testing and assessment of learning rates and levels, and student placement based on diagnoses of their learning problems rather than their achievement levels came to dominate the conceptualization of educational work—and the institutional mission of the school as an agency for socializing youth into a democratic polity and a capitalist system emerged to make schooling a complex social enterprise. As a result, conceptions of how to improve school productivity began to focus on the development of scientific process and product knowledge that would make learning outcomes predictable from the implementation of research-based educational programs. The abiding legacy of this period is a conception of schools as complex social organizations influenced by a broad range of social, demographic, and structural variables, all of which have to be considered in the design of fair, equitable, democratic, and economically viable outcomes.

The fourth stage in the evolution of educational administrative thought (which we call the Institutional Productivity Era) is still unfolding, but its broad outlines are already quite clear. Attention has shifted from technical complexity to political and social power relationships as the most important focus of scholarly inquiry and professional practice. Persistent inequalities in educational outcomes, the negative effects of student labeling and assignment to specialized educational programs, an awareness that most educational assessments are more important for their political than their technical utility, and the marginalization of teacher and parent influence over school programs and practices have combined to emphasize the importance of understanding the allocation and utilization of social and political capital within the public education system. As a result, the management of educational work has moved (federal efforts to the contrary notwithstanding) from an emphasis on the control of resources and specification of system operations to efforts to a belief that sociopolitical and moral commitments influence the perception of problems and the willingness to adopt or implement technical solutions that might be available to address them. Indeed, the very concept of educational productivity is shifting toward a belief that it is based on the accumulation of social and political capital and the development of moral purpose rather than the application of universally effective techniques. As a result, educational administration has come to focus on leadership and community building, establishment of compelling cultural visions, and practices that expose abuse of the powerless and commitment to community and public service. The abiding legacy of this era will almost certainly be its recognition that schools are political institutions where power is inevitably exercised for good or ill moral purposes, and that clarification of these purposes and mobilization of commitment to higher rather than baser purposes is a central element in effective leadership.

With this broad introduction to key concepts, we turn now to sketching out the four evolutionary stages in educational administration scholarship.

EVOLUTIONARY STAGES IN ADMINISTRATIVE SCHOLARSHIP

Educational administration began as a purely practical art. School teachers who appeared suitably adept in the eyes of their local boards of education were asked to shoulder the added responsibilities of administration, first at the school site level then at the district level. As school systems became larger and their infrastructure became more expensive, more technically sophisticated, and more socially and politically convoluted, administrative complexity outstripped the capacity of individuals unschooled in management techniques, and was too politically risky to be undertaken casually. Beginning in the late 1870s, universities were drawn into the business of training, and state governments initiated the practice of certifying for service a cadre of professional administrators. At the beginning, most of the training consisted of passing along the folklore and folk wisdom acquired by one generation of practicing administrators to the next.

Even before the nation's universities entered into the process, however, administrative leaders began to call for the development and application of social-science-based administrative strategies and techniques. We should probably date the beginning of the first stage in American educational administration scholarship with the publication of William H. Payne's *Chapters on School Supervision* in 1875 (to be followed by his *Contributions to the Science of Education* in 1886). These two publications bracket his movement from Superintendent of Schools in Adrian, Michigan to take the newly created chair of the Art and Science of Teaching at the University of Michigan in 1879. As H. G. Good (1956) reported, the University of Michigan was the first major U.S. university to give a prominent place to the training of educators. He indicated that University of Michigan President James B. Angell pointed out to his Regents that:

> Many young graduates were at once appointed as principals of large schools or to superintendences [sic] of city schools. Before they went to their new duties, he thought they should have been taught something of the work of organizing, managing, teaching, and governing a school. "Experience alone can thoroughly train them. But some familiar lectures on these topics would be of essential service to them." (pp. 330–331)

Thus began the first stage in the development of educational administration scholarship, the engagement of major universities in providing core training in school organization and management. In order to move beyond folklore, the universities had to find their own voice. This was done by turning to what by the beginning of the 20th century was clearly identified as the scientific management of complex productive processes.

Stage 1: The Scientific Management Period, 1875 to 1925

In the preface of his 1875 book, Payne called for the development of a scientific understanding of educational administration. He noted that, up to this point, no work, "not even the most elementary," had yet been published on analyzing the art of educational administration, "on an art whose importance can scarcely be over-estimated" (p. vi). In his introduction to Payne's book, William Harris, then Superintendent of Schools in St. Louis, concurred with the thrust of Payne's work, and argued that a science of education and management was needed and could be achieved. Both Payne and Harris were self-educated superintendents, but their work initiated a call for university involvement in the training of a new generation of school leaders. Payne realized that educators possessed empirical or practical knowledge but lacked scientific theory regarding their practice and their organization. He arrived at several areas where science would be necessary: guiding students' development, helping teachers achieve effective instruction, understanding the organization of schools, and determining the purpose of school and ideals of education.

Harris (Payne, 1875) held a somewhat different view. He emphasized the interconnections between education and other domains of urban life, reflecting on how social theory and social practice interacted with urban and industrialized contexts. As a member of the American Social Science Association (ASSA), he studied health, education, jurisprudence, and social economy. Among the social science departments identified by the ASSA for inclusion in its membership were two in education: elementary and higher education. Harris included within the elementary department's central concerns: courses of study, method, discipline, and plan of organization or management. He emphasized the view that education is linked to family, state, civil society, and church and that the science of education had to account for these relationships.

For Payne, educational science was largely deductive, although he allowed that inductive methods would be necessary to determine education's purpose. Harris, in contrast, rejected the positivist views of both Auguste Comte and Herbert Spencer, assigning to "speculative reason a higher role in the study of human institutions and processes" than "predictive science" (cited in Culbertson, 1988, p. 5).

In combination, these two practicing school administrators challenged the adequacy of practical experience in the preparation of school leaders and launched the search for scientific management theories and techniques for the public schools. Their work provided the major tenets of a science of educational administration, which have continued to influence university teaching and professional practice for more than a century.

Shortly after the University of Michigan created the education faculty chair initially occupied by Payne, the Teachers College at Columbia University began what was to become one of the nation's premiere education schools. Having created the first doctoral program, Teachers College granted eight doctoral degrees by 1905. Two of the initial graduates of this program were Elwood Cubberly and George Strayer, the most important university scholars of their generation—Strayer served with distinction at Columbia, whereas Cubberly gave prominence to Stanford University's emerging School of Education.

The conception of science grew slowly during the last quarter of the 19th century. Whereas the positivism of Comte and Spencer was gathering strength throughout the social sciences, except for a few stalwarts following Payne's lead, educational administration remained firmly rooted in the realm of practice. Part of the problem lay in Comte's explicit linkage of scientific thought with secular philosophy. He argued that a science evolved through three stages: the theological, the metaphysical, and the scientific. During the theological stage, causality is attributed to deities whose attitudes of pleasure and displeasure toward humanity and nature were seen as motivating them to control both human and natural events. In the second, metaphysical, stage the deities with their attitudes disappear, and are replaced by invisible but still active entities that animate human and natural activities— often in irregular and unpredictable ways. With the emergence of the positive scientific era, mankind presumes that the animating forces are natural, rational, and lawful in character. Although not always easily discerned, these animating forces become the focus of an active investigation. Indeed, the Comtean positivism sees any apparent phenomenon that cannot be directly encountered and measured to be essentially unreal and not worthy of study.

It was a physician, J. M. Rice, who first brought Comtean positivist science to the study of education. During his medical practice years, Rice became more and more interested in the education of children. By 1912 he had produced a research work that he claimed to be the "first of its kind" ever to be published (Rice, 1912, p. vi). This research involved visiting 36 school systems and collecting data on 50,000 students. He found little correlation between the time spent on teaching a subject and the learning that resulted. As Culbertson (1988, p. 8) summarized, "After having clearly described the essential tenets of Comtean science, [Rice] had used them successfully in inquiry."

Nevertheless, the secular emphasis that juxtaposed science and religion as cultural enemies did not sit comfortably with most school people because education was rapidly becoming what Laurence Iannaccone (1967) called the "secular religion" of America. The leaders of these secular religious institutions saw themselves as "managers of virtue" (Tyack & Hansot, 1982) and thus in need of attending to many human experiences that are both inaccessible to the positivist scientists' methods and denigrated by them as irrelevant to understanding personal and social realities. By the end of the first decade of the 20th century, however, the outlines of an accommodation between secular science and the quasi-religious character of education had been forged. Science was reduced from the Comtean status of global philosophy to become the handmaiden to practical action. That is, rather than seeing science as a worldview denying the reality of transcendental principles and experiences, educators began to see it as the source of refined professional practice—as the arbitrator of "what works," but not of broader claims to knowledge of ultimate, particularly moral, reality.

On the theoretical side, this accommodation was being given philosophical justification by John Dewey and the American pragmatists. On the practical side it prepared the way for a sweeping revolution in professional practice by embracing the human and social engineering ideology of Frederick Winslow Taylor and other prominent scientific interpreters of effective and efficient organization and management techniques (see, e.g., Fayol, 1944; Gulick & Urwick, 1937). The emerging rapprochement also accounts for the prominence of Cubberly and Strayer, who retained this emphasis on science as a means of improving professional practice throughout their long careers.

Taylor's *Scientific Management* (1911), detailed by Shipps in chapter 8 of this volume, became the archetype of this first stage in the evolution of education administration and policy sciences. This archetype preserved a place for the predominant view that public education is a moral enterprise pursuing the good life for individual citizens and the nation as a whole. It focused attention on improving the effectiveness and efficiency with which those moral ends are pursued and put collecting and analyzing data squarely at the center of educational research and scholarship. It responded with robust energy and a practical work agenda to Charles Adams (1880, p. 71), who harshly criticized the public schools for making it necessary for American citizens to "turn over our children to those whom we would never dream of entrusting with our potato patch."

Wayne Hoy and Cecil Miskel (1987, p. 11) summarized the central emphases of the scientific management approach to building a science of education. The basic features of this administrative model are contained in the following list:

1. Time and motion studies: The task is carried out in a way that minimizes time and effort.
2. Division of labor and specialization: Efficiency can be attained by subdividing any operation into its basic components to ensure workers' performance.
3. Standardization of tasks: Breaking tasks into component parts allows for routinized performance.
4. Unity of command: To coordinate the organization, decision making is centralized, with responsibility flowing from top to bottom.
5. Span of control: Unity of command and coordination are possible only if each superior at any level has a limited number of subordinates (5–10) to direct.

6. Uniqueness of function: One department of an organization should not duplicate the functions performed by another.

7. Formal organization: The focus of analysis is on the official organizational blueprint; semiformal and informal structures created by the dynamic interaction of people within the formal organization are not analyzed.

Once these broad principles of organizational design and managerial control processes had been developed, this scientific management conception of how to improve public education shifted focus from school organization and operations to the functions of executive action and leadership beginning in the mid-1920s.

Stage 2: The Executive Leadership Period, 1925 to 1945

The scientific management stage was transcended more by its successes than by its failures. As Callahan (1962, p. 246) summarized, "By 1925 the business-management conception of administration was firmly established and efficiency seemed to have been accepted as an end in itself." Time and motion, production processing, and school survey studies had been widely employed, leading to an impressive variety of school organization and program changes. Writing in 1930, Teachers College professor George D. Strayer saw this as 25 years of steady progress yielding not only vast improvements in school organization and program design, but also "a relatively powerful and able group" of school administrators who had become converts to the scientific management approach to school improvement (cited in Tyack, 1974, p. 182). But Callahan disagreed sharply with Strayer's assessment of the quality of administration that had been produced. According to Callahan, the overall result was:

> that educational questions were subordinated to business considerations; that administrators were produced who were not, in any sense, educators; that a scientific label was put on some very unscientific and dubious methods and practices; and that an anti-intellectual climate, already prevalent, was strengthened. (p. 246)

The limited ability of these administrators was not the result of there being too few of them to provide for adequate management. As Tyack (1974) documented in some detail, the number of administrators grew rapidly during the scientific management period. He cited with approval the summary by Robert and Helen Lynd that by the 1920s there had been created between the teacher and the superintendent "a whole galaxy of principals, assistant principals, supervisors of special subjects, directors of vocational education and home economics, deans, attendance officers, and clerks, who do no teaching but are concerned in one way or another with keeping the system going" (cited in Tyack, p. 185). Moreover, most states had replaced certification licenses based on tests for ones based on completion of professional training courses.

Pressures to rethink the production function focus of the scientific managers arose from at least three different directions. First, the progressives, led by John Dewey, attacked the goals of the scientific managers, accusing them of failing to grasp either the nature of the educational process or the goals of schooling, and thus defining efficiency entirely in cost-reduction terms rather than providing guidance for more effectively attaining the real goals of the public school system. Dewey's 1929 volume, *The Sources of a Science of Education*, laid out the broad outlines of this argument.

Second, though the dominant themes of research and training continued to focus on efficient practices, some leading scholars began to recognize and articulately analyze the links between schools and the larger sociopolitical communities within which they are embedded. Perhaps the best of these works was George S. Counts' (1932) *Dare the Schools Build a new Social Order?* Willard Waller's (1932) classic, *The Sociology of Teaching*, also underscored the sociopolitical dimensions of school operations.

The third source of pressure on the scientific management framework was a shift in the conception of management responsibility. An earlier emphasis on specification of production techniques (produced by time and motion study specialists) gave way to the study of what decision-making processes helped administrators to recognize and implement these techniques appropriately. This pressure came largely from the study of private sector industries and thus had the legitimacy to command immediate attention. The archetypes of this new focus on executive leadership were Chester Barnard's (1938) *The Functions of the Executive*, and the human relations studies of Elton Mayo and his colleagues, especially the famous Hawthorne studies (Roethlisberger, Dickson, & Wright, 1939). The result was a growing focus on decision making, employee motivation, leadership, and the importance of intelligent executive action and control.

During this period a second generation of education school research scholars came on the scene (e.g., Arthur Moehlman, Paul Mort, Jesse Sears) who continued to emphasize scientific management practices but also borrowed heavily from private sector researchers in order to move beyond the narrowly technical focus of works by Strayer and Cubberly. By the end of this period, in the mid-1940s, leadership and decision making had become central concepts in the lexicon of educational administration, but the focus remained internal to the schools themselves—little attention was given to the insights of Dewey, Counts, and Waller who sought to draw attention to the ways in which schools had been created as creatures of public

policy and were embedded in the social fabric of the communities that supported them.

Stage 3: Organizational Sociology
and the Theory Movement, 1945 to 1975

The executive emphasis of the second stage gradually gave way in the late
1940s and 1950s to an awareness of the sociological and political character
of schooling. Linking social and political themes of the sort emphasized by
Dewey, Counts, and Waller to the executive management emphasis of the
1930s and early 1940s, Herbert Simon's (1945) watershed volume, *Administrative Behavior*, brought a much more sophisticated conception of the
social sciences to bear on topics being addressed in the leadership and executive management studies that had emerged during the previous two
decades. The positivism of Comte (1974), which emphasized direct access
to knowledge of the lawful regularities of human and natural phenomena,
was replaced by the logical positivism of the Vienna Circle. The Vienna Circle philosophers saw Comte's positivism as entirely too optimistic in its expectation that scientific work would lead directly to knowledge of natural
laws. Instead, this revision of positivism emphasized the dynamics of hypothetico-deductive inquiry in which theories had to be developed and hypotheses regarding their implications for observable phenomena carefully
worked out in order to guide the collection and interpretation of data.
Thus, for the logical positivists, whose epistemological commitments were
central to Simon's work, theory rather than technique is the primary result
of successful scientific inquiry. Rather than focusing on the specification of
particular strategies of action and identification of "what works" (the core
emphasis of both the older Comtean positivism and the most recent federal
education policy), the logical positivists saw research scholarship as leading
to theories that explain the dynamics of organizational and social processes. These explanations would empower effective action by providing
criteria for evaluating strategic and tactical options rather than by prescrib-
ing specific actions. This led quickly to the belief that if organizational leaders were to be effective they would need to develop understanding, not just
acquire a repertoire of guidelines for action. Leadership came to be defined as acting knowledgeably to adapt organizational programs and practices to fit a growing understanding of the underlying dynamics of social
and technical processes.

The result of this subtle but profound reinterpretation of the nature of a
positive science of educational techniques and organizational processes was
the birth of the theory movement in educational scholarship. Beginning
with Simon, organizational scholars gradually moved from prescription to
analysis, formulating theoretical frameworks and testing whether their the-

ories could interpret and predict organizational dynamics. Education scholars did not lead this movement, however. As Griffiths (1988, p. 29) noted, the 1946 yearbook of the prestigious National Society for the Study of Education (NSSE) devoted to *Changing Conceptions of Educational Administration* (Henry, 1946) was devoid of references to theory and held few references to research. As Griffiths put it:

> The 1946 tome can best be described as the high-water mark of insularity in educational administration. The authors were all educationists, men who had spent their lives as professional educators. They gave no evidence of being influenced by the work of scholars in philosophy, history and the behavioral sciences. References to theory were completely missing, references to research nearly so. (p. 29)

Emergence of broad-based university and professional commitments to theoretical research and scholarship in educational administration came about over a decade-long process characterized by the historical convergence of the Vienna Circle's reconstructed logic of inquiry and massive growth in the appreciation of, and demand for, expanded schooling for the nation's children (on the importance of societal expectations, see McClelland, 1960; on expansion of school enrollment, see Tyack, 1974). This emergence, with its sweeping impact on the field, was brought about through the dedicated efforts of a small but potent band of university professors and can be tracked through a number of seminal events.

One of the most important individuals in this story is Daniel E. Griffiths. Griffiths' career spanned four decades from the early 1950s through the early 1990s. His scholarly credentials were solid, but his pivotal role in the emergence of the theory movement resulted more from his energy, skill, and prodigious effort as an organizer and promoter of the new behavioral sciences than from the power of his own scholarship. Lutz (2000, p. 2), on the occasion of his death in 1999, summarized Griffiths' impact as having "changed an entire profession." Griffiths became excited about the potential contributions to educational administration to be made by the positivist theoretical model of science set forth by the Vienna Circle as early as 1954, and never wavered in enthusiasm throughout his long career. Although he knew (Griffiths, 1978, p. 82) that educational administration is "largely an art and reflects the personal style of the administrator and the environment in which the person functions" and easily acknowledged that "much lies beyond the reaches of theory as we know it," Griffiths expected the theoretical analysis and research stimulated by logical positivism to transform and empower administrative leadership.

When, in 1964, Griffiths took responsibility for editing the NSSE's yearbook entitled *Behavioral Science and Educational Administration*, he assembled a virtual who's who of contributors to the theory movement to author chapters for the volume (R. Callahan & W. Button, R. Campbell, R. Carlson, W. W. Charters, J. Culbertson, W. R. Dill, B. M. Gross, L. D. Haskew, J. K. Hemphill, L. Iannaccone, J. M. Lipham, R. C. Lonsdale, and H. A. Moore). To this list, Culbertson (1988) and Griffiths (1988) would add only a few names—A. Coladarci, A. Halpin, J. Getzels, and M. Scriven and maybe one or two more. Griffiths' leadership in pulling together the theoretical arguments presented in the 1964 NSSE yearbook had been preceded by two decades of scholarly and professional work on questions of theory building and theory application. Even as he was being initially exposed to the logical positivist perspective by Getzels, Coladarci, and Halpin at the 1954 annual meeting of the National Conference of Professors of Educational Administration, he was already the one organizing and moderating the discussion of theory movement ideas. His *Human Relations in School Administration* (1956) was an early call for application of scientific theory principles to educational administration problems, and his 1959 volume, *Administrative Theory*, saw the maturing of his commitment to the application of the logical positivist principles underlying the theory movement. Griffiths was also active in the organization and promotion of the University Council for Educational Administration (UCEA), which was formed in 1954 with support from the Kellogg Foundation to enhance the training of administrators—committed from its inception to the behavioral science approach that came to be known as the theory movement.

Taken together, the essays found in the 1964 NSSE yearbook (Griffiths, 1964) present a view of sweeping confidence in the possibility of progressive reforms flowing from successful theoretical interpretation of educational administration problems and practices. Three central ideas are woven into the diverse chapter themes. First, educational administration, for all of its practical and idiosyncratic elements, was seen as susceptible to systematic empirical inquiry in ways that yield broadly relevant theories of action to improve the educational system. Second, the authors shared the view that administrators working in very diverse types of organizations share a common set of problems and tasks; hence the study of business, government, military, or civic organizations can be expected to yield useful insights into problems confronted by school administrators. Third, unlike the technical focus of the preceding generations of scholars responsible for developing the scientific management and executive leadership approaches to educational administration theory and training, these scholars focused on the social dynamics of group relationships, emphasizing sociological and political theories rather than psychological or engineering approaches to research and analysis.

Beyond its emphasis on the virtues of behavioral science research, the theory movement gained widespread support and legitimacy through organization, publication, and financial support. The formation of the UCEA in 1954 and formal endorsement of the logical positivist conception of science by the National Conference of Professors of Educational Administration have already been mentioned. Far more important than the organizational support provided by these professional associations, however, was the substantial financial support from the Kellogg Foundation that created and sustained the Cooperative Program in Educational Administration (CPEA) at eight of the nation's most prestigious universities. Initially proposed in 1946 by Paul Hanna, Ralph Tyler, and Maurice Seay, this program began supporting advanced graduate studies in five universities in 1950 (Chicago, George Peabody College, Harvard, Texas, and Teachers College at Columbia). Three additional universities (Ohio State, Oregon, and Stanford) joined the program in 1951. This program not only provided graduate student support and research funding, but also created opportunities for interaction among the seminal scholars at these major universities and gave visibility and legitimacy to their call for theoretically grounded research and scholarly analysis of educational organizations and administrative processes.

At the University of Chicago's Midwest Center a new publication, the *Administrator's Notebook*, was created to facilitate dissemination of the theory movement's research findings to professional educators and to scholars in other universities. The *Educational Administration Quarterly*, published by the UCEA, became one of education's most prestigious scholarly journals and thus played a significant role in dissemination of the theory movement perspective. The UCEA also encouraged and supported theory movement scholars, releasing, for example, a collection of papers edited by Andrew Halpin in 1958.

Events in the mainstream political and civic life of the nation also conspired to reinforce the importance of the theory movement with its progressive vision of improved school organizations and smarter educational policy and management decisions. The *Brown v. Board of Education of Topeka* (1954) decisions overturning *de jure* racial segregation in the public schools were followed by deep scientific interest in the nature and extent of social class and racial inequalities in the nation's schools. In his landmark study, *Equality of Educational Opportunity*, James Coleman (1966) brought the most sophisticated research methods available at the time to bear on the most detailed data set yet amassed to try to build a theory of how school, family, and community factors interacted to shape children's life chances. Earlier, the 1957 launching of the Russian Sputnik satellite led quickly to another massive infusion of federal resources and aggressive regulatory activity into the public schools to support the development of new science and mathematics programs—programs built on the presuppositions of the logical positivist conception of science. President Kennedy's executive order of

1960 (Mitchell, 1981) mandating that a percentage of federal money for educational programs be set aside for evaluation of program effectiveness created a cornucopia of fiscal resources and public legitimacy for the theory movement researchers seeking to discover how programs work and what could be done to improve their effectiveness.

By the early 1970s, however, optimism regarding theory-movement-driven reforms began to fade. Rather than explaining how to generate continuous progress, theory movement researchers seemed to find problems to be more intractable than expected. Interracial and interclass achievement gaps could be documented, but not easily overcome. English language fluency rates among new immigrant populations were proving stubbornly slow to change. Special education services were found wanting in both availability and quality. Continuous and highly controversial litigation was required to secure the *Brown v. Board of Education of Topeka* (1954) decision's promises of desegregation. Studies were undertaken to discover when and how social policymakers were (and more frequently were not) utilizing social science research findings to guide their decision making. Rather than producing broad consensus on theories of action, virtually every major research study was greeted with dissenting challenges regarding the adequacy of the data, the appropriateness of the analyses used to summarize it, or the theoretical framework used for its interpretation. One important result of this dissent was, as Nash documented in chapter 1, the creation of frankly partisan research agency "think tanks" tasked with marshalling theory and data in support of particular political interests.

Nor were the schools placid bastions of progressive rationality during this period. The 1960 teacher strike in New York City started a two-decade struggle by teachers (and in some places administrators) to unionize and secure collective bargaining agreements elaborating worker rights and workplace rules. Federal and state policymakers adopted categorical budgeting policies to redirect school expenditures away from local priorities and on to the priorities being established by centralized governments. And local citizen groups were activated to pressure school boards and administrators for implementation (or abandonment) of specific programs or curricular materials, and to prevent (or demand) desegregation plans. Not surprisingly, the Politics of Education, founded by theory movement scholars in 1969, grew within a decade to become the American Educational Research Association's largest special interest group.

By the mid-1970s the epistemological underpinnings of the theory movement came under direct attack. Culbertson (1988, p. 3) cited a provocative paper by Thomas Greenfield (1975) presented at the International Intervisitation Program in Bristol, England as the pivotal event bringing an end to the intellectual dominance of educational administration scholarship by representatives of the theory movement. In his paper entitled "Theory

About Organization: A New Perspective and Its Implications for Schools," Culbertson argued, Greenfield presented "a searching critique of inquiry in educational administration," concluding that "investigators using quantitatively oriented science to study educational organizations were traveling on a deadend highway" (p. 3). Culbertson went on to say that Greenfield's paper:

> argued that educational organizations are not "objective" phenomena regulated by general laws; rather, they are mental constructs that reflect the perceptions and interpretations of their members. Students of organizations should turn their backs, then upon logical positivistic science and adopt interpretive modes of inquiry. (p. 3)

One could certainly find other examples of the rising resistance to the scientific epistemology of the logical positivists, but Greenfield certainly tapped a sensitive nerve and drew Daniel Griffiths into a continuing debate over the merits of the theory movement's central tenets. The result was movement into a new stage of educational administration theory and research.

Stage 4: Institutional Productivity and Theoretical Diversity, 1975 to the Present

By the late 1970s the organizational sociology and the intellectual agenda of the theory movement scholars was not so much intellectually challenged or abandoned as it was overrun by at least three intellectual and political currents that set quite different priorities for research and action. These three powerful forces included: (a) a virtual explosion of theoretical frameworks for interpreting schooling, (b) shock waves of political, economic, and cultural change that challenged the legitimacy as well as the form of public education, and (c) a split between neoconservative political forces embracing the earlier form of Comtean positivism with its promise of proven techniques rather than explanatory theories, and new left forces emphasizing the use of critical theories to expose established power structures and relationships.

Competing Theoretical Frameworks.   By concentrating as it did on the development of alternative theories of school effectiveness, the theory movement opened the way for scholars to advance divergent and competing theories of action to account for the school operations and impacts. Had the progressive vision of continuous improvement held by the founders of the theory movement been realized, this framework would probably have continued to dominate the development of research and policy theories. By

1979, however, the longtime leader of the movement, Daniel Griffiths, recognized that educational administration was in "intellectual turmoil" (Griffiths, 1979, p. 43). His remark came on the heels of the more dramatic assertion made by McCall and Lombardo (1978, p. xi) that:

> It is no secret that the dissatisfaction with results is rampant among social scientists across a wide spectrum of content areas. . . . There is a feeling of disillusionment and an urge to throw the captain overboard. No captain can be found . . . only a yellow document . . . spelling out the canons of experimental science.

And this confession had followed the dramatic epistemological announcement by philosopher of science Karl Popper that "everybody knows nowadays that logical positivism is dead" (cited in Culbertson, 1988, p. 18).

Two intellectual developments were causing a rethinking of the promise of theory-driven scholarship. First, the distinction between professional practice and scholarly inquiry began to be recognized as an intellectual challenge, not just a problem of properly applying research findings to organizational design or managerial decision making. James Coleman (cited in Culbertson, 1988, p. 19) found it important to contrast theory-based with policy-oriented research. He emphasized that policy research is dominated by the "world of action"—that it originates in action and is fed back into action. Theory-driven research, in contrast, originates in a social science discipline and feeds back into the discipline. This means that the findings of policy research tend to shift the balance of political power, enhancing the position of some at the expense of others. Hence, Coleman concluded, policy research is best conducted by agencies free to express their political interests directly, not by universities.

By 1964, Joseph Schwab, a widely respected philosopher of education, was bluntly criticizing as inappropriate the theory movement's conception of science, asserting that it could never provide a proper foundation for either research on human organizations or the training of their leaders. He asserted that only physics had ever managed to utilize the logical positivist framework to advance understanding. The hypothetico-deductive model was, he asserted, "viciously abstract," leading scholars to pursue a "will-of-the-wisp" holy grail that could never provide an adequate interpretation of human actions and organizations (cited in Culbertson, 1988, p. 19).

The second intellectual challenge came from developments in research methodology and theory construction. Anthropological methods of qualitative or interpretive scholarship, utilizing intensive field observation and description of single cases, were widely adopted by the critics of the positivist framework. For many, Harry Wolcott's *The Man in the Principal's Office* (1973) came to represent the kind of richly textured, in-depth study needed to offset the tendency for quantitative, positivist research to gloss over complex affective and meaning-making aspects of administrative work.

As important as the methodological dissents were, however, the dominance of the theory movement framework was even more troubled by the emergence of multiple and largely incompatible approaches to theory construction. Picking up on the work of the Frankfort School, critical theorists brought Marxist and neo-Marxist ideas to the table—insisting that the primary purpose of theory building was to critique established power relations, to identify contradictions in the fabric of social systems, and to coordinate the liberation of individuals and social groups from systems of social dominance and exploitation. Critical theorists insisted that one must begin investigations of social organization and public policy by recognizing the centrality of power relationships, and recognize that societies are divided by race, class, gender, clan, culture, and other social factors that serve to privilege some groups at the expense of others. Social constructionists carried this argument to the point of asserting that the whole idea of utilizing positivist research to identify "real social relations" was impossible and served only to turn researchers utilizing these methods into the handmaidens of established power relations. One result was a breakdown in the capacity of scholars using different critical perspectives to resolve differences in their interpretations of social dynamics. Critical race theorists, for example, made common cause with feminists when it came to critiquing the positivist framework, but otherwise produced quite different explanations of the source and possible strategies for resolving persistent social problems.

Paradigm change—the central idea of Thomas Kuhn's *The Structure of Scientific Revolutions* (1962)—fed into the cacophony of competing theoretical frameworks, making the lack of agreement among competing scholarly interests seem to be the natural result of scientific development, rather than evidence of a serious intellectual crisis. Kuhn's idea was developed in the context of his study of the evolution of theory in the natural sciences. His historical analysis led him to argue that competing conceptual paradigms were characteristic of progress in science and that the competition between paradigms involved social conflicts among groups of scientists as well as intellectual arguments about how best to interpret available data. This idea seemed to justify reliance on clearly incompatible theories and to seek political rather than intellectual vindication for the conclusions they produced.

Social constructionist and postmodern theories went even further, arguing that contemporary social organizations exist as purely symbolic creations, stabilized and sustained by social agreement rather than by any natural laws or physical structures. Hence the social position and political biases of researchers came to be seen as key determinants of the focus of their work and the conclusions they reached. Moreover, the social progressivism of theory movement scholars came to be seen as a crucial defect in their intellectual framework, dooming them to naive misunderstanding of the real dynamics of social conflict and contradiction.

Within the theory movement tradition, the most important development was the reconceptualization of schools as institutions rather than organizations. Beginning with the seminal essay of John Meyer and Brian Rowan (1977), institutional theory evolved to solve two of the most intractable problems undermining confidence in the theory movement's grand design. First, institutional theory argued that social legitimacy is a vital prerequisite to productivity (not just the result of effective and efficient organizational activities). Without legitimacy in the eyes of their members, clients, governing agencies, and attentive publics, institutional theorists argued, schools and other complex social organizations are vulnerable to penetration and disruption of the routines and techniques needed to produce appropriate outcomes. Thus, it became important to recognize and evaluate activities aimed at generating social acceptance and support independent of those devoted to producing expected organizational outcomes.

A second problem finessed through the use of institutional theory was how to incorporate core public values into an analysis of schooling. The logical positivists had eschewed values analysis, and denied that their research would be able to specify what administrators ought to do, leaving this aspect of administrative work up to professional ethics and insights. Institutional theory, in contrast, recognized that organizations are cultural systems with embedded values specifying both the proper relationships among participants and the social purposes of the organizations' activities. Thus, studying institutional value systems and the use of potent symbols to express them acquired a central role in this expanded theory of schooling. Indeed, institutional values form the bedrock on which legitimacy is built and thus are the proper business of institutional leaders. Moreover, changing institutional values leads to changing the logic of organizational production just as fundamentally as do changing technologies, evolving organizational structures, or innovations in program design.

Shock Waves of Political, Economic, and Cultural Change.   As noted earlier, the 1970s, 1980s, and 1990s saw the public schools buffeted by dramatic changes in the larger social order. Social conflicts over race, ethnicity, gender, language, and religion spilled over into school policy debates, and in many communities led to the redirection or termination of administrative careers. Globalization of the economy and of cultural icons and ideals focused attention on the schools as the bulwarks of democracy and prosperity at an unprecedented level of intensity. Federal policy became dramatically more intrusive in the daily lives of school administrators as both the judicial and executive branches raised expectations and threatened sanctions. Initial guidance in the form of desegregation guidelines and National Defense Education Act (1958) support for curriculum development gradually gave way to harsher, more challenging policies aimed at enforcing accountability for attainment of politically adopted goals. Whereas the 1966 Coleman report saw children's achievement and life chances grounded in family and community structures with the schools playing an important role in ameliorating the most debilitating of these conditions, the 1983 *Nation at Risk* report castigated the schools in shrill and harsh terms for mediocre services and little or no accountability for results. By the time the No Child Left Behind Act was passed in 2002, federal policy had moved from trying to articulate goals and support school improvement to a stance of demanding uniformly high performance of all schools and creating a system for dismantling any schools that could not or would not meet expectations. During this same period, a new wave of immigration, and suburbanization of elites and middle-class families left what William Julius Wilson (1987) called "the truly disadvantaged" isolated in the great urban centers of the nation. Industry also tended to abandon the central cities, often seeking lower costs by moving operations to developing countries. The economic function of education began to be seen as more important than its civic functions, with measurable achievement becoming the almost singular yardstick of school quality. In this environment, educators displayed the characteristic American impatience with intellectual complexity and theoretical research agendas. They have increasingly come to see the university as too slow, too inept, and too biased to produce the guidance needed to take effective action.

Neoconservatism Versus the New Left.   The neoconservative political ideology dominating recent federal- and much state-level education policy sees administration as a kind of social engineering activity utilizing technical skill and coercive control systems to secure high performance. This view, as Dorothy Shipps argues in chapter 6 of this volume, can be traced back to the Comtean version of positivism, where the results of research are specifications for action, documentations of "what works," and discoveries that gradually pull back the veil of ignorance and expose the true nature of the "really real." Alternative theories are thought to be unnecessary and misleading, because properly conducted research will uncover the natural and social order of things as they are, just as we might imagine them to be. For its part, the contending new left politics framed by critical and postmodern theories of knowledge has no patience with what is seen as a strategy for domination and an unwillingness of scholars who hold positions of privilege and power to acknowledge their biases and prejudices. Not surprisingly, school administrators are caught in a withering cross-fire. On the one side stand the neoconservatives demanding accountability for results produced by techniques identified using a theory of knowledge that has not been credible in the nation's universities for nearly a century; on the other side are the critical theorists and postmodernists demanding a sensitivity to the domination and exploitation of children presumably documented by applying theories of knowledge to which administrators have not been exposed and that they do not understand.

CONCLUSION

As we come to the end of this review, it may seem that this chapter has been misnamed. We seem to have suggested that administrative knowledge was never very good and that it has tended more to deteriorate than to accumulate or evolve during the most recent stage. The point of this review, however, was to show that educational administration scholars are now able to trace the evolution of their own thinking and to recognize that competent professional practice is informed and transformed more by understanding what counts as useful knowledge than by the individual elements that might constitute a repertoire of reliable research findings. In that regard, the field stands ready to move forward, aware of the alternative claims to knowledge and ready to evaluate their potency in shaping and empowering professional practice. We urge close attention to the analyses provided in the remaining chapters of this volume. Brian Rowan (chap. 3) seeks to rehabilitate the positivist science of the theory movement; Paul Green (chap. 4) introduces us to the unique character of legal knowledge construction; Ronald Heck (chap. 5) and Gail Furman (chap. 6) explore the foundations of administrative theory; Kenneth Wong (chap. 7) and Dorothy Shipps (chap. 8) try to give systematic interpretation to the politics of education; and Douglas Mitchell returns to the central epistemological issues in chapters 9 and 10.

REFERENCES

Adams, C. F., Jr. (1880). The development of the superintendency. *Addresses and Proceedings of the National Educational Association, 18,* 61–76.

Barnard, C. S. (1938). *The functions of the executive.* Cambridge, MA: Harvard University Press.

Brown v. Board of Education of Topeka, 347 U.S. 483 (1954).

Callahan, R. E. (1962). *Education and the cult of efficiency: A study of the social forces that have shaped the administration of the public schools.* Chicago: University of Chicago Press.

Coleman, J. S. (1966). *Equality of educational opportunity.* Washington, DC: U.S. Department of Health, Education, and Welfare, Office of Education.

Comte, A. (1974). *Discours sur l'esprit positif* [Discourse on the positive spirit]. Paris: Librairie Philosophique J. Vrin.

Counts, G. S. (1932). *Dare the school build a new social order?* New York: Harper.

Culbertson, J. (1988). A century's quest for a knowledge base. In N. J. Boyan (Ed.), *Handbook of research on educational administration* (pp. 3–26). New York: Longman.

Dewey, J. (1929). *The sources of a science of education.* New York: Liverright.

Fayol, H. (1944). *General and industrial management.* London: Sir Isaac Pitman & Sons.

Good, H. G. (1956). *A history of American education.* New York: Macmillan.

Greenfield, T. B. (1975). Theory about organization: A new perspective and its implications for schools. In M. G. Hughes (Ed.), *Administering education: International challenge* (pp. 71–99). London: Athlene.

Griffiths, D. E. (1956). *Human relations in school administration.* New York: Appleton-Century-Crofts.

Griffiths, D. E. (1959). *Administrative theory.* New York: Appleton-Century-Crofts.

Griffiths, D. E. (1964). *Behavioral science and educational administration: The 63rd yearbook of the National Society for the Study of Education.* Chicago: University of Chicago Press.

Griffiths, D. E. (1978). Contemporary theory development and educational administration. *Educational Administration, 6*(2), 80–93.

Griffiths, D. E. (1979). Intellectual turmoil in educational administration. *Educational Administration Quarterly, 13*(3), 43–65.

Griffiths, D. E. (1988). Administrative theory. In N. J. Boyan (Ed.), *Handbook of research on educational administration* (pp. 27–51). New York: Longman.

Gulick, L., & Urwick, L. (Eds.). (1937). *Papers on the science of administration.* New York: Institute of Public Administration.

Halpin, A. W. (1958). *Administrative theory in education.* Chicago: Midwest Administration Center.

Henry, N. B. (1946). *Changing conceptions of educational administration: Yearbook of the National Society for the Study of Education, Part 2.* Chicago: University of Chicago Press.

Hoy, W. K., & Miskel, C. G. (1987). *Educational administration: Theory, research, and practice* (3rd ed.). New York: Random House.

Iannaccone, L. (1967). *Politics in education.* New York: Center for Applied Research in Education.

Kuhn, T. S. (1962). *The structure of scientific revolutions.* Chicago: University of Chicago Press.

Lutz, F. W. (2000). Daniel E. Griffiths: He changed an entire profession. *UCEA Review, 51*(3), 1–4.

McCall, M. W., & Lombardo, M. M. (1978). *Leadership: Where else can we go?* Durham, NC: Duke University Press.

McClelland, J. E. (1960). Theory in educational administration. *School Review, 68,* 210–227.

Meyer, J. W., & Rowan, B. (1977). Institutional organization: Formal structure and myth and ceremony. *American Journal of Sociology, 83,* 340–363.

Mitchell, D. E. (1981). *Shaping legislative decisions: Education policy and the social sciences.* Lexington, MA: Lexington Books.

National Defense Education Act, U.S. Congress (PL 85-864, 1958).

No Child Left Behind Act, U.S. Congress (PL 107-110, 2002).

Payne, W. H. (1875). *Chapters on school supervision.* New York: Wilson, Hinkle.

Payne, W. H. (1886). *Contributions to the science of education.* New York: Harper.

Rice, J. M. (1912). *Scientific management in education.* New York: Publishing Printing.

Roethlisberger, F. J., Dickson, W. J., & Wright, H. A. (1939). *Management and the worker: An account of a research program conducted by the Western Electric Company, Hawthorne Works, Chicago.* Cambridge, MA: Harvard University Press.

Simon, H. A. (1945). *Administrative behavior.* New York: Macmillan.

Taylor, F. (1911). *Principles of scientific management.* New York: Harper.

Tyack, D. (1974). *The one best system: A history of American urban education.* Cambridge, MA: Harvard University Press.

Tyack, D., & Hansot, E. (1982). *Managers of virtue: Public school leadership in America: 1820–1980.* New York: Basic Books.

United States. National Commission on Excellence in Education. (1983). *A nation at risk: The imperative for educational reform: A report to the Nation and the Secretary of Education, United States Department of Education.* Washington, DC: The Commission: [Supt. of Docs., U.S. G.P.O. distributor].

Waller, W. (1932). *The sociology of teaching.* New York: Wiley.

Wilson, W. J. (1987). *The truly disadvantaged: The inner city, the underclass, and public policy.* Chicago: University of Chicago Press.

Wolcott, H. (1973). *The man in the principal's office.* New York: Holt, Rinehart, and Winston.

Chapter 3

Truth or Consequences?
Reflections on the Theory Movement
and Its Aftermath in Education

Brian Rowan
University of Michigan

Discussions about educational research and its role in improving practice
tend to revolve around one of two things: truth or consequences. By *truth* I
mean the classic epistemic goal of acquiring justified true belief. By *consequences* I mean the pragmatic goal of using research for the betterment of
practice. There is both optimism and skepticism about these ends in the education literature. On one hand, many researchers embrace the enlightenment view of research—they believe that truthful statements can be arrived
at through systematic research and that such statements can be used to improve educational practice. But many others actively reject this view, questioning the veracity of the justification practices used to generate so-called
scientific knowledge and pointing to the lack of relevance of such knowledge to the improvement of practice. In between these extremes lie a host
of other views as well, as exemplified, for example, by researchers who believe in truth but do not necessarily see its consequences in practice, or researchers who believe in the consequences of research for practice but do
not necessarily search for truth as defined conventionally.

One goal of this chapter is to sort through these varying perspectives.
But in doing so, I want to take a stand on the issues of truth and consequences in educational research by standing with those who initially advocated for a theory movement in educational administration. In doing this, I
argue that: (a) It is possible to create a body of scientific knowledge about
educational practice and (b) that this body of knowledge can be used to
bring about change and improvement in education. In part, the argument I

make is a matter of personal belief, so at the outset of this chapter I make a brief biographical statement to give the reader a sense of the possible biases I bring to thinking about issues of truth and consequences in the field of education. But after that, I also try to make a substantive case that there are many instances where fairly robust truthful statements have been made about educational processes, as well as many cases where scientifically based knowledge has (in fact) resulted in the improvement of practice. The problem I address at the end of this chapter is how to make such results more prevalent, especially in the aftermath of the education paradigm wars. Here, I draw on arguments from the emergent field of social epistemology (Goldman, 2001) to argue that the enterprise of educational research should be organized in society to promote a pluralism of theoretical conceptions that optimize society's chances of discovering truth while at the same time promoting the social good in the field of education.

BACKGROUND

Several years ago, a critical theorist in the field of education advised me that it was good practice to begin my scholarly works by clarifying my structural location in society and stating my possible biases. I assume he advised me of this because he viewed science (and especially social science) as mostly socially rooted ideology. Over the years, I confess that I have largely ignored my colleague's advice. But issues of personal biography seem relevant to the arguments I make in this chapter about truth and consequences in educational research and, as a result, I now take a moment to situate myself socially in the field of education and personally in terms of my commitments to a particular form of research practice.

Let me start by declaring myself to be a descendent of the theory movement in educational administration. To some, this might seem a stretch. I have never been a practicing teacher or administrator in K–12 education, I do not have a degree in educational administration, and I have no track record in writing about or defending the theory movement. Instead, I hold a doctorate in sociology and moved (in mid-career) into a position as a professor of educational administration. But that, in my view, is precisely what makes me a direct descendent of the theory movement, for if it had not been for the theory movement, I almost certainly would not have come to hold my current position as a professor of educational administration. It was the theory movement, as I see it, that encouraged administrators and faculty at the research-oriented universities where I have worked to appoint people like me to faculty positions in education, largely (I assume) because they believed people with social science training actually had something to offer to the field of education.

Being schooled in a social science discipline and moving into a professional school has definitely shaped how I think about educational research. As an undergraduate sociology major with a passion for doing research, I was steered by my mentor into a graduate program in sociology despite wanting to follow my parents into the field of education. So, without a lot of deep thinking, I entered a graduate program in sociology in the 1970s, where I was exposed to a steady diet of Karl Popper-style philosophy of science in which the role of the sociologist was seen as developing theory— complete with covering laws, scope conditions, and so on. Equally important, I was educated by a group of hard-core empiricists committed to quantitative and realist styles of social research. To be sure, I read literature on the sociology of knowledge and other social constructionist lines of work as a graduate student and found myself quite attracted to them. But I also came to the view that one could formulate testable propositions about social phenomena using the standard experimental and quantitative techniques of the day, and that such propositions represented, at least partially, the underlying reality of social phenomena.

It was not until I moved into education that I began to think about the consequences of my commitment to this brand of science for the improvement of practice. After all, the sociology departments where I worked as a young scholar were not much interested in problems of practice. But as I moved into education, I found that all of my education colleagues were committed to the pragmatic goal of improving practice, although only some were equally committed to the advancement of knowledge as I had learned to define it. This was also true of the students I began to teach, most of whom came to graduate school in education with the intention of doing some good by learning more about research and theory in the social sciences. Thus, the education schools where I worked turned out to be very different from the sociology departments where I got my start. In education, I found, researchers had to justify their work not only in terms of its contribution to knowledge, but also in terms of its contribution to the improvement of practice.

Now here is the personal rub. If you are a faculty member in a school of education (or if you are intending such a career), you simply cannot avoid questions about the kind(s) of knowledge you think you are building through your research and how your research is related to the improvement of practice. Students want answers to these questions, administrators evaluate your work on this basis, funding agencies sponsor your research based on the promises you make about these issues, and school administrators, faculty, and parents do not let you do research in their settings until you can give them at least a sense of the kinds of knowledge you seek and how it can be used to improve conditions in schools. As a result, for me, debates about the truth or consequences of educational research have become more than just a scholarly concern. I take the literature on social science and its contribution to educational practice quite personally. If I am not engaged in a search for truth in my own research, what is it that I am engaged in? And if my search for truth has no consequences (other than perhaps satisfying my own passion for doing research), how can I justify my role as teacher, scholar, and fiduciary agent of research sponsors? As a way of starting this chapter, then, let me urge readers to take these same questions seriously. They require more than the usual scholarly jousting. They are central to any scholar's raison d'être.

THE SEARCH FOR TRUTH IN EDUCATION

This brings me to the main body of the chapter. As I am sure most readers know, perspectives on truth in educational research have been debated widely and passionately for more than 20 years. It is beyond the scope of this chapter to review these perspectives in any detail, but the casual reader can browse the back issues of *Educational Researcher* from about 1980 to 1990 (as I did in preparing this chapter) in order to get a quick sense of the perspectives on truth that were advanced in the field of education during this time period.

One way to summarize this literature is as an attack on the fundamental premises of the theory movement in educational administration, as well the theory movements that occurred in the social sciences more broadly.[1] At the base of the theory movement in educational administration (and the social sciences more broadly) was a commitment to a particular view of how to arrive at justified true belief. Truth in this view was arrived at through the development of abstract theories taking the form of universal, lawlike statements with associated scope conditions, where verification of such statements resulted from the use of particular sets of well-established research procedures based on the experimental and quantitative traditions of social science research (Culbertson, 1983). To be sure, the movement was excessive in many respects—overly formalistic in its admiration for hypothetico-deductive schemes, overly ambitious in its monism (it was searching for

---

[1]Another way to view this literature would be as a series of developments in the foundational field of philosophy, paying special attention to developments in the philosophy of science, which became an important nexus of work informing more general discussions about epistemology. The philosophy of science is an intellectually exciting field, and one from which many of the arguments and criticisms of the theory movement reviewed here were drawn. But it would be a bit distracting in the present chapter to review the scope of these philosophical arguments in depth, or to take apart the exact philosophical underpinnings of each argument about how to do social research that I review. For a sense of the complexity involved in the underlying philosophical arguments, see Phillips (1983).

"the" theory of administration), and probably not attentive enough to the relationships of theory to practice (see, again, Culbertson). But the core commitments of the movement—to build theory, do empirical research, and thereby arrive at "justified true belief" in the area of educational administration—have been endorsed by many researchers past and present.

However, in the 1970s and 1980s, attacks on these core commitments were launched from a number of directions. One was social constructionism, as for example in Greenfield's (1975) classic attack on the theory movement in educational administration. Here, knowledge was seen as socially constructed and therefore nothing more than what was believed or institutionalized in particular communities, cultures, or social contexts at particular historical points in time. On this view, the truth is nothing more than what is believed, and the job of social researchers is to reconstruct how particular individuals, in particular settings, arrive at such beliefs, because the presence of some underlying, objective reality can never be found apart from its social interpretation.[2]

A related attack on the theory movement was launched by scholars intent on justifying the use of case studies in educational research. One aspect of this attack involved advocacy for qualitative research methods as the best means of understanding situated beliefs and actions, a position having a close kinship to the phenomenological attack just discussed. But another part of the attack was directed at the notion that science could develop highly generalized, lawlike statements. On this view, each local setting is uniquely constituted and operates according to its own set of determining processes. As a result, there is little sense in trying to formulate highly generalized covering laws of the form "x causes y" because the relationship of x to y will vary across each unique case in a sample, and perhaps even within the same case over time (for a form of this argument, see Tilly, 1984). A similar line of attack was developed in psychology by Cronbach (1975), who argued that relationships among variables in real-world settings typically de-

---

[2]A major problem confronting this version of social constructionism is the problem of how to know when one has developed a satisfactory account of others' beliefs. For, if all knowledge is nothing more than situated belief, and if we can never establish when or if beliefs are true, then we face the problem in social research of not having any way at all of verifying whether a particular account of situated beliefs is trustworthy. Harvey Siegel (1982) called this the "impotence" of relativism. Many proponents of the phenomenological approach in educational research recognize this problem, and they have addressed it in various ways. Some, like Guba and Lincoln (1981), tried to formulate some principles for qualitative research that parallel concerns with internal validity, reliability, and so forth found in quantitative research (see also Miles & Huberman, 1984). Others, like Eisner (1979), advocated for a view of educational research as an "artistic" endeavor where taste is the major way to adjudicate the virtues and utility of particular pieces of research. And scholars like Peshkin (2000) simply admitted of the uncertainties of their methodological approach, arguing in essence that the commendability of an interpretive account is ultimately in the beholder's eye.

pend on many other aspects of a social situation and are thus modified by complex interactions. Moreover, Cronbach believed that such relationships are characterized by extreme temporal instability so that the half-life of any lawlike statement is incredibly short. In this situation, Cronbach saw the search for general covering laws in psychology as fruitless.

Yet another critique sought to undermine the value-neutrality assumption lying at the core of the various theory movements in the social sciences. By setting themselves up to search for truth, this argument goes, educational researchers have assumed that there is a form of belief that can be separated from one's class or social position. In this attack, an interest-free or value-neutral view of knowledge is explicitly rejected through the argument that knowledge is never free of interest and through the assertion that, for the most part, mainstream educational research has been captured by or developed in the service of powerful interests and used to perpetuate inequality. This is both a radical attack on the very possibility of achieving justified true belief, and an argument about the inherent bounding of all knowledge within particular historic structures with specific arrays of interests (for a good discussion of this view, see Ladwig, 1996, chaps. 4 and 5).[3]

A final assault on the theory movement came in the form of arguments about the multiple forms of knowledge that might exist in a profession like teaching, and a renewal of the classical philosophers' concerns with differences between abstract and theoretical knowledge on one hand, and practical and craft forms of knowledge on the other. Here, a number of observers have remarked on the incommensurability of these different forms of knowledge, the implication being that scientific knowledge (characterized by its general and abstract nature) cannot be applied to a given practice even after progressive specification and conditionalizing. That is because practical knowledge contains its own logic of truth, and because such knowledge involves qualitatively different forms of understanding than scientific knowledge (for such arguments, see Fenstermacher, 1994; Kessels & Korthagen, 1996). Here, then, we see a qualitative break in the relationship of theory to practice, one that many critics argue is essentially unbridgeable.

This brief review does little justice to several features of the debate that occurred in education and other social sciences from the 1970s onward. It

---

[3]The philosophical arguments lying behind this view are well known, but as Ladwig (1996) noted, they were not explicitly stated by critics in the field of education. Nevertheless, it is Ladwig's view that the radical sociologists of education whom he discussed based their philosophy on Kuhn's (1962) discussion of scientific paradigms, where paradigms are seen as carried by specific groups and as containing fundamental assumptions that are metaphysical in nature (i.e., beyond verification). In Ladwig's view, however, radical sociologists cannot test this idea, because they see all research (including their own) as being at its core an ideological enterprise. For a contrasting, and empiricist, view of critical sociology, however, see Liston (1988).

fails to capture the sheer volume of activity in this area, the sometimes vitriolic and always passionate tenor of the debate, and the stunning uncertainties it raised about the search for truth in the social sciences. In the field of education, moreover, the debate had lasting effects. It launched a new era of theoretical pluralism, gave rise to an expanding set of legitimized inquiry practices, produced new journals and special interest groups in the field, created new political divides to be traversed by faculty and students, expanded the curriculum of education schools to the breaking point, and raised fundamental questions about how to adjudicate the value of particular pieces of research submitted to journals or as part of tenure bids by faculty. In short, it brought into question the unbounded faith of the theory movement in a unified science of administration.

THE CONSEQUENCES OF EDUCATIONAL RESEARCH FOR PRACTICE

At the same time as the theory movement experienced setbacks in its version of what it means to discover truth in education, it also suffered a withering attack on its ability to produce consequences for educational change and improvement. By the 1990s, in fact, it was widely argued that educational research had an "awful" reputation—in the eyes of practicing educators, in the eyes of policymakers and government funding agencies, and in the eyes of the public at large (for documentation, see Kaestle, 1993). Thus, it was concluded that education research was of little consequence to education practice.

How did this situation arise? Researchers often blamed the situation on their lack of voice in the formation of education policy. As Guthrie (1990) noted, after a decade of school reform activities in the United States, "no one . . . outside of isolated school of education faculty members and a few employees of research-oriented institutions has proclaimed a future role or made a forceful case for significantly expanding educational research and development" despite the fact that "throughout most of American society, scientific and technological research is viewed as an important strategic consideration in restoring the nation economically and securing its future" (p. 27). On this view, educational researchers have been given few chances to demonstrate that they can translate their findings into effective practices, largely because the policy system responds to political and other pressures, giving only passing notice to researchers and their discovered truths.

There are plenty of reasons, however, to think that educational researchers are (at least partly) responsible for the awful reputation of educational research and its divorce from practice. For example, many observers have remarked on the constant bickering among researchers over what is true in the vast body of educational research. In part, such bickering reflects the fact that there is fragmentation, jealously, and competition among researchers in the so-called production of knowledge, all of which leads to a certain amount of chest pounding and put-downs among members of the research establishment. But disagreements among researchers also reflect the fact that many researchers committed to the theory-building, empiricist agendas want to apply only the most justified knowledge to the improvement of practice and believe that some knowledge claims have more or less of a warrant than others. Under these conditions, it is not surprising to find the public and its policymakers taking the view that for every study demonstrating a point, another study can be found contravening that fact (Cooper, 1996). Science is in fact contested terrain, and its arcane machinery is often not well presented to or understood by the public.

But even when there is a great deal of scientific consensus in a domain of educational research, the bickering among scientists often continues. A particularly striking example has occurred in the area of reading research, where scientific research of the sort advocated by the theory movement has been conducted for over 100 years, and where a strong consensus exists among researchers about the elements of effective early childhood reading programs. In this domain, there recently occurred several vitriolic exchanges among researchers who, as far as I can tell, agreed at every substantive point about how to design an effective reading program, but nevertheless engaged in intense bickering about how this research has been interpreted by and communicated to individuals in the policy and practice communities (see Allington & Woodside-Jiron, 1998; Foorman, Fletcher, Francis, & Schatschneider, 2000; Mathes & Torgeson, 2000; Taylor, Anderson, Au, & Raphael, 2000).

Finally, educational researchers themselves actively developed some damning arguments about the irrelevance of educational research to the improvement of practice. During the 1970s and 1980s, for example, a number of studies concluded that "scientifically based" educational innovations are never faithfully implemented in schools. Thus, the Follow-Through demonstration project, which looked closely at the implementation and effectiveness of several early childhood education programs in schools, was seen as demonstrating (quite conclusively) that the variation in program implementation existing among schools implementing the same program was actually larger than the variation that occurred across schools implementing different programs. In the same vein, the RAND change-agent study gave rise to a view of innovation as mutual adaptation, which sees local teachers and administrators inevitably altering a particular innovation almost beyond recognition in order to suit local needs. Both these views were reinforced by arguments about the inherently conservative nature of educational practitioners (who resist reform), and about the loosely coupled nature of educational organizations (which adopt plenty of innovations, but only ceremonially), and by historical arguments about the ephemeral and cyclic nature of most education reforms. By the 1980s, then, most theorizing in education was bent on explaining why scientifically based reforms did not work in practice, rather than finding the conditions under which they did.

THE COUNTER-ATTACK

If, at this point, you have concluded that the theory movement died (without going to heaven), I will forgive you. But the simple fact is that advocates of the theory movement in education had strong allies (inside and outside the academy) and fought an effective rear-guard action from the 1970s through the 1990s, managing, by the year 2000, to have established once again a very strong (if not dominating) position in the field of educational research. If you doubt this assertion, explain to me why current federal education laws and many state court decisions now require local schools to adopt "scientifically based" educational practices, why there is now increased attention to and funding of large-scale randomized field trials in education, why the federal government's once moribund "joint dissemination review panel" that convened panels of researchers to distribute money to "educational programs that work" has been reincarnated in the recently established "what works" clearinghouse in education, and why this clearinghouse places a premium on screening the effectiveness of educational programs using criteria that only the most committed empiricist could love? Also explain why the National Academy of Education, the National Research Council, and the National Research Policies and Priorities Board all have launched major activities to define the role of educational research in improving educational practice. Does it make sense to assume that these developments signal the triumph of critical theorists in the field of education, or the triumph of phenomenologists, case study advocates, loose coupling theorists, and so on? I rather doubt it.

So how could the theory movement have survived the withering critique it was subjected to for more than 20 years and rationalized the continuing search for truth? One way was by carefully marshalling evidence of its successes. Particularly noteworthy in this regard are the kinds of arguments empiricists like Gage (1996; Gage & Needels, 1989) made about the scientific yield and practical impact of education research. Over the years, Gage and others have argued (quite persuasively in my view) that educational research has discovered hundreds of statistically significant and substantively important empirical relationships between educational processes and student outcomes, that these relationships can be treated as main effects in research using the general linear model, and that when such research is done, main effects are not overwhelmed by interaction effects. Moreover, as Gage and others have shown, when knowledge of these relationships is used to design interventions that are put into practice in classrooms, research-based interventions end up having substantial impacts on teaching practice and student learning.

Gage (1996) was not alone in his defense of the knowledge generated by educational researchers. During Robert Donmoyer's term as editor of *Educational Researcher*, for example, panels of past American Educational Research Association (AERA) presidents were convened to comment on the future of educational research. For the most part, each of these presidents asserted that we "know" a great deal about education in K–12 schools, and most meant by this that education had accumulated the kind of knowledge that the theory movement set out to construct long ago. This might not be surprising given the careers of AERA presidents, which were built mostly during the reign of the theory movement. But even as arch an enemy of the education research establishment as Chester Finn (1988, p. 8), widely credited for attempting to disembowel the federal education research infrastructure (Kaestle, 1993), was moved in an essay entitled "What Ails Education Research" to point to 10 areas "where research is likely to make a significant impact on school and classroom practices over the next five years."

Add to this rosy picture the recent sea change in researchers' views about the possibility that research-based innovations can positively impact educational practice. There is an emerging consensus among those currently studying school improvement efforts that educational reform initiatives do have real and positive impacts on educational practice when certain conditions prevail. Among these are that the innovations are properly specified (not vaguely defined such as those enacted in the Follow-Through demonstration), that real incentives and sanctions are put into place to encourage faithful implementation of designs, that sustained attempts are made to provide teachers with the professional development they need to implement new practices, and that all of this takes place in a coherent—as opposed to fragmented—system of educational governance (for good discussions of this perspective, see Cohen & Ball, 2000; Cohen & Hill, 2001; Cohen & Spillane, 1992).[4]

---

[4]A large-scale study I am conducting of the design, implementation, and instructional effectiveness of three of America's largest Comprehensive School Reform programs has led me to a similar conclusion. In this study, we are finding that school reform programs with the most specified designs and most intensive professional development activities are indeed producing changes in teaching practice and improved student achievement. Moreover, these are not short-term effects. Changes in teaching practice and improvement in student achievement appear to occur quickly and to be sustained over a number of years in the schools undertaking well-specified programs in our study, largely as a result of intensive professional development.

The theory movement has survived as a result of other developments as well. For one, it has been remarkable in its ability to absorb and incorporate attacking factions. Thus, qualitative and case study researchers have been folded into many empiricist research programs, and a lively literature showing how qualitative researchers can develop theory-building and theory-testing strategies of the sort advocated by the theory movement has developed to justify the use of cross-site case studies in theory-confirming, empiricist research (Firestone & Herriot, 1983; Miles & Huberman, 1984). There also exists a burgeoning literature on "design experiments" and their use in adapting theories to practice and in developing research-based intervention programs that can be brought to scale in more than one locality (Shavelson & Towne, 2003).

Advances in statistical methods also have helped to bolster the theory movement. Empiricists in education now have at their disposal meta-analysis techniques that allow them to move beyond subjective literature reviews and to present a formal, statistical analysis of theoretical assertions aggregated across numerous studies. There also have been important advances in empiricists' understanding of how to make valid causal inferences. The logic of causal analysis has been more clearly stated, the importance of randomization to the efficient building of knowledge claims asserted, and the development of more careful techniques for making causal inferences in studies lacking random assignment developed and put into wider use. All of this leads quantitative, empirical researchers beyond the older warning that "correlation does not imply causation" toward more forceful claims of causal connections in educational research.

Finally, the theory movement seems to have been aided by a noticeable détente in the paradigm wars that wracked education for more than 20 years. To be sure, many and varied views exist about the kinds of scholarship available to educators and how these can be used to inform education practice. But explications of new theoretical and empirical logics no longer seem to include what was once the obligatory attack on the theory movement. Apparently, we have learned to live with differences in perspectives that we cannot make commensurate.

NEXT STEPS IN THE THEORY MOVEMENT

If the theory movement survived (and benefited from) two decades worth of attacks, it still faces serious challenges as an approach to building knowledge and improving educational practice. Some of these challenges arise from the altered landscape of educational research—particularly the emergence and growing acceptance of theoretical and methodological pluralism. But another challenge arises from the growing recognition that educational research (like all science) is a public good, not just the private practice of cognitive agents using well-established justification procedures in a relatively unfettered search for the truth. Indeed, how to adjudicate scientists' competing claims to scarce resources in an era of theoretical and methodological pluralism and to do so in ways that optimize both the search for truth and the public good are pressing issues, not only in education, but in the broader fields of science and technology at large.[5]

The theory movement in education never anticipated or addressed these issues, however. Nor, in my view, has the writing about paradigm wars in education come up with any strong advice about what to do in light of theoretical and methodological pluralism in the field, or more to the point, tried to relate this problem to a conception of educational research as public good. For example, almost everyone in education today recognizes the fact of theoretical pluralism, but few have articulated a cogent perspective on what to do about it. Should we seek to reconcile competing perspectives or encourage their growth? In doing so, how are we to judge each perspective's contribution to society's efforts to find the truth, especially if each perspective presents different, and partial, representations of reality? Moreover, how can we allocate scarce research dollars to researchers with competing theoretical agendas in ways that not only advance the truth, but also produce a socially just net social benefit?

In this closing section, I make some comments about these issues. I begin with the question of how researchers predisposed to search for the truth in education in ways consistent with the original aims of the theory movement can accommodate the rise of theoretical and methodological pluralism in educational research. One place to start, it seems to me, is with a renunciation of theoretical monism—for example, the idea that we are searching for "the" theory of administration, and the further claim that this theory should somehow be congruent with other theories of educational phenomena so as to form a kind of unity of science embedded within a hierarchy of theories about education. Many scholars in the philosophy of science are working against this view of science, in part by likening theories and explanations to maps. On this newer view, theories aiming to explain

---

[5]In recent years, the field of social epistemology has grown up to address these questions (for a review, see Goldman, 2001). In this chapter, I focus on the issues addressed in recent works by Kitcher (2001) and Longino (2002a), which address the problem of how to assure that science is conducted for the public good in an era of theoretical pluralism. As a broader enterprise, however, social epistemology addresses many other issues that are relevant to improving educational research. Broadly construed, social epistemology takes up the problem of how to organize science so that there is an increased chance of generating truth. In this regard, organizational problems emerge at many different levels of the social system and there is a discussion of many different problems that are directly relevant to questions about what ails educational research and what to do about them in ways that are comparable with the aims of the theory movement.

the same phenomena can end up being likened to maps of the same territory drawn up from different projections. They represent only a partial description of the target phenomena, and they do so from particular perspectives. In taking this view, there is no need to give up the idea of research (or science) as a search for truth (or the associated use of established verification procedures), nor must we forego our interest in formulating true statements that have practical consequences. Indeed, in taking this view we still need to carefully and rigorously assess the verification status of different theoretical perspectives, and there is room for critical experiments that seek to develop differential predictions from two or more theoretical perspectives, allowing their verification status to be tested against one another. But in this view, we are also admitting that fundamentally true and useful theoretical or explanatory statements can be made from a number of different perspectives that cannot be reconciled (at least for now, and perhaps for the foreseeable future).[6]

All of this accommodates a measure of theoretical pluralism in education research—even admitting into the scientific research community theoretical programs that are qualitative, phenomenologically oriented, and critically oriented, so long as these programs are conducted according to a verificationist agenda.[7] But now the question becomes which of the many competing perspectives we should encourage, especially in light of scarce resources for research. The classic answer in the philosophy of science was to use relevance criteria in assessing the worthiness of research programs— that is, to evaluate the contribution of research programs to the advancement of knowledge, where such advancement involved a steady and easily charted march toward a unified compendium of laws. On this view, science generated its own pressing problems as old theories came under challenge from new observations and as new theories were put into action to resolve these inconsistencies.

But purely scientific relevance seems difficult (if not impossible) to judge in domains where there are multiple theoretical agendas of roughly equal epistemic significance. So here is where the idea of consequences enters into the argument. I return again to the metaphor of theories as maps. Maps have both epistemic significance—they are either correct or incorrect descriptions of territory—and practical significance—some projections are

---

[6]It should be noted that this last assertion raises some sticky issues related to the commensurability of theoretical perspectives that trouble at least some epistemologists (see, e.g., the exchange between Kitcher, 2002, and Longino, 2002b).

[7]One could, I suppose, admit perspectives lacking a verificationist agenda into the community as well, for example, by including the kinds of qualitative, case study, and critical analyses that explicitly reject the possibility of finding truth. But this reduces the social sciences to social criticism. Although I admit there is value to such perspectives, for the moment I exempt these perspectives from my definition of science, which demands truth seeking.

useful for some purposes, whereas other projections are useful for other purposes. On this view of theory building, there is no way of "shielding epistemic significance from practical significance" in scientific endeavors, because representations of social phenomena, like maps, have both (Longino, 2002a, p. 3). So, an alternative way to examine the relevance of theories to the advancement of science is to assess particular theories in terms of their practical aims in addition to examining their scientific yield and promise.[8]

But now we have stumbled on the sticky problem of admitting value considerations into the realm of science. For it seems quite plausible that the worth of any set of practical aims is far from universal, varying instead across groups in different social situations (i.e., different social classes, ethnic groups, political parties, or any of a host of other interest groups we might consider). For those whose careers were formed in the era of scientific autonomy, where the goal of social agencies was to sponsor nondirected research—that is, research subjected only to the scrutiny of the scientific community—the admission of social significance into scientific deliberations is perhaps threatening.[9] But what is needed is a way to bring values and practical aims into scientific deliberations in ways that simultaneously produce good science and social justice in the achievement of practical aims. This surely will not be easy.

So, how can we think about building such a system of science? Kitcher (2001), following the lead of several other social philosophers, drew on democratic theory to discuss this process. He argued for creating a deliberative process that fully (and in his view, proportionally) represents diverse interests, involves the open deliberation of preferences among decision

---

[8]Even in a world of theoretical pluralism, it should be possible to screen competing theoretical agendas in terms of their scientific yield and promise. We can ask, for example, as we generally do in grant applications, what past findings have been generated by a theory, and what the likely yield to knowledge will be of funding continued work in the area. Thus, the argument I am making does not ignore the problem of epistemic significance in scientific work so much as conflate it with practical significance. Put differently, in a situation where two competing perspectives make a strong case for epistemic significance, an additional criterion that can be used for judging their worth would be practical significance.

[9]Some educational researchers, for example, surely will recall the era when Republicans introduced a "two-tiered" system of review into the Office of Educational Research and Improvement's grants programs. The basic idea was that the first tier of review consisted only of a review of the scientific merits of a proposal conducted by the scientific community, and the second and final tier admitted considerations of practical significance into deliberations through the inclusion of nonscientists on review panels. Many educational researchers (myself included) found this procedure totally unacceptable, and from personal experience on the final review panels, I also saw how flawed this system was. As I discuss later, however, the main flaws were (following Kitcher, 2001) failures of representation and the tyranny of ignorance. As I discuss later, these flaws (in principle, at least) might be overcome in a well-ordered scientific community.

makers whose preferences have been tutored, and makes decisions based on a calculation of net social benefit in a Rawlsian sense. Such a system, he admitted, must guard against several problems, including inadequate representation (i.e., the exclusion of some interests from deliberations), the tyranny of ignorance (in which decision makers or those they represent have little ability to examine issues of epistemic import), false consciousness (where deliberations cater to a social benefit that does not advance science), and parochial application (where many competing theoretical programs could contribute equally to a pressing problem, but only a few are selected). Though utopian, this view at least presents some criteria for building a system of scientific activity that addresses the advancement of both epistemic and practical aims in research.

More to the point, the well-ordered system of science that Kitcher (2001) outlined seems more sophisticated and socially responsive than the agenda drawn up in the early days of the theory movement in education. Whereas science was once seen as the exclusive province of value-neutral cognitive agents working toward a unified theory of education in ways that were insulated from social control, we have here a vision of scientific activity that seems far more suited to the situation of educational research in a post-paradigm-wars era. This newer view admits of multiple research programs and perspectives, incorporates an interest in both truth and consequences, and presents an overtly democratic vision of scientific decision making that opens the door to critical reflection and action as regards the use of science to further particular interests.

What remains, in my view, is for those researchers who embrace the goals of truth and consequences in educational research to begin to take steps to implement this vision. This involves tutoring the public, policymakers, and ourselves about the processes and aims of educational research (in its search for both truth and consequences). It also involves active scrutiny of scientific governance, and especially constant vigilance and positive actions to guard against the governance flaws that Kitcher (2001) outlined and to build a democratic community of scientific decision makers. And, finally, it involves a recognition by educational researchers that their own role as cognitive agents seeking the truth should be governed socially, for educational researchers are producing a public good and, in a democratic society, should be committed to social justice.

REFERENCES

Allington, R. L., & Woodside-Jiron, H. (1998, Spring). Decodable text in beginning reading: Are mandates and policy based on research? *ERS Spectrum*, Spring, 3–11.

Cohen, D. K., & Ball, D. L. (2000). *Instruction and innovation: Reconsidering the story*. Consortium for Policy Research in Education, Study of Instructional Improvement. Ann Arbor: University of Michigan.

Cohen, D. K., & Hill, H. K. (2001). *Learning policy: When state education reform works.* New Haven, CT: Yale University Press.

Cohen, D. K., & Spillane, J. P. (1992). Policy and practice: The relations between governance and instruction. *Review of Research in Education, 18* 1–49.

Cooper, H. (1996). Speaking power to truth: Reflections of an educational researcher after 4 years of school board service. *Educational Researcher, 25*(1), 29–34.

Cronbach, L. J. (1975). Beyond the two disciplines of scientific psychology. *American Psychologist, 30,* 116–127.

Culbertson, J. (1983). Theory in educational administration: Echoes from critical thinkers. *Educational Researcher, 12*(10), 15–22.

Eisner, E. (1979). *The educational imagination.* New York: Macmillan.

Fenstermacher, G. D. (1994). The knower and the known: The nature of knowledge in research on teaching. *Review of Research in Education, 20,* 3–56.

Finn, C. E. (1988). What ails education research. *Educational Researcher, 17*(1), 5–8.

Firestone, W. A., & Herriot, R. E. (1983). The formalization of qualitative research: An adaptation of soft science to the policy world. *Evaluation Review, 7,* 437–466.

Foorman, B. R., Fletcher, J. M., Francis, D. J., & Schatschneider, C. (2000). Response: Misrepresentation of research by researchers. *Educational Researcher, 29*(6), 27–37.

Gage, N. (1996). Confronting counsels of despair for the behavioral sciences. *Educational Researcher, 25*(3), 5–12, 22.

Gage, N. L., & Needels, M. C. (1989). Process-product research on teaching: A review of the criticisms. *Elementary School Journal, 89,* 253–300.

Goldman, A. (2001). Social epistemology. In *Stanford encyclopedia of philosophy* Retrieved October 22, 2004, from http://plato.stanford.edu/entries/epistemology-social

Greenfield, T. B. (1975). Theory about organization: A new perspective and its implication for schools. In M. Hughes (Ed.), *Administering education: International challenge* (pp. 71–99). London: Athlone Press.

Guba, E. G., & Lincoln, Y. S. (1981). *Effective evaluation.* San Francisco: Jossey-Bass.

Guthrie, J. W. (1990). Education R&D's lament (and what to do about it). *Educational Researcher, 19*(2), 26–34.

Kaestle, C. F. (1993). The awful reputation of education research. *Educational Researcher, 22*(1), 23–31.

Kessels, J. P. A., & Korthagen, F. A. J. (1996). The relationship between theory and practice: Back to the classics. *Educational Researcher, 25*(3), 17–23.

Kitcher, P. (2001). *Science, truth, and democracy.* New York: Oxford University Press.

Kitcher, P. (2002). The third way: Reflections on Helen Longino's *The Fate of Knowledge. Philosophy of Science, 69,* 549–559.

Kuhn, T. (1962). *The structure of scientific revolutions.* Chicago: University of Chicago Press.

Ladwig, J. G. (1996). *Academic distinctions: Theory and methodology in the sociology of school knowledge.* London: Routledge.

Liston, D. (1988). *Capitalist schools: Explanations and ethics in radical studies of schooling.* London: Routledge.

Longino, H. E. (2002a). *The fate of knowledge.* Princeton, NJ: Princeton University Press.

Longino, H. E. (2002b). Science and the common good: Thoughts on Philip Kitcher's *Science, Truth, and Democracy. Philosophy of Science, 69,* 560–568.

Mathes, P. G., & Torgeson, J. K. (2000). A call for equity in reading instruction for all students: A response to Allington and Woodside-Jiron. *Educational Researcher, 29*(6), 4–16.

Miles, M. W., & Huberman, A. M. (1984). *Qualitative data analysis: A sourcebook of new methods.* Beverly Hills, CA: Sage.

Peshkin, A. (2000). The nature of interpretation in qualitative research. *Educational Researcher, 29*(9), 5–10.

Phillips, D. C. (1983). After the wake: Postpositivistic educational thought. *Educational Researcher, 12*(5), 4–12.

Shavelson, R., & Towne, L. (Eds.). (2002). *Scientific research in education.* Washington, DC: National Academies Press.

Siegel, H. (1982). Relativism refuted. *Educational Philosophy and Theory, 14*(2), 47–50.

Taylor, B. M., Anderson, R. C., Au, K. H., & Raphael, T. E. (2000). Discretion in the translation of research to policy: A case from beginning reading. *Educational Researcher, 29*(6), 16–25.

Tilly, C. (1984). *Big structures, large processes, and huge comparisons.* New York: Russell Sage.

Chapter 4

Legal Inquiry and Equal Opportunity

Paul Green
University of California, Riverside

> *Brown I itself did not need to rely upon any psychological or social-science research in order to announce the simple, yet fundamental truth that the government cannot discriminate among its citizens on the basis of race. . . . As the Court's unanimous opinion indicated: "In the field of public education the doctrine of 'separate but equal' has no place. Separate educational facilities are inherently unequal." . . . At the heart of this interpretation of the Equal Protection Clause lies the principle that the government must treat citizens as individuals, and not as members of racial, ethnic or religious groups. It is for this reason that we must subject all racial classifications to the strictest scrutiny.*
> —*Justice Clarence Thomas quoted in Missouri v. Jenkins* (1995, p. 78)

The Supreme Court interpretations of Fourteenth Amendment equal protection principles have provoked some of the most interesting debates over constitutional law in our nation's history. One allegation frequently voiced is that the Court, in recent years, has abandoned the American ideal of equal opportunity and has embraced the goal of securing more "equal results" in the distribution of social wealth and opportunity among citizens. A classic essay by scholar Daniel Bell (1972) mapped out the logic of this fashionable claim. "What is today at stake is the redefinition of equality," he argued dramatically. The principle of equality of opportunity, which once was the primary weapon for changing the nation's social system, "is now seen as leading to a new hierarchy," one requiring "the reduction of all inequality, or the creation of *equality of result* in income, status, and power for all men in society" (p. 40).

Some scholars have concluded that the theory of equal results has, in fact, come to dominate judicial policy. The commitment to affirmative action that now prevails in public life, argued Robert K. Fullinwider, "is really a conception of equal results applied to groups" (1980, p. 110). Favorable in their attitude toward it, some liberals have accepted this characterization of trends in constitutional interpretation by the high court (Jencks, 1972). Those who press this claim are often conservatives critical of legal decisions interpreted as expanding government authority over marketplace freedoms. They purport to speak on behalf of citizens who are alleged to have never suffered any legal injury. The conservative analyst Thomas Sowell exclaimed, "Many Americans who supported the initial thrust of civil rights . . . [have] felt betrayed as the original concept of equal individual opportunity evolved toward the concept of equal group results" (1984, p. 37).

Conservative scholars like Sowell have hardly been alone in advancing this charge. Conservative political actors at every level—judges, bureaucrats, elected officials—have decried those trends as unjust, imprudent, socialistic, and, in Chief Justice Rehnquist's words, even "Orwellian." During the Ronald Reagan administration, federal pundits aimed to eliminate these purportedly harmful policies and return to more traditional conceptions of equal opportunity as the guiding light for public policy. "We offer opportunity at the starting line of life, but no compulsory tie for everyone at the finish," President Reagan pledged for over three decades (Wills, 1979, p. 223). In fact, Attorney General Edwin Meese made opposition to the allegedly prevailing judicial goal of equal results one of the most important priorities of his tenure: "We are battling for the moral principle of equality that has guided our political thinking since we began as a nation. . . . What we seek is a true equality *before* the law; not a distorted and unattainable equality by the law" (Meese, 1985, p. 14).

Their claims appeared to be on solid ground in at least one sense. American political thought has confirmed the near canonical status of the equal opportunity ethic in our inherited national creed (Dorn, 1979; Fishkin, 1983; Pole, 1978; Racowski, 1991). After all, equality of opportunity was the animating ideal behind democracy in the United States about which Alex de Tocqueville (1988) so eloquently wrote during the Republic's early years. Indeed, that ethic was passionately advocated by the most influential antebellum political leaders, such as Thomas Jefferson, Andrew Jackson, and Abraham Lincoln. The key promise of capitalist expansion into the western territories praised by each was, to quote Lincoln, "to afford all an unfettered chance, and a fair chance, in the race of life" (cited in Williams, 1957, p. 162). The dramatic revolution wrought by the corporatization of social production in the post–Civil War decades ironically only intensified the appeal of the ethic. "We owe it to each other to guarantee rights," insisted social theorist William Graham Sumner. "Rights should be equal, because they pertain to chances, and all ought to have equal chances so far as chances are provided or limited by the action of society" (1974, p. 141).

This same public pledge to make good on, or at least do better for, the dream of greater and more equal opportunity was invoked by Franklin Delano Roosevelt to sanctify the New Deal social contract over a half-century later: "If the average citizen is guaranteed equal opportunity in the polling place, he must have equal opportunity in the market place" (cited in Wills, 1979, p. 223). Yet, despite a sharp decline in support for political liberalism, the equal opportunity ethic has continued to animate main-stream politics. The recent conservative interpretations of the equal oppor-tunity ethic as being in opposition to equality of results are built on a long-established tradition in the United States (Friedman, 1985).

This chapter's primary focus is to discuss the means by which claims about constitutional doctrine are created and sustained. The objective is to examine the conceptual foundations of what the Supreme Court has said about equal protection principles and the implications of those legal ideas for challenging social inequality. The chapter's central thesis is that popu-lar allegations that judicial intent has been to interpret the Fourteenth Amendment as mandating more equal results, however rhetorically power-ful, are conceptually confused and interpretively inaccurate. The argument is organized into three sections. First, a brief exploration of the place of fact in a world of judgment is provided. This exploration shows that separating questions of fact from questions of law obscures their social connections and distorts the understanding of both. The second section discusses in for-mal analytical terms the primary concepts of equality, opportunity, and re-sults within the larger framework of arguments concerning the principles of distributive justice. The third section applies these understandings to an analysis of modern constitutional equal protection doctrine as it has evolved primarily in race, ethnicity, and sex discrimination cases. The aim in this discussion is to demonstrate that prevailing constitutional construc-tions contain a very narrow range of equal opportunity ideals and almost no concern for unequal results. The concluding section reflects on the impli-cations of this analysis for understanding and challenging the linkages of law, politics, and social opportunity in modern America.

LAW AND SOCIAL INQUIRY

The substantive argument about Fourteenth Amendment principles ad-vanced here relies on an "ideological" approach to legal analysis (Brigham, 1984; Friedman, 1985; Kelly, 1992; Scheingold, 1974). In this view, constitu-tional lawmaking is understood as neither the neutral application of objec-tive rules nor the subjective opinions of individual judges. Rather, the focus is on general, open-ended, but rationally bounded traditions of legal discourse structured around complex constellations of core ideas and formal patterns of judicial logic. In this framework, the operative test of legality is not the inherent rightness, certitude, or even predictability of judicial opinions so much as their plausibility and coherence, or, as John Brigham (1984, p. 31) put it, their capacity to "make sense" within the inherited legacy of constitutional discourse. Moreover, although this bounded subjectivity sustains the relative autonomy of the legal system from instrumental manipulation by independent political actors, the logic of law contains basic structures of bias in favor of status quo social relations—a bias strongly reinforced by the legal concept of precedent and the tradition of respect for constitutional and legal histories. Public law neither simply "reflects" nor "mystifies" underlying social reality, as Marxists often suggest, but it does act as a conceptual grid that selects, sorts, orders, and reorders the dominant elements of public discourse in ways highly supportive of prevailing social structure (Kairys, 1998; Nieli, 1991; Posner, 1997).

Of course, this role of law in legitimating social practice can have progressive as well as conservative implications. The intrinsic claim to impartiality, however imperfectly realized in practice, renders law a potentially useful tool for challenging the injustice of specific laws, practices, or policies. But invoking the law as a tool of reform often ends up supporting the logic of existing power relationships against fundamental social change as seen in the analysis of contemporary equal protection discourse developed later.

LAW AS AN INTERPRETED REALITY

The law is more than a set of rules to be applied in the process of making judicial decisions. Clifford Geertz, in his Storrs Lecture at the Yale Law School in 1981, highlighted this point as he examined "the place of fact in a world of judgment" (1983, p. 173). He argued that separating questions of fact from questions of law obscured their inseparable connection. Geertz urged readers to consider how intimately descriptions of the social world are linked to normative judgments about the world. Whatever else law might be, Geertz asserted, it could not be merely "a bounded set of norms, rules, principles, values, from which jural responses to distilled events can be drawn." Law is also "part of a distinctive manner of imagining the real" (p. 173).

Rather than seeing the law as a unitary imagining, as the quoted passage from Geertz (1983) might be understood to imply, legal institutions are arenas where many different ways of "imagining the real" compete for dominance. Recognizing this, Geertz acknowledged that his comparative perspective in "local knowledge" has the effect of flattening the internal variation of each of the legal systems he discussed, making it appear unitary and unproblematic. Still, the tone of his other writings suggest that he would be opposed to think first of legal institutions as places where power is exercised through judgments about facts (Geertz, 1973). His point appears to be that legal concepts and factual determinations are always inescapably linked.

The distinctive reality constructed by legal institutions results from some imaginings winning out over others, and the process through which some people's stories are accepted as fact, whereas others are dismissed as nonfact, need to be examined not as some manifestation of a deeper culture, but as the result of the exercise of power in a site of contested meaning. Power, absent from Geertz's (1983) conceptualization of the law, is evidenced not only through the enforcement of clearly prejudicial laws but also in the blunting of privilege through adjudicating grievances brought by members of various social underclasses (Thompson, 1975). Thompson discovered that laws enacted to reinforce the privileges of a dominant class also present opportunities for the working class to make arguments that blunt the raw exercise of arbitrary power. This analysis gave rise to his often-quoted homage to the rule of law. For this reason, the law has distinct advantages over ordinary political processes, though it is far from the neutral instrument in service of equality it is so often represented as being. Power, as Foucault (1997) made clear, operates through fields of knowledge, through the construction of beliefs about the factual, the natural, the inevitable, and other useful fictions. Courts are producers of knowledge in this sense, and they exercise power in an important way through providing official judgments about which statements are facts and which are not.

Though juridical models have some significant strengths and equal protection has sometimes been used in the service of the subordinated, juridical models can, and often are, used against subordinated groups by ruling inequality officially nonexistent, and by using apparently neutral effects. Rhetorically, liberal principles of law espouse universality and equality. But, though formally pretending to innocence about discrimination, their operations often reproduce and legitimate the very discrimination they seek to attack. As Kim Lane Schepple noted, for a person of poverty or of color, and for women, what everyone knows:

> turns out to be surprisingly hard to prove under conventional rules of evidence. You knew he was going to rape you by the look in his eyes? men ask women. You thought that the confederate flag was saying something about you? whites ask blacks. We understand that women suffer indignities every day that interfere with their abilities to work, managers say, but aren't you a little sensitive when this poor guy was making a joke. (1990, p. 42)

Reliance on formal rules of evidence to constrain the definition of acceptable proof allows courts to claim that they are enforcing the rules of an egalitarian society while still perpetuating the very social divisions that laws promising equality for all were designed to undermine and eliminate. We are all in favor of equality in the court system, such practices proclaim. However, the court does not often see inequalities, real inequalities that would justify the remedy the allegedly subordinated are seeking. In a system where everyone is formally equal, it becomes difficult to establish material inequalities as fact, especially when cases are decided one by one, often obscuring our ability to recognize patterns.

Law, contrary to liberal pretense, is expressive of the accrued history and self-identity of particular cultures, not of universal norms. As Clifford Geertz fittingly remarked, "Law, as I have been saying . . . is local knowledge, local not just as to place, time, class, and variety of issue, but as to accent . . . vernacular characterizations of what happens connected to vernacular imaginings of what can" (1983, p. 215).

EQUALITY OF OPPORTUNITY: A CONCEPTUAL ANALYSIS

Mapping out the conceptual framework or grammar of equality discourse within the larger context of moral debate over principles of distributive justice provides a case analysis of the link between law and reality construction. Drawing on a host of philosophical treatises by political theorists, this analysis reveals that most equality claims neither presume a de facto lack of differences among persons, nor seek, de jure, to force persons into a mold of dull uniformity. Rather, equality claims typically constitute a normative revolt against specific social differentiations that support domination or subordination of some persons by others and hence are deemed unjust. In this sense, as Michael Walzer noted, "the root meaning of equality is negative; egalitarianism in its origins is an abolitionist politics" (1983, p. xi). But this is also misleading, he added, in that the elimination of unjust subordination aims also to liberate, enrich, and ennoble persons. In other words, equality may promote as well as impede liberty, as Alex de Tocqueville contended long ago. To understand the paradoxical character of equality claims, it is necessary to make a variety of analytical distinctions among different components within traditional equality discourse.

We can begin by recognizing that legal equality claims usually refer to the allocation of specific social benefits or burdens. Hence the distributional problems involved in most debates over equality have a context specific character (Friedman, 1985; Walzer, 1983). Arguments on behalf of increased equality typically address the joining of two fundamental issues.

First, they deal with the fact that social goods being equalized are diverse in kind and largely incommensurate; they include income, capital, jobs, status, respect, authority, training, and other services or primary goods. Second, distribution of these social goods is overseen by different institutional spheres presided over by independent authoritative agents. These spheres differ in their relative public or private status and diverge yet further in their workings among more specific sites of social interaction affecting families, workplaces, or specific government agencies. These two issues are joined in what Douglas Rae (1981) termed a "domain of allocation," specifying the class of social goods that a given agent or agency controls within a given institutional sphere.

The joining of these issues reveals two rather different levels at which disputes about the substantive criteria of equality take place. One concerns the relative distribution of resources among the different authoritative spheres within society, and hence among the various domains of allocation. Decisions at this level thus are fundamentally redistributional and concern less the allocation of goods among specific persons or groups than choices about the type and relative amount of various goods to produce and the institutional mechanisms of investment, production, and exchange. For example, decisions at this level address difficult questions concerning how much of the total social resources should be allocated to military defense, public education, public arts, health care, private consumer wealth, and so on, and how to structure authority spheres for agencies administering allocations. Such decisions about differential social resource allocation are matters of macroeconomics, metapolitics, and grand ethical theory; they find justifications in competing global principles of utility, moral piety, simple equality, and the like (Dorn, 1979; Kelly, 1992; Rae, 1981).

By contrast, much ethical debate concerning relative equalities focuses on less grand and more manageable patterns of assignment within specific spheres of institutional authority, and hence within relatively stable and limited domains of resource allocation. These domain-specific assignment processes are, of course, highly interdependent with, and continuously subject to, changes in the overall structure of allocation among institutional spheres. But even if such structural interdependence does determine the relative amounts and kinds of goods constituting a particular domain of allocation, the procedural and normative patterns of assigning those goods within each sphere usually retain a considerable degree of autonomy (Kelly, 1992).

OPPORTUNITIES VERSUS RESULTS

We turn now to the central question of how the concepts of opportunity and result are incorporated into equity theory. Most philosophers and educational researchers tend to agree that the term *opportunity* refers to citizens' chances of attaining desired allocational outcomes (Coleman, 1973). Such chances generally depend on two factors: procedural access to register demand for the desired goods or roles and possession of the characteristics needed to qualify for these allocations. The term *results*, by contrast, refers to the actual allocation of goods among persons who qualify for and desire them.

We can immediately identify some problems arising from efforts to treat these related activities as separate phenomena. For one thing, the interdependence among allocational spheres means that the results of goods allocations in one area affect opportunities in other spheres. For instance, allocation of special training to selected students in early grades can sharply enhance their opportunities for advancement in later grades, which in turn can enhance college prospects, which in turn promote opportunities for employment, the results of which shape opportunities for position, status, income, and so on.

Opportunities do not always lead to desired results, but outcomes at every level of goods allocation tend to either restrict or expand subsequent opportunities. This is why the image of a competitive race so often invoked by advocates of meritocratic, individualistic conceptions of equal opportunity is fundamentally misleading. There is no singular, competitive race in society, at least not in modern complex societies such as ours. Modern liberal societies are more like endless tournaments held in multiple arenas, where everyone runs a myriad of different races simultaneously. Some have discernible ends with definite results, but the results tend to flow together into a complex of resources and opportunities that determine the distribution of role, status, and power relationships in society. As James Rosenbaum (1976, p. 40) put it, "When you win, you win only the right to go on to the next round; when you lose, you lose forever." There are other races to run, of course, but many allocation outcomes have permanent effects. The line between opportunities and results in the overall scheme of complex interdependent interactions in modern competitive society is difficult to keep in focus or determine.

The alleged opposition between equalities of opportunities and results tends to break down under conceptual scrutiny in a more fundamental sense. Even where specific allocations can be isolated in time and space, commitment to an ethic of equal results is conceptually problematic. Traditional discourse tends to use the term *equal results* in situations where all subjects seeking access to social goods are allotted an essentially identical share. This requires that the domain of allocation be large enough (which requires a macro-level structural commitment) and the social goods themselves sufficiently divisible to be distributed in an undifferentiated way. An egalitarian income scheme providing identical incomes to all citizens would exemplify this type of policy.

Such cases are rare. In most contexts, goods are not fully divisible and are scarce relative to demand, requiring allocation on an unequal and exclusive basis. In typical cases where relative zero-sum scarcity requires differentiated distribution, a de facto inequality of results is virtually unavoidable. Some subjects will receive some goods, and others will not; however equal the shares for those who do qualify, the results are inherently unequal.

The key question at the micro level of domain allocation thus is not how to secure the impossible goal of equal results but to create opportunity structures for differentiating access and allocation that are defensibly fair. For example, most legal challenges alleging racial discrimination in job hiring or professional school admissions are directed not to providing more jobs or more schools to meet surplus demand (or redividing resources through job sharing or part-time enrollments, etc.), but rather to imposing more just criteria specifying who does and does not qualify for the limited, exclusive goods. The alleged choice between more equal results or more equal opportunities thus is largely irrelevant in most practical, domain-specific contexts.

EQUALITIES OF OPPORTUNITY: STRUCTURAL VARIATIONS

Viewed in these ways, most debates over the relative equality of social goods allocation within specific domains (employment, income, education, political influence, and others) concern the legitimacy of different types of opportunity-allocation structures built into authoritative decision-making processes rather than the creation of schemes to secure more equal outcomes. This is so because truly equalizing outcomes will almost always depend on controlling macro-level redistribution decisions.

Opportunity structures and their resulting patterns of unequal outcomes are distinguished in three ways: (a) by the criteria used to determine individual and group eligibility, (b) by the values used to set specific allocation levels, and (c) by the degree to which compensation for historical inequities is embraced. As far as eligibility is concerned, a distinction articulated by Rae (1981), separating "individual-regarding" from "bloc-regarding" criteria is important. Individual-regarding equality exists where a single class of equals is defined, and every member of that class is treated equally. Bloc-regarding equality is emphasized when: (a) subjects are divided into two or more subclasses and (b) allocation decisions seek parity between the subclasses (blocs) but not within them (Fiss, 1976; O'Neil, 1981; Rae). The latter point highlights the fact that even in cases where goods are scrupulously allocated in one sense according to bloc group membership, individuals within those groups may still be discriminated against in the actual distribu-

tion of scarce goods. In other words, bloc- (or group-) oriented and individ-
ually oriented allocations must both be analyzed in evaluating the equity of
an assignment process.

Differentiating allocation values, the second major variable distinguishing among opportunity structures concerns criteria employed to differentiate allocations among eligible subjects. A variety of value criteria can be
identified; three deserve special note. It is possible, for example, to avoid
embracing any particular value system by avoiding human choice altogether, and refusing to identify any personal basis for allocating goods—relying on chance mechanisms such as a lottery. A second general approach
to formulating criteria for differential allocations is to rely on such inherited characteristics as birth, color, race, ethnicity, sex, class, or social status—criteria over which individual subjects have no direct control. Criteria
of this type are widely used and are typically legitimated by reference to the
will of God, the order of nature, tradition, or some other transcendent authority. A third type of criterion for selective allocation relies on some measure of merit—a qualitative evaluation of citizen achievement or performance using some standard of individual desert or social utility. Merit criteria
are far less uniform, reliable, or objective than often is assumed when they
are endorsed. As John Schaar (1964) eloquently put it, "The usual formulation of the doctrine-equal opportunity for all to develop their capacities is
rather misleading. . . . Out of the great variety of human resources available
to it, a given society will admire and reward some more than others." When
these admired characteristics are used to allocate opportunities, "it becomes clear that commitment to the formula implies prior acceptance of
an already established social-moral order" (p. 42). Indeed, over time societies have valued differentially a host of merit-oriented standards: courage in
war, religious piety, artistic creativity, academic achievement, political loyalty, social productivity, and money-making ability, to name a few.

Compensation for historical inequities is the third major distinction
among opportunity structures. Purely formalistic opportunity structures
are restricted to narrow procedural differentiation among citizens at the
level of access and allocation determination. That is, formal models seek to
promote impersonal fairness through uniform treatment regardless of past
circumstances (Schaar, 1967). Compensatory opportunity structures, by
contrast, recognize and attempt to mitigate historical obstacles that have
impeded citizen efforts to meet the primary criteria of goods allocation. In
the case of meritocratic opportunity structures, compensatory models require not merely uniform treatment in evaluating citizen performances but
also what James Fishkin (1983) labeled recognition of the "specific life
chances" citizens have had to develop measured skills, talents, and aspira-
tions. Hence, the compensatory version of meritocratic equal opportunity
affirms the need to accommodate for "background inequalities" in re-

sources that limit citizen abilities to compete effectively in various social races for power and position (Fishkin).

There are several justifications for compensatory models, including support for the primary social ends of individual reward, social utility, social pluralism, and self-development. Two strategies for institutionalizing compensatory policies have evolved: a domain-specific strategy of balancing allocation criteria with consideration of background inequalities, and a cross-domain strategy of directly redistributing social goods from one domain to another to offset unmitigated background inequalities. These strategies highlight the important ways in which compensatory opportunity structures depart from purely formalistic structures (Joseph, 1980; Rawls, 1973; Walzer, 1983).

On a hypothetical continuum with purely formal opportunity at one pole and radical compensatory opportunity structures at the other pole, we thus can envision several alternative interim guidelines for compensatory action, including remedies for state-imposed obstacles, remedies for specific socially imposed obstacles, and fulfillment of basic human needs even in the absence of any clear impediment or injury-causing deprivation. At the formal end of this scale, any movement toward equalizing opportunities will remain largely domain specific and produce only marginal improvements in results; some long-deprived citizens may do better absolutely, but relative structural inequalities in the control of goods among groups will generally remain unchanged (Dorn, 1976; Rae, 1981).

As equalities of opportunity become more compensatory in character, sharply differentiated allocations within specific domains or substantial macro-level redistribution of resources among domains becomes necessary, often requiring radical reconstruction of key social institutions. As Fishkin (1983) pointed out, for example, most versions of radical equal opportunity would require extensive social reorganization in the realms of family and property ownership long revered as appropriately "private" and autonomous by liberal theory.

Several points are worth keeping in mind regarding the three key factors that serve to distinguish among opportunity structures. First, they are relatively independent in character. Although it may be true that formal meritocratic structures tend to be individual and ascriptive status distinctions (e.g., birth characteristics) are often used to create bloc-regarding allocational patterns, neither pattern is logically necessary. Moreover, it must be reemphasized that such variables can be employed to advance or to secure unequal, even exclusively monopolistic, allocational structures leading to permanent opportunity inequalities as well as to greater equality of opportunity among subjects. And, finally, we must not lose sight of the fact that even the most radical cases of compensatory opportunity structures rarely lead to substantially equal outcomes. More fair decision processes and equal life chances may alter the distributional patterns (of who gets scarce social goods) within specific domains, but advances toward reducing hierarchies of global difference in social goods allocation depend on different types of macro-level redistributional decisions about the kind of society that ruling citizens desire (Michelman, 1969; Rawls, 1973).

EQUALIZING OPPORTUNITIES:
THE (RE)EVOLUTION OF EQUAL PROTECTION

This outline of philosophical equality discourse provides a framework for analyzing contemporary equal protection legal doctrines. Above all, it is important to emphasize the restricted, abolitionist character of equal protection entitlements. Indeed, the courts have been careful in most instances not to impose any single model of equality on state officials. Rather, the justices have aimed primarily only to establish general standards of review ranging from a minimal rationality test to the strictest scrutiny by which to assess the relative legitimacy of those criteria employed to discriminate among citizens in the allocation of access to public position, wealth, and other goods (*Gulf, C. & S.F. R. v. Ellis*, 1987). However, even such a limited abolitionist review posture still implies affirmative support for certain types of differentiation over and against other less favored types. In short, equal protection doctrine turns on an identifiable if minimal theory of just distributive processes.

In this light, it is easy to demonstrate that the variable standards of judicial review in Fourteenth Amendment cases have been defended by the Supreme Court primarily in terms of advancing the equal opportunity ethic rather than an ethic of equal results. As historian J. R. Pole argued, "Equality of opportunity was the chief meaning that Americans could hope to extract from a tradition which has been handed down to them as equality of rights" (1978, p. 129). Indeed, allegiance to this ethic was voiced in many landmark equal protection cases. For example, however objectionable his unique rendering of the principle, Justice Brown argued for a majority in *Plessy v. Ferguson* (1896, p. 551) that the goal of legal equality is to secure "to each of its citizens . . . equal opportunities for improvement and progress" wherever the state is responsible.

The logic of "separate but equal" authorized by *Plessy v. Ferguson* (1896) was overruled half a century later in *Brown v. Board of Education* (1954, p. 495) with the same promise that all citizens are legally entitled to "substantial equality in educational opportunity." As the majority in the subsequent *Bakke* case acknowledged, "When a classification denies an individual opportunities or benefits enjoyed by others solely because of his race or ethnic background, it must be regarded as suspect" (cited in Pole, 1978, p. 130).

Even later, judicially approved affirmative action plans were justified by reference to an opportunity rather than an outcomes ethic. To quote Justice Thurgood Marshall: "Today, by upholding this race-conscious remedy, the Court accords Congress the authority to undertake the task of moving our society toward a state of meaningful equality of opportunity" (*Fullilove v. Klutznick*, 1980, p. 522). The same promise was repeated in a variety of cases involving employment, education, political access, and other areas of public allocation.

Merely to cite often-repeated phrases selected from judicial decisions does not get us very far, however. After all, despite occasional references to "equal opportunity," the primary language of constitutional discourse is that of rights to "equal protection" and "equal treatment," of determining "suspect" classifications and "invidious discrimination," and so on. At the very least, some interpretive work is necessary to translate formal legal language into the terms of abstract philosophical equality talk. Moreover, to cite repeated references to "equal opportunity" ignores the highly variable contextual and normative nuances signified by different usages of the term; we thus remain in doubt as to what kind of opportunity structures are implied by these references and how they have or have not changed over time.

Importantly, it has yet to be demonstrated that, despite its formal rhetoric to the contrary, the Court has not edged toward a reconstruction of the Fourteenth Amendment synonymous with the logic of equal results rather than that of equal opportunity. In short, we must subject the discourse of equal protection opinions to more subtle, rigorous, and systematic scrutiny to make the case concerning its narrow opportunity-oriented logic. Four aspects of judicial interpretations of constitutional equality discourse deserve elaboration: (a) the domain boundaries of state action, (b) the formal definition of state neutrality, (c) the construction of standards for judicial review, and (d) definitions of legal subjects of judicial action. These four issues are analyzed, in turn, in the following sections.

State Action Boundaries: Limited Spheres and Domains

The first significant factor determining the reach of equal protection emerged quickly in the nation's judicial history, in the *Civil Rights Cases* of 1883. These decisions are important because they invalidated the public accommodation sections of the 1875 Civil Rights Act prohibiting racial discrimination by operators of restaurants, inns, theaters, and public conveyances. The key argument by the eight-justice majority opinion rested on the emerging principle limiting constitutional protection against racial discrimination to the acts of state officials, thus excluding from legal concern the broader range of social acts of racial discrimination by institutions, groups, and individuals in private discourse and market relations. Under the Fourteenth Amendment, Justice Bradley held, "It is state action of a particular character that is prohibited. Individual invasion of individual rights is not the subject-matter of the amendment. . . . It does not authorize congress to create a code of municipal law for regulation of private rights" (*Civil Rights Cases*, p. 11).

According to this view, African Americans excluded from private institutions and relationships suffer denial not of legally defined civil or political rights but only of their social rights, for which there was no constitutional guarantee. Such is the ordinary mode of legal treatment for all full citizens, which prohibits the alleged request of African Americans to be the special favorite of the laws governing social life (*Civil Rights Cases*, 1883; Kluger, 1975).

The obvious implications of this doctrine were to restrict greatly the institutional spheres, and hence the specific domains, of allocation to which constitutional equality claims were held to be applicable. Its impact was soon felt in cases upholding a variety of private discriminatory practices against African Americans ranging from Ku Klux Klan organization to restrictive covenants among property owners (*Burton v. Wilmington Parking Authority*, 1961; *Corrigan v. Buckley*, 1926; *Norwood v. Harrison*, 1973; *United States v. Harris*, 1882). Despite some specific reversals, these same basic principles continue to limit the reach of constitutional equal protection obligations in many important domains.

Although these restrictions were significantly weakened by post–New Deal judicial interpretations extending the definition of state action to private individuals and institutions that perform public functions, receive state aid, or have other significant state involvement (*Marsh v. Alabama*, 1946), the right to private discrimination remains intact. Likewise, although the relatively expansive commerce clause in the 1964 Civil Rights Act extended statutory protections against invidious racial and sexual discrimination to many areas of commercial and workplace activity as well, judicial review remains limited to public transactions. Moreover, neither of these legal routes to expanding state authority over market behavior has seen significant progress in recent years. Indeed there were significant retrenchments during the 1970s, 1980s, and 1990s.

In a series of oft-ignored cases, the Burger Court retreated from liberal standards by finding inapplicable state involvement and public performance standards that once had bound social institutions by constitutional obligations (*Moose Lodge v. Irvis*, 1972; *Rendell Baker v. Kohn*, 1983). What is more, the logic of limited state authority has been used to restrict significantly the range of governmental responsibility for affirmative action policies in domains where only private social discrimination is found to explain existing racial inequalities. As Justice Powell stated in *Wygant v. Jackson*

Board of Education (1986, p. 274), the "Court never has held that societal discrimination alone is sufficient to justify a . . . racially classified remedy." Only denials of social goods allocation by formally public institutions define a potential legal injury under the Fourteenth Amendment, and only a wrong committed by the state deserves remedy.

The state action doctrine thus retains an important conceptual line between public responsibility and private freedom, and gives greatest constitutional voice to the latter in ways that significantly restrict government advancement of citizen opportunities and welfare, particularly within capitalist societies where private wealth can be used to substantially harm targets of private prejudice.

State Neutrality: The Formalist Ethic

The second defining component of the prevailing doctrine derives from the principle that state action under the "Constitution is neutral as to persons" (Pole, 1978, p. 287). The promise of this formalist commitment is that the state should treat all individual persons alike within the terms of general differentiation among categorical groups and that these classifications themselves should not discriminate on arbitrary grounds such as biological or social inheritance. This grant of impersonal treatment from the state long ago proved beneficial for a majority of White "common men" against the inherited inequalities of aristocratic society, and more recently for racial and ethnic minorities, women, and other groups long subordinated to unequal status by such men.

Important limitations on this position were apparent in the 1883 *Civil Rights Cases* when the high court refused the demands of African Americans to bar societal discrimination as a plea for status, "as special favorites of the law." The infamous case of *Plessy v. Ferguson* (1896) even more dramatically displayed the exploitive possibilities of this new legal logic. In upholding the constitutionality of a Louisiana statute requiring separation of African American and White travelers on an intrastate railroad line, the Court interpreted the Fourteenth Amendment to mean that segregationist policies did not inherently deny "equal protection" to persons of color. Drawing on Justice Shaw's distinction in *Roberts v. City of Boston* (1849) between the "principle" of equal protection and its differential "application," as well as the Court's holding in *Strauder v. West Virginia* (1880), the majority behind Justice Billings Brown rejected the argument inferring that "separation of the two races stamps the colored race with a badge of inferiority" (*Plessy v. Ferguson*, p. 551).

In other words, state discrimination among persons on the basis of color that does not deny the enjoyment of basic opportunities for property owner-

ship, political participation, and so on, is not an injurious discrimination prohibited by the Constitution. Affirming the established difference between political and social equality, he explained that the Fourteenth Amendment
"could not have been intended on color" that arise from "the nature of
things" in civil society (*Plessy v. Ferguson*, 1896, p. 551). As long as the state did
not initiate such distinctions, therefore, the mere legal recognition of existing social practices does not offend its neutrality toward persons (Bell, 1992;
Civil Rights Cases, 1883; Kluger, 1975; *Plessy v. Ferguson*; *Strauder v. West Virginia*, 1880).

This specific position concerning the formalistic neutrality of the state in
the equal treatment of persons survived until 1954 when *Brown v. Board of
Education* declared that "separate but equal" is a contradiction in terms.
However significant this reversal of precedent, though, the *Brown* decision
did not challenge the principle of neutrality so much as redefine equal protection in terms more compatible with changing societal conceptions of
fairness. The unanimous Court invoked scholarly research to dispute earlier assumptions that racial segregation does not inherently brand persons
of color with a stigma of inferiority and the "badges of slavery."

The Court in *Brown* could have, if it had chosen, defined the legally relevant fact at the case-specific level. In this scenario, future litigants would
have been required to demonstrate actual injury caused by segregation. But
in constitutional law, even case-specific facts, ones that do not specifically
apply to future cases, have important values attached to them. Facts that are
particular to a case—such as whether the light was red or green when the
plaintiff crossed the street—are called "adjudicative facts." These facts are
jurors' determinative responsibility. Robert Carter had initially defined the
facts in *Brown v. Board of Education* (1954) as adjudicative in nature limited
only to what was happening in Topeka. In constitutional cases, however,
adjudicative facts implicate basic constitutional values and thus have far-
reaching implications. Even the most case-specific factual questions in the
constitutional context have broad policy implications.

At the same time, there is always a substantial factual component to constitutional fact questions. It necessarily follows, then, that either the facts
themselves or knowledge of them might and indeed are likely to change
over time. If a constitutional principle is truly tied to a factual premise, then
perhaps lower courts should be permitted to hear new evidence that the
facts are different from those on which the constitutional rule was based. In
short, if *Brown v. Board of Education* (1954) was actually premised on the fact
that African Americans were disadvantaged by segregated schools, then
subsequent and better research that African Americans were advantaged by
separate schooling should lead to reconsideration of the constitutional
rule. The truth, however, is that we know that the facts in *Brown v. Board of
Education* were merely a proxy for a judgment made on moral grounds. No

new set of facts would change the decision. Not all constitutional cases that depend on factual premises will be so readily resolved.

Brown v. Board of Education (1954) and subsequent cases gave expression to the evolving position of the Court that all racially conscious discrimination is immediately "suspect" and thus "subject to the most searching scrutiny" (*Korematsu v. United States*, 1944, p. 216). This scrutiny for invidious discrimination extends beyond the prima facie language of official statutes or actions to the very intentions and motives of their authors as well. In other words, though seemingly neutral on their face, various forms of discrimination among persons (e.g., in educational placement) may be scrutinized to determine any covert manifestations of racial prejudice in either unequal administration or biased design of state rules and procedures. In so doing, the emerging doctrine of equal protection declared that neutrality to persons requires a formal posture of nondiscrimination on the basis of race, color, and ethnicity except where there exists a compelling state interest. Recalling the dissent of Justice Harlan in *Plessy v. Ferguson* (1896), Justice Robert Jackson reaffirmed the idea that justice in the United States remained blind and therefore applied equally to all citizens regardless of race, creed, or religion (Kull, 1992, p. 363). The great deficiency in this formal posture of colorblind neutrality is that it remains mostly insensitive to the persistent effects of past state-supported discrimination that continues to limit opportunities for people of color. After years of limiting remedies focused on the termination of racist policies in schools and other public sector enterprises, in the late 1960s the Court required more affirmative actions aimed at redressing the continuing effects of past discrimination. As Chief Justice Burger stated, "The presumption must be made that past discriminatory systems have resulted in present economic inequalities" (*Fullilove v. Klutznick*, 1980, p. 465). But, contrary to the interpretations of many conservatives, affirmative action mandates to remedy past wrongs aim less to violate than to fortify the principle of state neutrality by overcoming the limits of a historically insensitive antidiscrimination ethic. The crucial point in the affirmative action stance is that it still does not establish a constitutional obligation to take remedial steps based on historical discrimination. Affirmative action is required only after purposeful (de jure) invidious racial discrimination has been proved, and even then "the nature of the violation determines the scope of the remedy" (*Swann v. Charlotte Mechlenberg Board of Education*, 1970, p. 16). Thus, remedies are closely tailored to narrow allocational domains within specific institutional settings for limited periods of time.

This logic has prevailed since the earliest of equal protection cases. The Court has narrowly interpreted Fourteenth Amendment authorization of appropriate congressional legislation for enforcement of equal protection entitlements to include only corrective measures for wrongful past acts undertaken by state officials (Kluger, 1975). The public accommodation remedies, rejected in these early cases, sought to mandate direct and primary action aimed at social reorganization where no proof of explicit state wrongdoing was proved. The same principle of right to remedial action limited solely to discriminatory actions by government officials has governed opinions regarding public school integration, employment preference, statutory state contract awards, and other affirmative action policies. As the majority ruled in *Swann v. Charlotte Mechlenberg Board of Education,* "Once a right and violation have been shown, the scope of . . . equitable powers to remedy past wrong is broad. . . . [But] it is important to remember that judicial powers may be exercised only on the basis of a constitutional violation" (1970, p. 15). Not surprisingly, this logic has been employed to arguments seeking to restrict as well as to expand remedial state action. It has justified decisions limiting remedies to ever narrower allocational spheres (within rather than among school districts), more specific aspects of allocation (distinguishing seniority in hiring from firing), and shorter periods of domain-specific remedial obligation (*Milliken v. Bradley,* 1974; *Pasadena Board of Education v. Spangler,* 1976).

In short, affirmative action actually aims to restore state neutrality by mandating reflexive redress only against past incidents of racially non-neutral official action in allocating scarce goods. As affirmative action policies are said to achieve a certain wholeness for wronged persons, so do they promote a sense of wholeness to impersonal legal authority. Formally, then, the Court has not moved to secure more equal results, but only more equal opportunities. Contending claimants may benefit or suffer differently from changed allocational guidelines created by affirmative action mandates, but increased allocations (by redistribution among spheres) to reward all claimants equally have almost never been required (Karst, 1977).

A narrow majority on the Court has edged only modestly from a purely formal, ahistorical, equal opportunity ethic prohibiting invidious discrimination toward a moderately compensatory opportunity ethic requiring only limited remedies for past violations to a few categories of persons in specific public institutions. Indeed, such compensatory action limited to narrow remedies for state wrongs constitutes only the smallest step from the most historically detached formal model of opportunity on the continuum described earlier. As Allan Sindler concluded, "Such affirmative actions square thoroughly with the popular view of equal opportunity because they serve to enlarge the competition by removing inappropriate disadvantages for some potential applicants, while leaving all else intact" (1983, p. 3). Even the most progressive efforts by some members of the Court to liberalize the standards of proof used to determine purposeful state wrongdoing—by including "foreseeable" impact or discounting to "remoteness in time"—have not departed from this basic logic of quasi-formal posture in securing legitimate citizen opportunities through remedial action (*Keyes v. School District No. 1*, 1973, p. 211).

State Neutrality: Standards for Review

We have seen that the cornerstone of equal protection is that citizens will be treated impartially by the state. But this characterization of liberal state neutrality and nondiscrimination is misleading in a very important sense. Judicial reviews of purported violations of this neutrality are not all held to the same standard; different types of discriminatory action have received different levels of review, conferring on them very different degrees of legal legitimacy. Whereas classifications made on the basis of race and ethnicity (and to a lesser degree gender, alienage, and illegitimacy) have been subjected to a highly rigorous review, allocational differences arising from evaluations of citizen performance, skill, merit, and other marketplace measures of worth are typically subjected to minimal review requiring only reasonable relation to a legitimate state interest. Moreover, violations of state neutrality with regard to managing allocations across domains often go unnoticed and unchallenged.

This treatment has been well illustrated by legal challenges to competence tests as measures of discrimination among persons in both public and private spheres (Green, 1981). In *Washington v. Davis* (1976), for example, a majority of seven justices upheld a District of Columbia police department's standard personnel test (measuring verbal skills) administered to all applicants for officer positions even though it disproportionately excluded African Americans from contention. The logic of the decision was clear: Absent clear proof of intent to discriminate on racial grounds, exclusion of persons on the basis of inability to demonstrate basic skills on ostensibly neutral performance tests meets the rationality test required by traditional equal protection.

The legitimacy of discrimination according to ability or merit is yet more evident in cases involving the more rigorous standard ostensibly mandated by the Civil Rights Act (1964). Although the Court found in *Griggs v. Duke Power Co.* (1971) that this employer's use of high school diplomas and intelligence test scores to screen job applicants was an impermissible violation of Title VII, it explicitly upheld the principle of merit discrimination. In saying that "what is required by Congress is the removal of artificial, arbitrary, and unnecessary barriers to employment when the barriers operate invidiously to discriminate on the basis of racial or other impermissible classifications" (*Griggs v. Duke Power Co.*, p. 431), the Court declared that unequal racial impacts remain permissible where the criteria used are substantially "related to successful job performance" (p. 426). In other words, far from challenging the impact or intrinsic character of meritocratic discrimination among citizens, the Court's most rigorous scrutiny has simply held various processes of applicant evaluation to their own rational standards of marketplace justification. The touchstone is business effectiveness or efficiency (*Griggs v. Duke Power Co.*).

Reflection on these points reveals much about the logic of opportunity implied by equal protection principles. Indeed, the fact that meritocratic or performance-based criteria generally are exempted from strict scrutiny calls attention to the underlying criteria determining suspectness itself. The most common reason given by experts on and off the bench is that most suspect characteristics are immutable and natural in essence. Because they are "determined solely by the accident of birth," persons have no choice about them and hence should not suffer before law because of them (*Frontiero v. Richardson*, 1973, p. 686).

Though plausible in itself, this logic fails to explain why personal strength, beauty, and intelligence are not treated as suspect as well. Also, the frequent charge of past stigmatization alone is similarly insufficient because it fails to reveal why penalizing persons for a history of treatment based on ugliness, stupidity, or clumsiness also is not suspect. The additional point at stake in this logic is that stigmas attached to race, color, ethnicity, and religion are understood not to derive from the objective personal performance of persons in social or marketplace interaction. Because discrimination on the basis of race is unrelated to one's ability to achieve, to one's display of creative talent, to one's merit as defined by prevailing standards of social utility and moral worth in the social marketplace, the Court has deemed that it must be justified by a very compelling state interest (Bell, 1972, 1992; Green, 1981).

This logic is implicit, if not explicit, in a host of cases. Justice Brennan, for example, articulated it for a plurality in *Frontiero v. Richardson* (1973, p. 686), saying that what distinguishes race (and sex) from such nonsuspect statuses as intelligence and physical disability, and aligns it to the recognized suspect criteria, is that it "bears no relation to ability to perform or contribute to society." Nearly every justice on the high court during the 1970s joined opinions invoking this same position. Examples are Justice Burger's majority opinion in *Fullilove v. Klutznick* (1980) to uphold congressional policy advancing the "century-old promise of equality of economic opportunity by granting preferential treatment in building contract awards to remedy past barriers impairing access . . . not related to lack of capable and qualified minority enterprises" (p. 463); Justice Powell's rejection in *University of California Regents v. Bakke* (1978) of racial quotas perpetuating "stereotypes holding that certain groups unable to achieve success" and "having no relationship to individual worth" (p. 298); and Justices Stewart, Stevens, and Rehnquist's frequent opposition to all classifications "made according to race—rather than according to merit or ability" (*Fullilove v.*

Klutznick, p. 532). After centuries of struggle against stigmatizing myths, classifications based on race, ethnicity, and gender have been deemed morally suspect as well as departures from the meritocratic logic of entitlement esteemed by liberal philosophy, American capitalist culture, and, at least through deference, constitutional law.

Court decisions elevating compensatory action for past wrongs above simple measures of current citizen performance have continued to allow state use of defensibly neutral measures of performance or merit, however, and have stopped far short of recognizing a basic constitutional right to compensatory considerations. Approved affirmative action remedies continue to support the meritocratic logic of opportunity rather than the equality of outcomes principle of equal results. Not only are supported remedial guidelines necessarily limited in scope and time, but they still allow meritocratic differentiation among the members of groups accorded compensatory preference. Most programs approved by the Court still require minimum standards of performance for all recipients of goods such as employment, advancement, or admission to higher education (Rae, 1981).

Even more important, most approved compensatory policies can be understood not to supersede merit considerations but to create more rational processes for evaluating citizen talent and potential, particularly when potential exceeds short-term performances that have been stifled by the impact of past laws, policies, and practices. In short, affirmative action programs that take the effects of past racial (or sexual) discrimination into account often improve on traditional assessments of ability or merit in an effort to restore the claims to objectivity, utility, and fairness esteemed in liberal market society and granted a presumption of constitutionality. This was a large part of the logic developed by Powell's majority opinion favoring Harvard's model of multidimensional evaluation for student applicants: "An admissions program operated in this way is flexible enough to consider all pertinent elements of diversity in light of the particular qualifications of each applicant, and to place them on the same footing for consideration, although not necessarily according them the same weight" (*University of California Regents v. Bakke*, 1978, p. 317). The basic point is that recent judicial constructions of equal protection aim only at prohibiting specific types of differentiation in domain-specific opportunity structures rather than at promoting anything approaching equal results in public goods allocation. Claims to the contrary simply are confused and misleading, even if rhetorically effective. To take one classic example, the Court has interpreted equal protection law (and the Civil Rights Act, 1964) not "to guarantee a job to every person regardless of qualification" (*Griggs v. Duke Power Co.*, 1971, p. 430) but only to provide for a basic fairness in individual competition for opportunities (Title VII of the Civil Rights Act) to qualify for unequal allocations of scarce public jobs (varying in wages, status, authority, and so on;

Griggs v. Duke Power Co.). Indeed, the highest authoritative interpreters of the Constitution have long shown much tolerance, even approval, for inequalities in public allocation, which can be traced to allegedly neutral evaluations of performance and ability. Such a posture remains largely blind to substantial biases in the actual criteria of merit routinely applied in our modern corporatized political economy. Nevertheless, the courts' formal deference to most standards of unequal allocation of goods in specific domains, and even more their acceptance of existing unequal macro-level distribution of social resources among spheres, remains a guiding principle of contemporary constitutional policymaking.

The Legal Subject: Abstract Individualism

The fourth and most often misrepresented aspect of judicial interpretation of the equal protection doctrine concerns the identification of the legally entitled individual persons to be protected. The logic of individual protection is manifest in the very words of the Fourteenth Amendment, which reads that no state shall deny to any "person" the equal protection of the laws. This individualistic principle has been affirmed in numerous cases. For example, *Shelley v. Kraemer* (1948, p. 1) found that "the rights ceated [sic] by the first section of the Fourteenth Amendment are, by its terms, guaranteed to the individual. The rights established are personal rights." This bias is hardly surprising, of course, given the commitment to private life and property long at the heart of our constitutional tradition. Indeed, the evolving equal protection logic not only respects the autonomy of the marketplace, it incorporates the basic premise of competitive exchange relations among individuals within the logic of duty binding state officials and institutions. As John Schaar (1967, p. 237) put it, "The [prevailing] doctrine of equality of opportunity . . . is a precise symbolic expression of the liberal-bourgeois model of society, for it extends the marketplace mentality to all spheres of life. . . . Individualism, in de Tocqueville's sense, is the reigning ethical principal [sic]." (See also Cohen, 1979; Green, 1981.)

The most notable aspect of this individualist principle is its peculiarly abstract and limiting manner of dealing with what are essentially group-based, structural inequalities (McCann, 1986). On one hand, the bias of the prevailing equal protection antidiscrimination logic is to place the focus of attention on the violations that Alan Freeman (1978) called official "perpetrators." The result is that constitutional injury is restricted not only to formal public domains of allocation but to verifiable transgressions by specific officials or laws on whom to pin the blame for injustice. "It is a notion of racial discrimination as something that is caused by individuals, or individual institutions, producing discrete results that can be identified as discrimination and thereafter neutralized" (Freeman, pp. 98–99; see also

Green, 1981; O'Neil, 1981; Pole, 1978). Although transcending the color-blind and amnesiac biases of older doctrines, the obligatory remedial actions thus still remain myopic and selective in memory regarding the complex, multifaceted structural dimensions of institutional racism that transcend individual agency and control. The perpetrator perspective focuses on the official wrongdoing rather than on the needs of the victim, on remedying the act of purposeful discrimination rather than the pervasive sufferings and injustices of racially specific citizen deprivation.

Moreover, by singling out specific laws and wrongdoers as offensive, the individualist perpetrator perspective promotes the perception of racism as an anomalous disease curable by selective surgery and remedial therapies to restore an otherwise healthy body politic composed of innocent citizens. This is the logic of the majority in *University of California Regents v. Bakke*. Those members of the majority White race who are not guilty of discrete official wrongdoing are understood as innocent victims with rights equal to those of minority racial victims, freed of responsibility for advantages they have derived from centuries of White domination simply because they themselves did not initiate it (Green, 1981).

Attempts to remedy inequalities created by official acts affecting groups of citizens over extended periods of time can generate their own equity problems. As conservatives are quick to point out, many programs for remedying violations have extended preferential treatment for an indefinite time to members of stigmatized groups who themselves were not directly victimized by past acts of official wrongdoing. In the most extreme cases, the use of racial (and other group-based) quotas to rectify imbalances resulting from past invidious discrimination has promised to provide benefits not only directly to selected individual group members, but also indirectly to the larger group in the form of resource redistribution, group-specific role models and leadership, and a collective sense of esteem (Dorn, 1979). This hardly constitutes a shift to policies promoting equal group results. Where unbounded remedies have been attempted they have been rejected by the courts. As we have seen, since *University of California Regents v. Bakke* (1978), the Court has consistently ruled that bloc-regarding quotas are contrary to the spirit of equal protection except where they are strictly remedial in intent, limited in duration, and flexible in implementation (*Fullilove v. Klutznick*, 1980; *U.S. Steelworkers of America AFL-CIO-CLC v. Weber*, 1979; *Wygant v. Jackson*, 1986). Limited quotas of this type neither trample the individualistic logic of entitlement nor promote greater substantive equality of result in public goods distribution. Although some short-term bloc-regarding, nonmeritocratic components for some selected opportunity structures have been adopted, they all allow for differentiated allocation of goods within those blocs on individualistic, meritocratic criteria with predictably unequal results among group members and nonmembers alike. In short, the opportunities of a few victimized-group members may be improved by affirmative action, but the large majority of members can expect no more than marginal improvements in their prospects for attaining increased allocations of desired goods from existing legal mandates (Dorn; Freeman, 1978).

On the other hand, the alternative to bloc-regarding quotas endorsed by a majority since the mid-1970s is even more individualistic in character. Expressing preference for a program that "treats each applicant as an individual in the admissions process" (*University of California Regents v. Bakke*, 1978, p. 318), Justice Powell argued for the majority in the case that it is only "the individual who is entitled to judicial protection against classifications based upon his racial or ethnic background because such distinctions impinge upon personal rights," not "because of his membership in a particular group" (p. 299). In Powell's majority view, race may be considered as only one of many factors, and then only to the degree that it is presumed to have been an obstacle to development of skills or demonstration of talent. Such an approach does allow for greater equity in competitive evaluation processes. It also tends to reduce the complex structural sources of citizen background inequalities to idiosyncratic, random hardships discernible in discrete life histories. Remedies are constitutionally limited to mandates for more flexible and socially sensitive discretionary processes of domain-specific evaluation among claimants contending for scarce goods.

Coordinated policies of macro-level resource redistribution to mitigate continuing group-based sources of social deprivation or to meet citizen developmental needs may be legislated, but none is required by the Fourteenth Amendment nor created by court decrees. The classical liberal union of faith in individual responsibility and antistatism rarely has found clearer expression than in this legal opportunity-oriented logic. Such constructions of equal protection affirm the perception that, as Green (1981, p. 264) noted, "in liberal society people get generally what they deserve, and what they deserve is purely and simply a consequence of their own individual character and actions, and nothing else" (Fiss, 1976; O'Neil, 1981).

CONCLUSION

The central aim of this analysis has been to demonstrate that recent trends in equal protection construction have not contributed substantially to a constitutional mandate for more equal results. Far from orchestrating a more equal distribution of resources, the Court instead has limited itself to reviewing only a few of the suspect classifications historically employed to discriminate among citizens within existing domains of limited and typically unequal goods allocation. In such cases, the Court has explicitly and consistently adhered not only to an ethic of equal opportunity but to a version of that ethic that is narrowly public in reach; individualistic in subject eligibility; highly deferential to, and supportive of, unequal distributions of access and allocation justified by meritocratic standards; and consistent with our long cultural and legal tradition of limited state authority over marketplace transactions. This analysis does not deny that significant shifts have occurred in judicial constructions of equal protection since the historic *Brown v. Board of Education* (1954) decision. Rather, it contends that changes that have occurred are merely minor conceptual revisions in the Court's understanding of the ethic of equal opportunity, particularly in public education following the *Brown v. Board of Education* decision.

The *Brown v. Board of Education* (1954) decision illustrates a phenomenon that became common in the late 20th century and appears to be a mainstay of 21st-century constitutional law. As science continues to evolve, it will produce an ever-expanding corpus of knowledge about the real world, a world of particular interest to the Supreme Court justices. Constitutional principles do not exist in a vacuum. They are both framed by and framed for the affairs of a modern state. Yet facts have the frustrating tendency to change, either because our understanding of facts change or the facts themselves change in an evolving and technologically advancing society.

This phenomenon has plagued the modern Court and remains an issue the Court continues to struggle with in the 21st century. As such, the Court's emphasis shifted from purely formal principles of anti-invidious discrimination to an emphasis on modestly compensatory versions of the traditional meritocratic opportunity ethic mandating limited remedial action where past incidents of invidious discrimination by the state have been documented. The relatively conservative character of this opportunity-oriented logic has been clarified in the preceding analysis. This logic, however, has barely addressed the deep structural effects of long-standing racial and sexual divisions, much less the class-based sources of those material inequalities that deny to many citizens both genuine opportunity and basic needs fulfillment. As Philip Green put it, "The strategy of formal 'equal opportunity' is a strategy for maintaining the position of African Americans, women, and similar minorities in the condition of stigma and relative exclusion; it is a strategy for keeping a plural society unequally plural" (1981, p. 264). But this nevertheless is the logic of modern constitutional law in our society.

This critical argument is not intended to suggest that equal protection litigation is inherently fruitless. Rather, my intent is to call attention to the important differences between constitutional debates relying on judicial analysis and other approaches to policymaking. Judicial methodologies instruct legal decision makers as to what materials, argumentation, and normative commitments can be admitted as the foundations of proper decisions and, by implication, to instruct those making legal arguments. For example, to be methodologically acceptable, an argument must be consistent with the principles of *stare decisis*—that is, apply the logic of precedent-setting decisions or, if not, appropriately explain why apparently controlling case law does not apply, or forthrightly set forth the principles on which a request is made to overrule that case law. Similarly, in interpreting and applying constitutional and statutory provisions, judicial methodology insists that an argument demonstrate that a proposed decision is faithful to both the legal text and the intent of the drafters. Legal methods require appropriate deference to the policy judgments of legislative bodies and administrative agencies, and proper standards of review to lower court fact finding. Proper legal arguments are also limited by the issues actually raised by the parties, and restrain the courts from unnecessary dictum. Above all, proper legal argument presents conclusions that are open and rationally explained. As the Supreme Court stated, "A decision without principled justification would be no judicial act at all" (*Planned Parenthood v. Casey*, 1992, p. 32).

Of course, such principles, even if assiduously applied, will never standardize decision making completely, for interpreting precedent, as well as constitutional and statutory text, requires judgment and reasonable judges can disagree. The result is that courts are confronted with a myriad of jurisprudential theories, and an even broader array of sociological, political, psychological, and anthropological theories of social context and dynamics claiming to properly interpret the law and show how it is to be applied in specific sociopolitical contexts. This splintering of theoretical perspectives weakens claims that law offers a unifying conceptual framework for guiding decision making as an objective process. Above all, conceptual clarity is crucial to avoid the rhetorical trap of labeling equal opportunity and affirmative action policies as equal results policies when they are not, and to expose the inequalities endorsed in the narrowly formalistic ideals advocated by conservative critics of the Court. Moreover, to the extent that advocates seek greater social equality through law, it is important to clearly identify how each proposed strategy reinforces or challenges prevailing doctrine.

For example, most advocates who argue for group-based remedies, who urge looking beyond state action to social sources of deprivation, and who direct attention to correcting background inequalities, tend to adopt a more liberal version of the opportunity ethic. Activists arguing for the goal of systemic wealth redistribution may do so, however, by endorsing policies promoting more just results as well as those aimed at creating fairer opportunities. Some approaches to legal change may opt to circumvent the language of opportunities and results altogether. Given the intrinsically conservative logic of our inherited Fourteenth Amendment discourse and the changing composition of the Court, however, it remains true that the most brilliant arguments on behalf of social justice are highly unlikely to generate more.

REFERENCES

Bell, D. (1972). On meritocracy and equality. *Public Interest, 84*(3), 35–49.
Bell, D. (1992). *Race, racism and American law.* Boston, MA: Little, Brown.
Brigham, J. (1984). *Wealth discrimination: An investigation into constitutional ideology.* Paper presented at the Western Political Science Association, Sacramento, CA.
Brown v. Board of Educ., 347 U.S. 493 (1954).
Burton v. Wilmington Parking Authority, 365 U.S. 715 (1961).
Civil Rights Cases, 109 U.S. 3 (1883).
Coleman, J. S. (1973). Equality of opportunity and equality of results. *Harvard Educational Review, 43,* 129–137.
Corrigan v. Buckley, 271 U.S. 323 (1926).
de Tocqueville, A. (1988). *Democracy in America.* Harper Perennial. HarperCollins Publishers.
Dorn, E. (1976). *Rules and racial equality.* New Haven, CT: Yale University Press.
Fishkin, J. S. (1983). *Justice, equal opportunity and the family.* New Haven, CT: Yale University Press.
Fiss, O. (1976). Groups and the equal protection clause. *Philosophy and Public Affairs, 5,* 107–177.
Freeman, A. D. (1978). Antidiscrimination law: A critical review. In D. Kairys (Ed.), *The politics of law: A progressive critique* (pp. 279–311). New York: Pantheon Books.
Friedman, A. D. (1985). *A history of American law.* New York: Simon & Schuster.
Frontiero v. Richardson, 411 U.S. 677, 686 (1973).
Fullilove v. Klutznick, 448 U.S. 448 (1980).
Fullinwider, R. K. (1980). *The reverse discrimination controversy.* Totowa, NJ: Rowman & Littlefield.
Geertz, C. (1973). Ideology as a cultural system. In *The interpretations of cultures* (pp. 4–20). New York: Basic Books.
Geertz, C. (1983). Local knowledge: Fact and law in comparative perspective. In C. Geertz (Ed.), *Local knowledge: Further essays in interpretive anthropology* (pp. 35–57). New York: Basic Books.
Green, P. (1981). *The pursuit of inequality.* New York: Pantheon Books.
Griggs v. Duke Power Co., 401 U.S. 424 (1971).
Gulf, C. & S.F. Ry v. Ellis, 165 U.S. 150 (1987).
Jencks, C. (1972). *Inequality: A reassessment of the effect of family and schooling in America.* New York: Basic Books.
Joseph, L. (1980). Some ways of thinking about equality of opportunity. *Western Political Quarterly, 33,* 394–399.
Kairys, D. (1998). *The politics of law: A progressive critique.* New York: Basic Books.
Karst, K. L. (1977). Foreword: Equal citizenship under the fourteenth amendment. *Harvard Law Review, 91,* xi–12.
Kelly, J. M. (1992). *A short history of western legal theory.* New York: Oxford University Press.
Keyes v. School District No. 1, 413 U.S. 189 (1973).
Kluger, R. (1975). *Simple justice: The history of Brown v. Board of Education and black America's struggle for equality.* New York: Knopf.
Korematsu v. United States, 323 U.S. 214 (1944).
Kull, A. (1992). *The color blind constitution.* Cambridge, MA: Harvard University Press.
Marsh v. Alabama, 326 U.S. 501 (1946).

McCann, V. (1986, April). *Equal protection and unequal wealth: The economic foundations of constitutional ideology*. Paper presented at the annual meeting of the American Political Science Association, Washington, DC.

Meese, E. (1985, September 17). *Address to the students and faculty of Dickinson College.*

Michelman, F. (1969). On protecting the poor through the Fourteenth Amendment. *Harvard Law Review, 83*, 7–69.

Milliken v. Bradley, 418 U.S. 717 (1974).

Missouri v. Jenkins, 515 U.S. 70 (1995).

Moose Lodge v. Irvis, 407 U.S. 163 (1972).

Nieli, R. (1991). *Racial preference and racial justice: The new affirmative action controversy.* Washington, DC: National Book Network.

Norwood v. Harrison, 413 U.S. 455 (1973).

O'Neil, T. (1981). The language of equality in a constitutional order. *American Political Science Review, 75*, 626–635.

Pasadena Board of Educ. v. Spangler, 427 U.S. 424 (1976).

Plessy v. Ferguson, 163 U.S. 537 (1896).

Pole, J. R. (1978). *The pursuit of equality in America.* Berkeley: University of California Press.

Posner, R. A. (1997). *The problematics of moral and legal theory.* Cambridge, MA: Belknap Press.

Racowski, E. (1991). *Equal justice.* New York: Oxford University Press.

Rae, D. (1981). *Equalities.* Cambridge, MA: Harvard University Press.

Rawls, J. (1973). *Theory of justice.* Cambridge, MA: Belknap Press.

Rendell v. Baker v. Kohn, 457 U.S. 830 (1983).

Roberts v. City of Boston, 59 Mass. 198 (1849).

Rosenbaum, J. E. (1976). *Making inequality: The hidden curriculum of high school tracking.* New York: Wiley.

Sarat, A. (1997). *Race, law, and culture: Reflections on Brown v. Board of Education.* New York: Oxford University Press.

Schaar, J. (1964). Some ways of thinking about equality. *Journal of Politics, 66*, 867–895.

Schaar, J. (1967). Equality of opportunity and beyond. In J. R. Pennock & J. W. Chapman (Eds.), *NOMOS IX: Equality* (pp. 228–249). New York: Atherton Press.

Scheingold, S. A. (1974). *The politics of rights.* New Haven, CT: Yale University Press.

Schepple, K. L. (1990). Facing facts in legal interpretation. *Representations, 30*, 30–45.

Shelley v. Kraemer, 334 U.S. 1 (1948).

Sindler, A. P. (1983). *Equal opportunity: On the policy and politics of compensatory minority preferences.* Washington, DC.

Sowell, T. (1984). *Civil rights: Rhetoric or reality?* New York: Morrow.

Strauder v. West Virginia, U.S. 303 (1880).

Sumner, W. G. (1974). *What social classes owe to each other.* Caldwell, ID: Caxton.

United States v. Harris, 106 U.S. 629 (1882).

United Steelworkers of America, AFL-CIO-CLC v. Weber, 443 U.S. 193 (1979).

University of California Regents v. Bakke, 438 U.S. 265 (1978).

Walzer, M. (1983). *Spheres of justice: A defense of pluralism and equality.* New York: Basic Books.

Washington et al. v. Davis et al., 426 U.S. 229 (1976).

Weber v. Aetna Casualty & Surety Co., 406 U.S. 164 (1972).

Westen, A. (1982). The empty idea of equality. *Harvard Law Review, 95*, 537–585.

Williams, T. H. (1957). *Abraham Lincoln selected speeches, messages, letters.* New York: Holt, Rinehart, and Winston.

Wills, G. (1979). *Nixon agonists: The crisis of the self-made man.* New York: Mentor Books.

Wygant v. Jackson Board of Education, 476 U.S. 267 (1986).

CHANGING CONCEPTIONS OF ADMINISTRATION AND POLICY

The two chapters in part II summarize the state of knowledge in educational administration and outline two views of how the study of administrative policy should be organized in order to address school problems and the improvement of educational practice.

In chapter 5, Ronald Heck highlights the shift from an earlier emphasis on organizational analysis and administrative practices to scholarly interest in educational governance and policy. He examines the politicization of scholarship that has accompanied this shift, and argues that scholarship in this field stands at an important intellectual crossroads requiring tough intellectual decision making in order to reestablish confidence in the value of the knowledge claims being made. Heck traces the demise of confidence in overarching conclusions based on commonly accepted theoretical frameworks and research methodologies. He uses the metaphor of "big tent" scholarship to describe the increasingly popular practice of treating incommensurate and contradictory theories and research findings as representing equally legitimate claims to reliable knowledge. In the end, he concludes, the big tent simply will not sustain confidence in knowledge claims or adequately guide professional practice.

Gail Furman provides a very different take on the state of educational administration scholarship. She takes as her starting point the oft-repeated proposition within classical social sciences that questions of fact and questions of value belong to essentially different domains of inquiry, and that questions of fact are the central domain of empirical inquiry. Values, she notes, are studied within this framework as simply the variable opinions and beliefs of social actors, not as an attribute of the social action system itself. She insists, however, that questions of moral purpose and public value are absolutely central to understanding school programs and practices. As a result, she concludes, the entire enterprise of social-science-based research on school administration and administrative policy has to be called into question. She rejects positivism in the social sciences, asserting that it leads to both intellectual error and political bias. In place of the traditional model of social science research, she makes a spirited defense of postmodernism as the intellectual perspective from which school programs and practices can be fruitfully studied.

Chapter 5

Scholarship in Educational Administration: At a Crossroads or Dead End?

Ronald H. Heck
University of Hawaii at Manoa

Historical traditions exert a powerful, though at times unacknowledged, influence on ways that scholars pursue understanding and solving important problems in a field (Kuhn, 1970). Examining the progress in educational administration's development as a field has drawn the attention of numerous scholars during its 125-year history (e.g., Boyan, 1988a; Bridges, 1982; Culbertson, 1988; Donmoyer, 1999a; Erickson, 1967; Everhart, 1988; Getzels, 1952; Mitchell & Ortiz, chap. 2, this volume; Moore, 1964; Mort, 1935; Payne, 1875, 1886; Willower & Forsyth, 1999). Although the field has generated much scholarly interest, reviewers of the literature generally concluded that it has not been given to rigorous empirical investigation and knowledge accumulation. Since the field's scholarly genesis, writers have struggled to identify problems, subject matter, methods of inquiry, and a knowledge base that could inform administrative practices in schools. Perhaps because the natures of the problems scholars seek to understand are considerably more complex than in some other fields, scholarly directions in educational administration have been more affected by changes in politics and societal values (e.g., efficiency, equity) than by sustained programmatic research to resolve a set of well-defined disciplinary problems.

As Mitchell and Ortiz (chap. 2, this volume) note in their discussion of the evolution of educational administration theory, research, and practice, during the 1950s and early 1960s the theory movement became a significant intellectual framework in educational administration (e.g., Griffiths, 1959; Halpin, 1957). Proponents attempted to replace folklore and professional prescriptions for administrative practice with scientific analysis of the dynamics of educational organizations and the effects of administrator behavior. The results of this shift in disciplinary focus were expected to unify the field's fragmented, largely nonempirical scholarly efforts to create a comprehensive body of knowledge and provide a set of trustworthy outcomes that could be applied to problems of practice and inform the initial preparation and professional development of school administrators (Griffiths, Carlson, Culbertson, & Lonsdale, 1964).

The theory movement and quantitative analysis formed the dominant modes of inquiry in the field as it matured from the 1960s through the 1980s. The promise of a scientific knowledge base in educational administration, however, never fully materialized. Over the two decades following the theory movement's introduction, its intellectual underpinnings, methods of inquiry, and utility for improving practice were harshly criticized within the scholarly community (e.g., Bates, 1980; Erickson, 1967; Foster, 1980; Greenfield, 1978). Some went so far as to suggest that the theory movement had led scholars down the wrong intellectual road. The prolonged criticism notwithstanding, however, it is clear that programmatic empirical inquiry did provide cumulative knowledge in at least certain subfields of educational administration (e.g., policy and politics, school leadership, school effects on student learning, school improvement). The legacy of the theory movement lies more in its endorsement of theoretically informed study of administrative practice than in the content of its major research findings.

In its aftermath, serious divisions within the academic community surfaced regarding whether the theory movement had given too much emphasis to particular ways of looking at problems, methods of inquiry, and solutions. Scholars advanced a number of alternative ways of investigating problems (e.g., critical theory, humanism, phenomenology, postmodernism, pragmatism) and situating the field's disciplinary practices (e.g., craft, moral endeavor, advocacy). Donmoyer (1999a) described the growing disillusionment with the dominant rational-quantitative paradigm and the proliferation of alternative approaches metaphorically as a "big tent" that held opposing scholarly views without critique of intellectual stance, method, or the relevance of knowledge produced. Some of these alternative perspectives advanced very different views about epistemology, the use of research methods, patterns of discourse in research texts, and the role of the scholars and researchers in the production of knowledge (e.g., Donmoyer; Mitchell & Ortiz, chap. 2, this volume; Sackney & Mitchell, 2002; Willower & Forsyth, 1999). To date, however, proponents of emerging perspectives have extolled their promise more than documented what they have actually accomplished.

In contrast to the century-long quest for a scientific knowledge base that preceded it (Culbertson, 1988), the big tent conception of incompatible diversity has become the normative account of educational administration scholarship today. Uncritical acceptance of scholarly views, however, has led to intellectual relativism, a weakening of standards for inquiry and argument, and an inability to judge the merits of competing claims to knowledge. Moreover, the research community has largely abandoned a serious commitment to problems related to improving professional practice. At the same time, outside of the research community, political agendas have reshaped the federal role in education, altered the scope of educational research to be utilized in determining what works in affecting educational practice, dictated the resultant policy actions that should be used to improve schools, encouraged the development of public school alternatives, and promoted alternative preparation programs and certification for school leaders. This new political agenda regarding schooling is likely to change the way the public thinks about education and the ways in which the field's scholarship will inform future policymaking, school improvement, and educational leadership preparation and practice. Critics of current trends in educational research suggest it is of little use to policymakers, does not attend to important questions, is poorly conceived and conducted, cannot be replicated, and is seldom disseminated in ways that enable educators to put the results to use (Feuer, Towne, & Shavelson, 2002).

The theory movement and the big tent provide metaphoric bookends for the diverse ways scholars in educational administration have defined problems and inquiry during the past 50 years. Understanding the scholarly stories that are between the bookends may provide some insights for reorienting our scholarly efforts and pointing in new and more fruitful directions. The field currently faces a number of challenges regarding its future direction. Some of these include the relevance and utility of its research and scholarship for improving educational practice and addressing other important educational problems, the nature of its knowledge base and disciplinary outcomes, and the quality of its preparation of new administrators. There is a certain amount of urgency in meeting some of these challenges head-on and making some headway, because we face a crisis of credibility and relevance.

In this chapter, I consider the tension that has resurfaced between the scientific and normative views and its implications for reestablishing some scholarly direction. First, I briefly characterize reaction against the shortcomings of early scholarship in the field that led scholars to call for a more theoretically informed and scientific study of educational administration. Second, I contrast this more uniform call for a science of educational administration with the diversity of scholarly perspectives (some scientific and some normative) that developed in the years following publication of Daniel Griffiths' (1964) landmark volume on the theory movement's agenda. Here I show that the big tent response is a reaction to the rigid view of theory and research method the theory movement proposed and is shaped by that movement's inability to address many educational problems of interest to scholars. Third, confronting the current lack of agreement on the field's scholarly direction and the absence of any means of arbitrating conflicting claims to knowledge, I argue that the field is now facing a dialectic crossroads in its scholarly pursuits. At this crossroads, one road beckons us toward more normative and political ends (i.e., Whose beliefs, values, and interests are served?), whereas the other leads toward renewed commitment to scientific ends (i.e., What knowledge can be utilized in alleviating educational problems?). If we are to regain some scholarly direction as a field that can produce disciplinary outcomes relevant to current political and social discussions of policy action and practice in education, we will need to find ways to finesse this scholarly Hobson's choice.

THEORY AND EDUCATIONAL ADMINISTRATION SCHOLARSHIP

To move the analysis forward, I need to summarize the history of educational administration scholarship briefly and place the theory movement in proper perspective. Initial scholarship in the field was preoccupied with taking efficient, practical action (Payne, 1875). Payne argued that a science could be developed to understand the "art" of running school systems and schools. To build a science of educational management, Payne concluded that scholars should borrow from the social science disciplines of "history, sociology, political science, and legislation" (1886, p. 4). Writings on scientific management in pursuit of organizational efficiency (e.g., Taylor, 1895) were eagerly embraced by educational progressives during the early 20th century as a means to improve educational efficiency. Despite rhetoric supporting the marriage of science and school administration, however, critics of the information collected (i.e., mounds of descriptive survey data) were skeptical of its utility in generating knowledge that could actually be used to improve educational practice (e.g., Mort, 1935). Outside of stories told by former administrators and their prescriptions based on what they believed, there was little to suggest a viable knowledge base. Hence, concerns were raised beginning in the 1930s and 1940s that scholarship in educational administration was faulty, unimaginative, and out of step with community needs and desires (Moore, 1964).

In response to this criticism, during the 1950s key scholars in a small circle of prominent university programs in educational administration began to call for disciplined scientific inquiry that went beyond anecdotes, individual stories of success, and normative prescriptions in preparing administrators to manage educational institutions. The goal of the theory movement was to make educational administration a field of scientific study by developing the complexity of its conceptual models, the rigor of its research methods, and the volume of its empirical studies. A comprehensive and optimistic view of this movement was captured in the National Society for the Study of Education's (NSSE) 1964 yearbook entitled *Behavioral Science and Educational Administration*, edited by Daniel Griffiths.

How the 1964 NSSE Yearbook Framed a Disciplinary Perspective

The NSSE volume (Griffiths, 1964) described the new disciplinary perspective for studying educational administration as consisting of: (a) a way of addressing phenomena scientifically rather than normatively, (b) a comprehensive body of knowledge, and (c) an orderly pursuit of new knowledge (Haskew, 1964). Major sections in the volume dealt with historical perspectives on educational administration, new scientific bases for guiding scholarly activity, and implications of proposed scientific research and scholarship for the profession (e.g., improving practice, training new administrators). In framing the NSSE yearbook's new perspective on scholarship, Griffiths et al. (1964, p. 3) emphasized, "Probably the most critical feature of past efforts in the study of administration was that there was no confrontation of evidence and principles. This resulted largely from the value orientation of the writers who felt that it was sufficient to assert that they believed in something." Griffiths et al. asserted that their effort was directed toward "operationalizing concepts, testing propositions, and developing theories based upon evidence" (p. 3). The integration of theory, research, and improved practice was possible, they contended, because management was best viewed as a generic concept applicable to all types of formal organizations (e.g., Bidwell, 1965).

Movement proponents emphasized the development of a generic type of administrative theory that could be applied across contextual settings, underpinned by mathematical relationships that could be empirically supported. Their definition of theory required a set of assumptions from which could be derived by purely logico-mathematical procedures a larger set of empirical laws (Feigl, 1951; Halpin, 1958). This body of knowledge would serve as a guide for improving educational practices in schools. Proponents of this paradigm had in mind that a set of theoretical assumptions could be logically proved or disproved, whether or not the actual analytic tools for testing it were available at the time the theory was formulated (Griffiths et al., 1964). They were confident that scholarly advances in the study of educational administration rested squarely on the ability to distinguish more from less powerful ideas about how schools work and how school administrators could influence their workings.

Despite this intense optimism for developing an overarching theory of educational administration, Halpin's (1958) definition of theory was quickly shown to be too rigid to apply to empirical investigation. Halpin (1960) himself noted that theorizing based on rational organizational models was often too limiting in examining school administration. Other scholars in Griffiths' (1964) volume also expressed reservations about the application of mathematical models to derive practical administrative actions in schools (Gross, 1964; Haskew, 1964). Gross concluded that Herbert Simon's (1945) mathematical models of administrative behavior were likely to have only limited applicability to the practice of school administration. Haskew noted that the use of scientific theory applied to management over the previous 15 years was rare and did not really meet the standards of scientific investigation in the natural sciences. He found that the volume of scientific investigation fitting this lofty standard was also extremely limited within the more established social science disciplines themselves, despite decades of advocating for high standards of investigation within those fields. In fact, he suggested that if "evidence is necessary for proof, it is extremely doubtful that scientism is the method for education" (Haskew, p. 338). Having said that, however, Haskew concluded empirical investigation represented a divergent method, promising and underused, in a field that had "been almost solely dependent upon folklore and revelation" (p. 339). Although the scientific beginnings were rudimentary and not applicable to the whole field, they represented a considerable step forward from the state of the field in the late 1940s.

SCHOLARSHIP FOLLOWING THE 1964 YEARBOOK

Reaction and Counterpoint

Although the 1964 yearbook (Griffiths, 1964) paid considerable attention to the need to organize scholarship in educational administration more scientifically, it did not provide even a glimpse of what the accumulated knowledge base from theory testing might look like. Neither did it describe very specifically the research methods and procedures that actually would be used to develop this knowledge. In truth, training in research methods was considerably lacking at the time, so it was an optimistic view that the quality of the field's empirical studies (both qualitative and quantitative) would be immediately upgraded by adopting a more scientific stance.

Scholarly review of the research produced and critique of the theory movement's underlying principles quickly exposed weaknesses in the development of an overarching, context-sensitive theory of administration; limited application of specific theories to the study of schooling; little or no programmatic research; and a serious lack of methodological rigor in conducting studies (Bridges, 1982; Erickson, 1967; Immegart, 1977). Reviewing research conducted from the mid-1960s to 1980, Bridges concluded that empirical studies of school administrators were "intellectual random events" (p. 23). He described the accumulated research in the following manner:

> Research on school administrators for the period 1967–1980 reminds one of the dictum: "The more things change, the more they remain the same." . . . Moreover these researchers persist in treating research problems in an ad hoc rather than a programmatic fashion. Despite the rather loose definition of theory that was used in classifying the sample of research . . . most of it proved to be atheoretical. Likewise the research seemed to have little or no practical utility. (pp. 24–25)

By the late 1970s, intellectual criticism began to challenge the philosophical underpinnings of the theory movement. Critics undertook construction of an opposing philosophical argument, asserting that the increasingly apparent complexity of the environment surrounding educational organizations, the dynamics of organizations themselves, and the complexity of administrators' roles and responsibilities required a more diverse set of epistemological approaches (e.g., constructivism, phenomenology, critical theory) and research methods for successful study (e.g., Bates, 1980; Foster, 1980, 1986; Greenfield, 1978, 1980). Bates and Greenfield (1978) argued that rational organizational and behaviorist models based on quantitative analyses were ill-suited to understanding the social constructions of school life. Instead, understanding shared meanings within school settings (i.e., tenets of constructivism) required process-oriented research methods (e.g., fieldwork). Bates and Foster (1986) contended that such rational and behavioral approaches failed to consider how political, ethical, and moral issues (e.g., social class and race, equity, social justice) might affect the practice of administration. Bates concluded that the pursuit of a knowledge base was ultimately a political, rather than an objective endeavor. Similarly, Anderson (1991) challenged researchers to find ways to study the invisible and unobtrusive forms of control exercised in schools; otherwise, how could school personnel hope to improve the lives of students who attend them?

**Research Compendia and the Scholarly Landscape
in Educational Administration**

In the years following the calls for a science of educational administration, several compendia of the field's scholarship appeared. Because they are extensive intellectual efforts, they provide one window to examine general scholarly trends, conflicts, and emerging issues in the field. They offer broad insights into the problems emphasized, the lines of inquiry pursued, and the issues contested (Willower & Forsyth, 1999). Unlike scholarly journals, which generally provide a forum for sharing the empirical results of individual studies conducted from a variety of epistemological and methodological stances on various aspects of educational administration, comprehensive research volumes bring together numerous scholars in an explicit attempt to assess the progress and directions in the field from a macro perspective. Whereas the knowledge gained from individual studies often breaks down relatively rapidly (e.g., through lack of scholarly citation, the existence of newer studies), these more extensive volumes invite individual chapters that attempt to synthesize research in various subfields of educational administration over a decade or more.

Key works in this genre are: (a) Boyan's (1988b) *Handbook of Research on Educational Administration*; (b) Murphy and Seashore-Louis's (1999) *Handbook of Research on Educational Administration*; (c) Leithwood, Chapman, Corson, Hallinger, and Hart's (1996) *International Handbook of Educational Leadership and Administration*; and (d) Leithwood and Hallinger's (2002) *Second International Handbook of Educational Leadership and Administration*. This is not to suggest that these volumes entirely hit the mark in assessing scholarly trends and progress. The editors' framing of the scholarly endeavors is open to criticism, and the quality of the individual chapters is somewhat uneven and subject to the specific views and interpretations of their authors, despite attempts by editors to provide some type of external review. They also are privileged accounts, because they represent choices among editors and advisory groups about which scholarly views should be heard and which ones neglected.[1] The University Council of Educational Administration also undertook a major project to define a knowledge base in the 1990s (Hoy, Astuto, & Forsyth, 1994). Hoy's (1994) own assessment of the participating scholars' ability to move the field forward in defining a knowledge base and fostering systematic inquiry was that they provided a modest step. They identified debates, contested topics of reform, and emerging issues of racism, sexism, and classism during the 1990s, but could not identify a reliable and robust technology of school practice.

The American Educational Research Association (AERA) handbooks (Boyan, 1988b; Murphy & Seashore-Louis, 1999), consistent with Griffiths'

---

[1]Numerous other volumes, chapters, and articles addressing progress in educational administration provide alternative ways readers can understand the dynamics of practice, research, and scholarship, as well as their surrounding political, historical, and cultural contexts (e.g., Anderson & Grinberg, 1998; Bridges, 1982; Donmoyer, Imber, & Scheurich, 1995; Evers & Lakomski, 1996; Foster, 1998; Greenfield, 1980; Gunter, 2001; Hallinger & Heck, 1996; Hoy, 1996; Lindle & Mawhinney, 2003; Marshall, 2004; Mitchell, 1984; Ribbins & Gunter, 2002; Richmon & Allison, 2003).

(1964) volume, framed trends in the field in more scientific (and progress-related) terms. This was not coincidental, for as Boyan (1988b) described in the preface of the first handbook, the genesis for the project began in the mid-1970s with an ad hoc advisory committee that consisted of a number of the contributors to Griffiths' book. The focus of the first handbook was largely dictated by Halpin's (1957) rubric for research on administrative behavior. Major substantive divisions in the volume included administrators, organizations, and the environment, with sections on methodology and special topics (i.e., economics and finance, politics and policy). Emphasizing the historical, rational, and objective underpinnings of the volume, Boyan (pp. ii–iii) argued:

> The straightforward and archival function of the *Handbook* has required telling where scholarship in educational administration has been as well as where it might be going. Ideology or belief about where a field ought to go cannot change the history of where the field has been and where it came from. So, if what have been the subjects and models of inquiry over the past 30 years do not fit readers' tastes, they will not be able to erase by dialectic, no matter how pervasive, what happened over the course of one-third of a century.

The first handbook (Boyan, 1988b) devoted considerable attention to describing progress in developing a science of administration within changing historical, social, and political settings. For example, individual chapters addressed the ongoing development of a knowledge base (e.g., Culbertson, 1988), the status of theory in educational administration (Griffiths, 1988), and the use of appropriate qualitative and quantitative methods of inquiry (Everhart, 1988; Tatsuoka & Silver, 1988). The piecemeal organization of the volume by several topical content areas provided as many dead ends as promising areas for further scholarly inquiry. Evident among the collection of chapters was growing scholarly fragmentation and concern with alternative philosophical and methodological perspectives in approaching inquiry in the field. As Willower (1988) summarized, "Inquiry in educational administration proceeds on many fronts, a state of affairs that reflects the diversity of problems and subject matter characterizing the field and the variety of approaches to those problems and subject matter" (p. 744). A common thread in the two research method chapters was the need for scholars to provide more specific explication of the methods and analytic techniques used in conducting empirical inquiry, as well as the need for a higher standard in judging the quality and appropriateness of research. As Griffiths concluded, however, despite changing social and political contexts and prolonged criticism of the field's dominant research paradigm in the 1970s and 1980s, there was little impact on the actual methods preferred by the majority of scholars through the mid-1980s (rudimentary as the investigative techniques used were).

In considering a number of organizing frameworks a decade later, the editors of the second handbook (Murphy & Seashore-Louis, 1999) noted that the archival function of the handbook was a necessary, but insufficient, function to describe the growing intellectual diversity present in field in the late 1990s. Some of the intellectual threads remained from the previous volume—a concern with the field's knowledge base (Donmoyer, 1999a; Leithwood & Duke, 1999) and the state of its scholarship (Hill & Guthrie, 1999; Willower & Forsyth, 1999). Besides the archival function, a number of chapters addressed some of the flux and emerging trends in representing knowledge that took place in the decade between the first and second handbooks (e.g., Cibulka, 1999; Heck & Hallinger, 1999; Seashore-Louis, Toole, & Hargreaves, 1999). The editors also acknowledged that their own choices about organizing frameworks brought some topics to the forefront, while deemphasizing others. One way this influenced the second handbook, for example, was to place topics of political relevance in the forefront—an increased emphasis on school leadership, the technical aspects of schooling (i.e., curriculum, teaching, student learning), and school improvement (e.g., site-level politics, school change).

Compared with the first volume, there was less emphasis placed on state and federal politics, finance, policy, and methods and techniques of conducting research. More discussion was directed toward conceptualizing problems from alternative frameworks (e.g., Cibulka, 1999; Firestone & Seashore-Louis, 1999; Reyes, Wagstaff, & Fusarelli, 1999; Rowan & Miskel, 1999; Seashore-Louis et al., 1999; Slater & Boyd, 1999) and less directed toward the use of systematic inquiry to provide definitive answers to educational problems, as proponents of the theory movement hoped. Also in contrast to the earlier edition, few of the chapters were organized around a thorough review and evaluation of extant studies in their subfield. For example, Seashore-Louis et al. likened the use of contrasting conceptual frames in examining school improvement problems to John Godfrey Saxe's (1963) poem, "The Blind Men and the Elephant." Each man describes the elephant in very different terms because he encounters a different part. Donmoyer's (1999a) chapter on the continuing search for a knowledge base in educational administration identified the field's emerging scholarly dilemma: Although scholars embraced changes in the larger intellectual landscape in academia (e.g., critical theory, social reproduction, postmodernism), they have not "redefined research and inquiry in the field in the direction scholars like Greenfield and Bates proposed" (p. 34). Donmoyer concluded that the complex and contradictory perspectives existing in the field confuse policymakers and practitioners looking for tools to improve practice.

In contrast to providing a macro view of progress in the field, the Leithwood et al. (1996) and Leithwood and Hallinger (2002) volumes focused more specifically on a growing subfield of educational administration—educational leadership. Underlying this focus was the editors' realization that since the early 1980s, when the educational context shifted from equity to quality and accountability, the role of leadership became more central to efforts to improve schools. Because of these changes, the field focused more closely on how leadership affects the more traditional aspects of educational administration (i.e., allocating resources, serving as a political intermediary between school personnel and the wider community context, participating in school change directed at improvement). Rather than emphasizing the canons of scientific inquiry and the accumulation of a knowledge base, these two volumes suggested that it might actually be futile to pursue a general theory of leadership (i.e., in the sense suggested by proponents of the theory movement), because it was generally accepted that context interacts with leadership's exercise. Instead, the editors suggested the need "to focus on building middle-level or domain-specific theories of leadership" (Leithwood et al., pp. 1–2). When this is done, they noted that "we find concepts of leadership that are actually quite concrete and sufficiently precise to offer significant guidance for practice" (Leithwood et al., p. 2).

The Leithwood et al. (1996) and Leithwood and Hallinger (2002) volumes also highlighted increasing scholarly diversity and tensions regarding disciplinary purposes, directions, and philosophical underpinnings; the role of scholarship and research in supporting practice; and the place of the field in contributing to the wider context of schooling and society. Importantly, however, the group of contributors represented a considerable step in the direction of engaging a larger, international community of scholars in discussing progress and emerging perspectives in the field. In the first volume, specific chapters examined leadership within changing community and social processes (Goldring & Sullivan, 1996), ethics and values (Begley, 1996), cognitive perspectives and problem solving (Allison, 1996), organizational learning (Cousins, 1996), cultural politics, and emancipatory practices (Anderson, 1996; Blackmore, 1996; Corson, 1996; Robinson, 1996; Smyth, 1996)—topics noticeably absent (or only discussed in broad terms) in the AERA handbooks (Boyan, 1988b; Murphy & Seashore-Louis, 1999). The second volume continued the scholarly debate over contextual influences (e.g., culture, communities, school variables), cultural politics, cognitive perspectives, organizational learning, and the explication of alternative intellectual perspectives and their proposed utility in addressing important problems of practice (e.g., Ah Nee-Benham with Napier, 2002; Fidler, 2002; Moos, 2002; Robinson, 2002).

From perusing the Leithwood et al. (1996) and Leithwood and Hallinger (2002) handbooks, it is evident that continued critiques of the field's lack of systematic research progress encouraged the development of several new approaches (e.g., critical theory, constructivism, phenomenology, neo-Marxism, feminism, and postmodernism) that emphasized alternative ways of constructing knowledge. The empirical evidence demonstrating the usefulness of these approaches in solving identified problems, however, is relatively scant. In contrast with scientific neutrality in producing knowledge, a number of authors suggested that empirical investigations should be used to promote alternative paradigms, for example, humanistic (i.e., emphasizing stories about the realities, dilemmas, and values underlying various leadership roles) or advocacy (e.g., Ah Nee-Benham with Napier, 2002; Anderson, 1996; Blackmore, 1996; Sackney & Mitchell, 2002; Smyth, 1996). The handbooks, in particular, illustrated the growing intellectual controversy within the field over the pursuit of scientific ends (i.e., providing accumulated scientific knowledge to improve schools) or political advocacy ends (i.e., identifying and removing oppressive educational structures).

Assessing the Adequacy of the Scientific Perspective on Inquiry

Examined at a distance through these sets of research handbooks, the theory movement came and went leaving scholars relatively unaffected, at least as measured by debate and discussion about it in texts published after the early 1980s. The abiding legacy of the theory movement, however, was its success in calling for the development of theoretical and conceptual lenses to inform the study of administrative problems and practices. Did the scholarly efforts of the theory movement amount to the wrong intellectual path? Not if we consider proponents' intent to move the field from one of folklore and prescription to one where empirical evidence and cumulative knowledge form the basis for improving educational practices. Has the empirical evidence accumulated in the field over the past 40 years amounted to a promised science of educational administration? Not if we peruse the diverse scholarly commentary on the field's growth and shortcomings over the past several decades. Evidence of the type of sustained programmatic research and cumulative knowledge Griffiths (1964) and his colleagues hoped for is decidedly lacking in most substantive areas within the field. Boyan (1988a) summarized this scholarly quest by questioning whether educational administration was really a field of scientific study or merely a field for study.

In retrospect, the scientific view of educational administration advanced in the Griffiths (1964) yearbook was inadequate to represent the field's problems and disciplinary practices on at least four different levels. First, despite its promise of providing elegant theories and rigorous investigation, it failed to produce reliable guidance for actions to improve schools. Having said that, however, few would argue that there are not viable research strands today (e.g., school effects, school leadership, organizational change) that have increased our understanding of, and ability to manage, the interplay between contextual and educational processes on school improvement. Second, its narrow definition of science considerably restricted the range of legitimate explanatory frames, emphasizing the rational and structural functional paradigms, without acknowledging such challenging frames of organizational analysis as critical, phenomenological, and feminist theories. Alternative lenses challenged this narrow view of conceptual modeling and methods of scientific inquiry and brought increased understanding about how various social and organizational structures and processes serve political as well as intellectual ends by socially advantaging some groups and individuals while marginalizing others. Some scholars also argued that the earlier research did not go far enough in changing educational practices or in identifying oppressive structures and working to replace them (e.g., Anderson, 1996; Bates, 1980; Robinson, 1996). Third, by emphasizing hypothesis testing through quantitative methods, it diminished the value of alternative, especially qualitative, methods of research, analysis, and interpretation. Finally, it suppressed the awareness of moral, ethical, and ideological elements that define schooling as a cultural institution.

SCHOLARSHIP IN THE BIG TENT

Although debate over the theory movement largely ended about 25 years ago (except as an occasional "straw person" to skewer), a deeper concern for the field is the lack of scholarly direction that continues to exist (for different interpretations of this history, see Rowan, chap. 3, and Shipps, chap. 8, this volume). Recent changes in global environmental conditions (e.g., revolutions in information and communications technology) and turmoil surrounding the purposes of public education and expectations for its reform have significantly impacted the intellectual focus of the field. In this context of complex and divergent expectations for education, it is important to engage in dialogue about the field's scope, essential problems, and methods of inquiry. These discussions can help clarify and organize the complexity of methodological and conceptual thinking in the field (Donmoyer, 1999b) as well as make future scholarly work more relevant to important educational debates. My examination of the research compendia discussed in the previous section suggests several emergent themes regarding how scholars currently view the state of knowledge and inquiry in the field.

Diversity (and Fragmentation) of Perspectives

One obvious theme is open embrace of the diverse approaches used to investigate problems and construct knowledge. It is clear that the type of more narrowly focused, quantitative inquiry Griffiths (1964) and his contemporaries envisioned as the field's disciplinary orientation has lost its exclusive hold on the field. Because of the complex nature of problems and interventions that interact with context, scholars are finding that multiple types of conceptual perspectives and methods of inquiry are useful in the investigation of educational problems. Although scholars have widened the manner in which they define problems intellectually (Cibulka, 1999), this intellectual diversity has not led to alternative programs of sustained inquiry directed toward their successful solution in the manner expected by earlier critics (Donmoyer, 1999a).

Each intellectual approach emphasizes different features and provides a contrasting explanation of events. There has been little discussion to date, however, about the bases for these differences, and we are not seeing exemplars of empirical studies and outlines of scholarly programs to demonstrate their usefulness in solving important problems. One core tenet of scientific explanation is that competing explanations be juxtaposed in order to rule out some rival explanations as inadequate on the basis of empirical investigation. Without adequate explication and testing, however, the explosion of contrasting theories has created a situation where the acceptance of an argument rests more on normative conceptions of proper aims of action than on contested interpretation of the empirical data.

Journals contribute to the fragmentation of scholarship in the field. Although they typically recognize and publish excellent examples of individual scholarly work within the diverse research traditions each represents, contributors are too often allowed to treat those with whom they disagree with benign neglect, as if they lacked the proper commitment to action or were promoting inappropriate conceptions of the problems under study, rather than illuminating and debating their differences (Donmoyer, 1999a). The tendency to suppress serious debate creates divergent schools of thought that go unchallenged and thus confuses, rather than clarifies, action alternatives. Lack of agreement about important problems to investigate encourages the submission of work that may be of personal interest to individual contributors but may have little likelihood of moving the field forward intellectually. This lack of clarity about problems and journal aims also makes it difficult for contributors to decide where to send their work. Moreover, because of academic tenure pressures, many new scholars are told to "start at the top, no matter what" and work their way down the journal ladder, instead of learning to hone their writing craft by working their way up to top-tier journals. This creates a morass of intersecting problems, manuscripts, reviewer opinions, and publication decisions. At worst, journals continue to publish work related to perspectives that were intellectually mined but abandoned years before. Readers are left to try to make their own sense out of the patchwork quilt of problems, methodological approaches, and findings presented from issue to issue.

Relativism

A second, related theme is that intellectual diversity has made it more difficult to judge the worth of scholarly efforts. Unfortunately, many concepts presented as new intellectual frameworks amount to little more than ideological beliefs. In contrast to scientific explanations, which seek to provide some type of interpretation of an action system based on assessments of facts, whether those facts are viewed as objective or as socially constructed, ideologies are interpretations based on normative values about how things ought to work, and how they would work if good actions were taken (Douglas Mitchell, personal communication, July 25, 2003; Willower & Forsyth, 1999). As Donmoyer (1999a) noted, rather than debating the legitimacy and utility of ideological and political conceptualizations, many scholars just adopt a relativist stance that the worth of ideas cannot be judged—all ideas are viewed as having legitimacy because someone advanced them. Undercurrents within the academic community have also challenged the goals and legitimacy of the research process itself and the privileged status of the researchers who present their results (e.g., Littrell & Foster, 1995). With this type of anti-empiricism based on topical argument, it becomes difficult to determine which, if any, viewpoints can be appropriately rejected as intellectually inadequate (Björk, Lindle, & Van Meter, 1999).

Acceptance of relativistic stances is seen in granting scholarly legitimacy, by making some topics more sacred through publication in scholarly journals and by endorsing their normative righteousness, despite problematic underlying logic or a lack of methodological rigor in conducting the investigations (Constas, 1998; Donmoyer, 1996). Journal editors can be reluctant to dismiss new approaches because there are no clear standards available for judging the quality and contributions of the work, nor is there enough textual space to provide contrasting scholarly viewpoints. To move forward intellectually, as scholars, editors, and reviewers, we need to establish some criteria for judging the quality of diverse academic work to alleviate some of the present confusion and disagreement.

Failure to Address Problems of Practitioners and Policymakers

A third theme is that scholarship in educational administration has often seemed oblivious to problems of concern to practitioners and policymakers (Ah Nee-Benham with Napier, 2002; Bridges, 1982; Everhart, 1988; Fidler,

2002; Moos, 2002; Richmon & Allison, 2003; Robinson, 2002). Gunter (2001) provided one conceptual framework for the investigation of problems in the field. She noted that policymakers and practitioners prefer the reliability and utility of knowledge generated within the scientific (i.e., knowledge about effects or what works) and instrumental (e.g., strategies that can be used to improve outcomes) intellectual stances. They view knowledge from the humanistic (i.e., accounts and descriptions of leadership realities, tensions, ethics) and critical (i.e., explanations of contexts and structures that marginalize students) stances as less legitimate (Gunter). As Woodhead (2000) echoed, the current attack on educational research in the United Kingdom characterizes much published scholarly work as simply "wacky theorizing" among academics (p. 13).

When scholars do address problems of practitioner concern, they often frame them in ways that are very different from how practitioners view them (Robinson, 1996). Robinson (2002) noted that there is currently less emphasis among scholars on knowing how to do something (i.e., the scientific view) than on knowing the interests and values that underlie why changes should be made (i.e., the normative view). Thus, although new and promising approaches may describe certain realities of life in schools, it remains to be seen exactly how this scholarship may recenter how practitioners perceive problems and practices in the field (Robinson, 1996).

Changing social contexts may affect priorities, definitions of important problems, and expectations for education, as well as alter the focus of research and scholarship, but divergent and unrelated claims backed more by moral commitment than scholarly inquiry do not provide answers for practitioners seeking help in solving problems (Donmeyer, 1999a). This is not to suggest that only scientific scholarship is beneficial to the field, but that scientific scholarship (conducted from a variety of conceptual and methodological perspectives) does have an important role to play in today's political arena. At the present, federal policymakers are attempting to overcome divergent and incommensurate claims of university scholars by imposing standards (i.e., randomized trials) for researchers seeking federal funds. This narrow, experimentally oriented research agenda provides one indication of the fallout from scholars' continuing debates over the field's purposes and disciplinary practices and the reality of criticism about the quality and utility of its scholarship.

Scientific or Advocacy Ends?

Finally, scholarship in the compendia suggests there is growing disagreement over whether scientific or political (advocacy) ends should frame the field's scholarship. At one end of the spectrum, the first AERA handbook

(Boyan, 1988b) attempted to document a clear linkage to knowledge accumulation through empirical investigation as proposed during the theory movement. This conceptualization was not adequate, however, to address the more open and complex environment surrounding schools. The second AERA handbook (Murphy & Seashore-Louis, 1999) focused primarily on multiple ways of understanding various types of problems in the field (reflecting the impact of greater environmental complexity and existence of messy problems). In contrast to empirical reviews of research, there was considerably more scholarly critique in the Leithwood et al. (1996) and Leithwood and Hallinger (2002) handbooks (e.g., critical theory, neo-Marxism, feminism, and postmodernism) that emphasized alternative ways of constructing knowledge and highlighted its role in creating and controlling political power. Recent scholarly trends, therefore, imply a diminished valuation of empirical work, at least as described in more rigorous, scientific terms, for resolving pressing educational problems. At the same time, however, the external policy environment is calling for greater commitment to scientific procedures and accumulated knowledge to achieve desired educational goals. To move forward, scholars are first going to need to address where the field's priorities should lie (e.g., providing evidence, pursuing ideological ends) and then pursue some sustained work that impacts education for children in light of the present policy environment.

REFRAMING SCHOLARLY DIRECTION

With intellectual diversity abounding, a weak empirical knowledge base, and little means of arbitrating conflicting claims to knowledge, we seem to have arrived at a crossroads in educational administration. There are no easy resolutions to the scholarly stalemate under the big tent. My opinion is that although progress has been uneven, over the past few decades empirical investigations have produced knowledge that is regularly incorporated into administrators' daily practices. It also seems that scholars have made the case convincingly that some aspects of educational administration (e.g., morals, values, and beliefs that underlie personal action) are not as amenable to traditional methods of scientific investigation (e.g., experimentation). As a field for study, therefore, educational administration may differ in some important ways from other established fields of scientific study (Boyan, 1988a).

First, the field does not seem to have a well-defined set of disciplinary problems that need to be resolved. Over time, reviewers have noted that scholars in educational administration seem to pursue their own interests in an ad hoc fashion. Moreover, evolving political contexts affect the nature of educational expectations and the structuring of educational activities. These changing contexts can also affect the direction of research. An example is the No Child Left Behind Act's (2001) focus on producing equal achievement outcomes across various student subgroups, even though previous research and federal policy emphasized the need to consider the differing rates at which students progress academically and the varying amounts of school resources it can take to produce similar student achievement outcomes across diverse community settings. Hence, scholars face the dilemma of producing sustained scientific inquiry about important problems (e.g., using a federal definition of *scientific*) within a political environment where the ways in which the problems are defined and solutions framed are constantly changing (of course, social, political, and cultural issues affect knowledge construction in other fields as well). Second, as a professional field, educational administration scholarship should speak to those who actually practice in the field. Third, as an applied research field, we should be concerned that the empirical results of our research produce some type of systematic knowledge that practitioners can use to improve what they are doing for children in schools. Previous reviewers of the field's progress, however, have lamented the dearth of sustained, programmatic research on educational problems that matter and the disconnect between research and practitioners' needs. Ways to bridge the gap between the results of scholarly inquiry and the needs of potential users of knowledge generated should be encouraged.

Although currently there are more ways to view problems, intellectual diversity without scholarly criticism points to the need to make some attempt to alleviate the crowding of ideas in our field. A number of scholars recently weighed in on the issue of how to provide some scholarly direction (e.g., Anderson, 2004; Donmeyer, 1999a, 1999b; Kahne, 1994; Marshall, 2004; Robinson, 1996; Willower & Forsyth, 1999). Kahne noted that traditional research methods are often so technically oriented toward efficiency that they lack the ability to examine the types of research questions related to emerging ideals such as democratic community and social justice. Marshall argued that scholars' pursuit of political ends such as social justice is more important than traditional research ends. Anderson went so far as to suggest that the field has become intellectually and morally bankrupt and needs to reorient its scholarship and relevance to the work of practitioners. These few examples illustrate the recurring tension in deciding among scholarly aims. My own view is to encourage scholars to take on problems of both practical and political importance, but to do so in more sustained manners and in ways that upgrade standards of inquiry and scholarship in our field. These are issues of quality and utility—and they represent bases on which scholarship in the field has been criticized throughout the past 40 years. To retreat from empiricism, however, would represent a giant step backward.

Addressing What Counts as Knowledge

One way forward involves finding ways to overcome the problem of arbitrating alternative claims to knowledge. It is one thing to celebrate the diversity of approaches and legitimacy of all ideas. It is another to judge the worth of ideas in providing solutions to persistent problems. Honoring all approaches in the big tent leaves scholars and practitioners hopelessly muddled with competing, irresolvable knowledge claims. The problem is a metatheoretical one: how to establish the criteria and standards of intellectually legitimate alternative explanatory frameworks.

Instead of granting uncritical acceptance of claims to knowledge from either normative or scientific ends, scholars must explore other ways of understanding their intellectual differences and then, before granting legitimacy, construct agreements regarding the need for new claims to provide demonstrations of their worth and utility in solving significant problems (Anderson, 2004; Gunter, 2001). If empirical inquiry and reasoned argument (tenets of determining truth) are granted no more privilege than ideological belief, intuition, or myth in commenting on human endeavors, it calls into question the whole meaning of our scholarship. If we demand less, we admit that we can progress no further than ideological commitment to imagined worlds, as opposed to explanations of documented realities. If that is the case, there will be few lasting disciplinary outcomes from the study of educational administration. Only if we come up with some criteria for testing whether knowledge claims are being made from within a reliable and valid framework for asserting some claim about schooling can we take identifiable paths to informed judgment and legitimate action.

There are several legitimate, contrasting strategies that can be used to assess claims to knowledge (for further discussion, see Mitchell, chap. 9, this volume). Although it is certainly the case that empirical evidence can be biased due to the agendas, assumptions, and decisions of researchers (as critics argue), one hallmark of empiricism is that alternative conceptualizations can be eliminated through one of several methodological means—the most powerful of which is replication. Quantitative methods are often used to find patterns in the data and to determine cause–effect relationships. Qualitative methods provide contextualized descriptions and interpretations of events and meanings in order to understand the contingencies that influence the manner in which such events evolve (Everhart, 1988). These claims can be arbitrated by the appropriateness and rigor of methodological techniques used to generate the empirical findings.

A second and sharply contrasting approach to knowledge construction is phenomenology (Eisenhart & DeHaan, 2005; Everhart, 1988; Mitchell, chap. 9, this volume; Rorty, 1982; Sackney & Mitchell, 2002), which focuses on understanding how social actors make meaning of their world and organize their lives in more desirable ways. From a phenomenological per-spective, the construction of proper categories of thought arises through a dialectical process as individuals move back and forth between lived mo-ments and reflective moments (Mitchell, chap. 9, this volume). Categories of understanding are embedded in and mediated through individuals' ex-periences and, therefore, are authentic to the extent they properly repre-sent the experienced world. Multiple interpretations are probable because people interpreting the data do so through different circumstances (e.g., social, cultural, political) and lenses. The primary criterion for arbitration of this type of knowledge claim lies in its ability to provide a coherent inter-pretation of experience.

The third approach is theoretical, or the extent to which a knowledge claim is sufficiently coherent, comprehensible, and comprehensive to ori-ent people to the world of action that it purports to explain (Mitchell, chap. 9, this volume). Theoretical knowledge provides an explanation of how things work in ways that allow individuals to use that explanation to antici-pate events and guide strategic action toward desired goals. The knowledge test of a good theory is its utility in explaining or predicting what it pur-ports.

As this short discussion of knowledge claims suggests, some theories, models, or arguments can be demonstrated to be superior to others in achieving desired ends by using methods and standards of inquiry, logic, and utility (Donmoyer, 1999a; Eisenhart & DeHaan, 2005; Mitchell, chap. 9, this volume; Willower & Forsyth, 1999). Clearly, the demand for knowl-edge from outside the field currently focuses on its validity, credibility, and utility.

Raising the Standards for Method

A second way to move the field forward is to require the use of evidence, as opposed to normative ideals, in establishing the legitimacy of empirical and political arguments. Previous scholarly reviews (e.g., Bridges, 1982; Boyan, 1988a; Erickson, 1967; Hallinger & Heck, 1996) identified the needs to im-prove methods of inquiry and to develop and sustain programmatic re-search on important problems. A wide array of methodological techniques is available, but the techniques have not always been put to full use (Heck & Hallinger, 1999). Scholars have not always been very clear about the meth-ods of inquiry and argument they use to advance their work. It is the appro-priate application of an inquiry approach to a particular problem, rather than the approach itself, that enables judgments about a study's merit (Feuer et al., 2002). In recent years, there has been a wider variety of both qualitative and quantitative methods available for investigating problems. Advances in methodology, however, do not necessarily lead to uniform improvement in the accumulation of knowledge, certainly when methods are not coupled with conceptual and theoretical advances (Heck & Hallinger).

As I suggested earlier, changing contextual conditions and historical traditions can exert a powerful influences on the way scholars think about epistemological and methodological issues. Over time, scholarly investigation in educational administration has become more inclusive. The scholarly mainstream has embraced more diverse means of inquiry and evidence collection. Yet, diversity of approach does not require the abandonment of methodological rigor. Even if some past research was a reflection of existing power structures or was used to advance particular political arguments, these misuses should not invalidate the possibility of conducting good research. We can require that scholars lay out their cases with both argument and evidence. Despite a broader set of theories of knowledge, reason and evidence continue to be relevant criteria in judging scholarship (Willower & Forsyth, 1999). Published scholarship should move the field forward substantively and serve as an exemplar for the type of inquiry it represents. Critical reviews of accumulated evidence should also be encouraged—in particular, reviews that assess how well competing explanations resolve the field's practical, professional, and intellectual problems.

Rethinking Our Relationship With Practitioners and Policymakers

Finally, renewing the focus on resolving problems of policy and practice will also help develop scholarly direction and relevance. In recent years, the field has been long on intellectual critique, but short on sustained action and demonstrated results about alternatives that will enhance schooling for all children. This has created a crisis of credibility about the field's scholarly inquiry, especially in the wake of the No Child Left Behind Act of 2001 (i.e., the underlying impact of this law in negating previous research on school effects and student learning should be a concern of scholars in our field). As scholars debate the knowledge base and methods of investigation, they should also be concerned with the meaning of these differences for contributing to our understanding of educational practice (Leithwood & Duke, 1999) and our commitment to demonstrating the impacts of unjust policies and school structures and working to remove them. Orienting the field's scholarship toward more utilitarian ends will be no simple task (Donmoyer, 1999a). It may require some reshaping of norms about scholarly focus and advancement within the academy, orienting scholars to the practical impact of their work, providing more substantial training for new professors, and creating opportunities for scholars, practitioners, and policymakers to engage in more fruitful conversations about problems.

It is obvious that the field needs concrete reference points to ground discussion and debate about the value of work from emerging intellectual genres. Few professional situations (e.g., annual meetings, journals) are currently structured to provide forums for the exchange of ideas (Donmoyer, 1999a). We can strengthen the requirement for scholarly work to demonstrate linkages to administrative practice or to alleviating social problems. We could also provide more syntheses of research for practitioners and policymakers framed in ways they perceive problems (e.g., Robinson, 1996, 2002). The use of structured abstracts may also provide further ways to link research to practice.

The prognosis for the future study of educational administration is by no means wholly optimistic. It seems as if we pay a considerable price in continuing to create a bigger tent to house our proliferation of scholarly views. Critique and exposition of alternative perspectives have served a useful purpose to date, but this will not suffice in moving the field forward intellectually in the future. Proponents of alternative orientations have a responsibility to make their case in a means that is accessible to both scholars and practitioners (Donmoyer, 1999a; Heck & Hallinger, 1999). Only in this manner can peers make informed judgments. Ultimately, if we do not attend to the field's direction, we run the risk of reaching a scholarly dead end because of blind neglect. By acknowledging some of the past intellectual differences, working toward conceptual clarity and standards of scholarship, and venturing outside the boundaries of academic settings to work with policymakers and practitioners on important problems, scholars can contribute to solutions that acknowledge cultural plurality and challenge educators to apply new combinations of ideas and practices that enhance the educational and life chances for all students.

ACKNOWLEDGMENTS

The author is grateful to Ed Bridges, Phil Hallinger, Cecil Miskel, Doug Mitchell, and two anonymous reviewers for insightful comments and suggestions for revision on earlier versions of this work.

REFERENCES

Ah Nee-Benham, M. K. P., with Napier, L. A. (2002). An alternative perspective of educational leadership for change: Reflections on native/indigenous ways of knowing. In K. Leithwood & P. Hallinger (Eds.), *Second international handbook of educational leadership and administration* (pp. 133–165). Dordrecht, The Netherlands: Kluwer Academic.

Allison, D. (1996). Problem finding, classification, and interpretation: In search of a theory of administrative problem processing. In K. Leithwood, J. Chapman, D. Corson, P. Hallinger, & A. Hart (Eds.), *International handbook of educational leadership and administration* (pp. 477–549). Dordrecht, The Netherlands: Kluwer Academic.

Anderson, G. L. (1991). Cognitive politics of principals and teachers: Ideological control in an elementary school. In J. Blase (Ed.), *The politics of life in schools: Power, conflict, and cooperation* (pp. 120–138). Newbury Park, CA: Sage.
Anderson, G. L. (1996). Cultural politics of schools: Implications for leadership. In K. Leithwood, J. Chapman, D. Corson, P. Hallinger, & A. Hart (Eds.), *International handbook of educational leadership and administration* (pp. 947–966). Dordrecht, The Netherlands: Kluwer Academic.
Anderson, G. L. (2004). William Foster's legacy: Learning from the past and reconstructing the future. *Educational Administration Quarterly, 40,* 240–258.
Anderson, G. L., & Grinberg, J. (1998). Educational administration as disciplinary practice: Appropriating Foucault's view of power, discourse, and method. *Educational Administration Quarterly, 34,* 329–353.
Bates, R. (1980). Educational administration, the sociology of science, and the management of knowledge. *Educational Administration Quarterly, 16,* 1–20.
Begley, P. T. (1996). Cognitive perspectives on the nature and function of values in educational administration. In K. Leithwood, J. Chapman, D. Corson, P. Hallinger, & A. Hart (Eds.), *International handbook of educational leadership and administration* (pp. 551–699). Dordrecht, The Netherlands: Kluwer Academic.
Bidwell, C. (1965). The school as a formal organization. In J. March (Ed.), *Handbook of organizations* (pp. 972–1022). Chicago: Rand McNally.
Björk, L. G., Lindle, J. C., & Van Meter, E. J. (1999). A summing up. *Educational Administration Quarterly, 35,* 658–664.
Blackmore, J. (1996). Breaking the silence: Feminist contributions to educational administration and policy. In K. Leithwood, J. Chapman, D. Corson, P. Hallinger, & A. Hart (Eds.), *International handbook of educational leadership and administration* (pp. 997–1042). Dordrecht, The Netherlands: Kluwer Academic.
Boyan, N. (1988a). Describing and explaining administrative behavior. In N. Boyan (Ed.), *Handbook of research on educational administration* (pp. 77–97). New York: Longman.
Boyan, N. (Ed.). (1988b). *Handbook of research on educational administration.* New York: Longman.
Bridges, E. (1982). Research on the school administrator: The state of the art, 1967–1980. *Educational Administration Quarterly, 18,* 12–33.
Cibulka, J. G. (1999). Ideological lenses for interpreting political and economic changes affecting schooling. In J. Murphy & K. Seashore-Louis (Eds.), *Handbook of research on educational administration* (2nd ed., pp. 163–182). San Francisco: Jossey-Bass.
Constas, M. A. (1998). The changing nature of educational research and a critique of postmodernism. *Educational Researcher, 27*(2), 26–33.
Corson, D. (1996). Emancipatory discursive practices. In K. Leithwood, J. Chapman, D. Corson, P. Hallinger, & A. Hart (Eds.), *International handbook of educational leadership and administration* (pp. 1043–1067). Dordrecht, The Netherlands: Kluwer Academic.
Cousins, J. B. (1996). Understanding organizational learning for educational leadership and school reform. In K. Leithwood, J. Chapman, D. Corson, P. Hallinger, & A. Hart (Eds.), *International handbook of educational leadership and administration* (pp. 589–652). Dordrecht, The Netherlands: Kluwer Academic.
Culbertson, J. A. (1988). A century's quest for a knowledge base. In N. Boyan (Ed.), *Handbook of research on educational administration* (pp. 3–26). New York: Longman.
Donmoyer, R. (1996). Editorial: Educational research in an era of paradigm proliferation: What's a journal editor to do? *Educational Researcher, 25*(2), 19–25.
Donmoyer, R. (1999a). The continuing quest for a knowledge base, 1976–1998. In J. Murphy & K. Seashore-Louis (Eds.), *Handbook of research on educational administration* (2nd ed., pp. 25–43). San Francisco: Jossey-Bass.

Donmoyer, R. (1999b). Paradigm talk (and its absence) in the second edition of the handbook of research on educational administration. *Educational Administration Quarterly, 35,* 614–641.

Donmoyer, R., Imber, M., & Scheurich, J. (Eds.). (1995). *The knowledge base in educational administration.* Ithaca, NY: State University of New York Press.

Eisenhart, M., & DeHaan, R. L. (2005). Doctoral preparation of scientifically based education researchers. *Educational Researcher, 34*(4), 3–13.

Erickson, D. A. (1967). The school administrator. *Review of Educational Research, 37,* 417–432.

Everhart, R. (1988). Fieldwork methodology in educational administration. In N. Boyan (Ed.), *Handbook of research on educational administration* (pp. 703–726). New York: Longman.

Evers, C. W., & Lakomski, G. (1996). Science in educational administration: A postpositivist conception. *Educational Administration Quarterly, 32,* 379–402.

Feigl, H. (1951). Principles and problems of theory construction in psychology. In W. Dennis (Ed.), *Current trends in psychological theory* (pp. 179–213). Pittsburgh, PA: University of Pittsburgh Press.

Feuer, M. J., Towne, L., & Shavelson, R. J. (2002). Scientific culture and educational research. *Educational Researcher, 31*(8), 4–14.

Fidler, B. (2002). Strategic leadership and cognition. In K. Leithwood & P. Hallinger (Eds.), *Second international handbook of educational leadership and administration* (pp. 613–652). Boston: Kluwer.

Firestone, W. A., & Seashore-Louis, K. (1999). Schools as cultures. In J. Murphy & K. Seashore-Louis (Eds.), *Handbook of research on educational administration* (2nd ed., pp. 297–322). San Francisco: Jossey-Bass.

Foster, W. (1980). Administration and the crisis of legitimacy: A review of Habermasian thought. *Harvard Educational Review, 50,* 496–505.

Foster, W. (1986). *Paradigms and promises: New approaches to educational administration.* Buffalo, NY: Prometreus.

Foster, W. (1998). Editor's foreword. *Educational Administration Quarterly, 34,* 294–297.

Getzels, J. W. (1952). A psycho-social framework for the study of educational administration. *Harvard Educational Review, 22,* 235–246.

Goldring, E. B., & Sullivan, A. V. (1996). Beyond the boundaries: Principals, parents and communities shaping the school environment. In K. Leithwood, J. Chapman, D. Corson, P. Hallinger, & A. Hart (Eds.), *International handbook of educational leadership and administration* (pp. 195–222). Dordrecht, The Netherlands: Kluwer Academic.

Greenfield, T. (1978). Reflections on organizational theory and the truths of irreconcilable realities. *Educational Administration Quarterly, 14*(2), 1–23.

Greenfield, T. (1980). The man who comes back through the door in the wall: Discovering truth, discovering self, discovering organizations. *Educational Administration Quarterly, 16*(3), 26–59.

Griffiths, D. E. (1959). *Administrative theory.* New York: Appleton-Century-Crofts.

Griffiths, D. E. (Ed.).(1964). *Behavioral science and educational administration: The sixty-third yearbook of the National Society for the Study of Education, Part II.* Chicago: National Society for the Study of Education.

Griffiths, D. E. (1988). Administrative theory. In N. Boyan (Ed.), *Handbook of research on educational administration* (pp. 27–51). New York: Longman.

Griffiths, D. E., Carlson, R. O., Culbertson, J., & Lonsdale, R. C. (1964). The theme. In D. E. Griffiths (Ed.), *Behavioral science and educational administration: The sixty-third yearbook of the National Society for the Study of Education, Part II* (pp. 1–7). Chicago: National Society for the Study of Education.

Gross, B. M. (1964). The scientific approach to administration. In D. E. Griffiths (Ed.), *Behavioral science and educational administration* (pp. 33–72). Chicago: University of Chicago Press.

Gunter, H. (2001). Critical approaches to leadership in education. *Journal of Educational Inquiry, 2*(2), 94–108.

Hallinger, P., & Heck, R. H. (1996). Reassessing the principal's role in school effectiveness: A review of empirical research, 1980–1995. *Educational Administration Quarterly, 32*(1), 5–44.

Halpin, A. W. (1957). A paradigm for research on educational administrator behavior. In R. F. Campbell & R. Gregg (Eds.), *Administrative behavior in education* (pp. 155–199). New York: Harper & Row.

Halpin, A. W. (Ed.). (1958). *Administrative theory in education.* Chicago: The Midwest Center, University of Chicago.

Halpin, A. W. (1960). Ways of knowing. In R. F. Campbell & J. M. Lipham (Eds.), *Administrative theory as a guide to action* (pp. 3–20). Chicago: The Midwest Center, University of Chicago.

Haskew, L. D. (1964). A projective appraisal. In D. E. Griffiths (Ed.), *Behavioral science and educational administration* (pp. 333–348). Chicago: University of Chicago Press.

Heck, R. H., & Hallinger, P. (1999). Next generation methods for the study of leadership and school improvement. In J. Murphy & K. Seashore-Louis (Eds.), *Handbook of research on educational administration* (2nd ed., pp. 141–162). San Francisco: Jossey-Bass.

Hill, P. T., & Guthrie, G. W. (1999). A new research paradigm for understanding (and improving) twenty-first century schools. In J. Murphy & K. Seashore-Louis (Eds.), *Handbook of research on educational administration* (2nd ed., pp. 511–523). San Francisco: Jossey-Bass.

Hoy, W. K. (1994). Foundations of educational administration: Traditional and emerging perspectives. *Educational Administration Quarterly, 30*(2), 178–198.

Hoy, W. (1996). Science and theory in the practice of educational administration: A pragmatic perspective. *Educational Administration Quarterly, 32*(3), 366–378.

Hoy, W. K., Astuto, T., & Forsyth, P. B. (1994). *Educational administration: The UCEA document base.* New York: McGraw-Hill.

Immegart, G. (1977). The study of school administration, 1954–1974. In L. Cunningham, W. Hack, & R. Nystrand (Eds.), *Educational administration: The developing decades* (pp. 298–328). Berkeley, CA: McCutchan.

Kahne, J. (1994). Democratic communities, equity, and excellence: A Deweyan reframing of educational policy analysis. *Educational Evaluation and Policy Analysis, 16*(3), 233–248.

Kuhn, T. (1970). *The structure of scientific revolutions* (2nd ed.). Chicago: University of Chicago Press.

Leithwood, K., Chapman, J., Corson, D., Hallinger, P., & Hart, A. (1996). *International handbook of educational leadership and administration.* London: Kluwer.

Leithwood, K., & Duke, D. (1999). A century's quest to understand school leadership. In J. Murphy & K. Seashore-Louis (Eds.), *Handbook of research on educational administration* (2nd ed., pp. 45–72). San Francisco: Jossey-Bass.

Leithwood, K., & Hallinger, P. (Eds.). (2002). *Second international handbook of educational leadership and administration.* London: Kluwer.

Lindle, J. C., & Mawhinney, H. B. (2003). Introduction: School leadership and the politics of education. *Educational Administration Quarterly, 39*(1), 3–9.

Littrell, J., & Foster, W. (1995). The myth of a knowledge base in educational administration. In R. Donmoyer, M. Imber, & J. Scheurich (Eds.), *The knowledge base in educational administration: Multiple perspectives* (pp. 32–46). Albany: State University of New York Press.

Marshall, C. (2004). Social justice challenges to educational administration: Introduction to a special issue. *Educational Administration Quarterly, 40*(1), 5–15.

Mitchell, D. (1984). Educational policy analysis: The state of the art. *Educational Administration Quarterly, 20*(3), 129–160.

Moore, H. B. (1964). The ferment in school administration. In D. Griffiths (Ed.), *Behavioral science and school administration* (pp. 11–32). Chicago: University of Chicago Press.

Moos, L. (2002). Cultural isomorphs in theories and practices of school leadership. In K. Leithwood & P. Hallinger (Eds.), *Second international handbook of educational leadership and administration* (pp. 359–394). Boston: Kluwer.

Mort, P. R. (1935). Organization for effective educational research in colleges and universities. *Teachers College Record, 36,* 541–558.

Murphy, J., & Seashore-Louis, K. (Eds.). (1999). *Handbook of research on educational administration* (2nd ed.). San Francisco: Jossey-Bass.

No Child Left Behind Act of 2001, Pub. L. No. 107-110 (2001).

Payne, W. H. (1875). *Chapters on school supervision.* New York: Wilson, Hinkle.

Payne, W. H. (1886). *Contributions to the science of education.* New York: Harper & Row.

Reyes, P., Wagstaff, L. H., & Fusarelli, L. D. (1999). Delta forces: The changing fabric of American society and education. In J. Murphy & K. Seashore-Louis (Eds.), *Handbook of research on educational administration* (2nd ed., pp. 183–201). San Francisco: Jossey-Bass.

Ribbins, P., & Gunter, H. (2002). Mapping leadership studies in education: Toward a typology of knowledge domains. *Educational Management and Leadership, 30,* 359–384.

Richmon, M. J., & Allison, D. J. (2003). Toward a conceptual framework for leadership inquiry. *Educational Management and Leadership, 31,* 31–50.

Robinson, V. (1996). Critical theory and the social psychology of change. In K. Leithwood, J. Chapman, D. Corson, P. Hallinger, & A. Hart (Eds.), *International handbook of educational leadership and administration* (pp. 1069–1096). Boston: Kluwer.

Robinson, V. (2002). Organizational learning, organizational problem solving, and models of mind. In K. Leithwood & P. Hallinger (Eds.), *Second international handbook of educational leadership and administration* (pp. 775–812). Boston: Kluwer.

Rorty, R. (1982). *Consequences of pragmatism.* Minneapolis: University of Minnesota Press.

Rowan, B., & Miskel, C. G. (1999). Institutional theory and the study of educational organizations. In J. Murphy & K. Seashore-Louis (Eds.), *Handbook of research on educational administration* (2nd ed., pp. 359–383). San Francisco: Jossey-Bass.

Sackney, L., & Mitchell, C. (2002). Postmodern expressions of educational leadership. In K. Leithwood & P. Hallinger (Eds.), *Second international handbook of educational leadership and administration* (pp. 821–847). Boston: Kluwer.

Saxe, J. G. (1963). *The blind men and the elephant: John Godfrey Saxe's version of the famous Indian legend.* New York: Whittlesey House.

Seashore-Louis, K., Toole, J., & Hargreaves, A. (1999). Rethinking school improvement. In J. Murphy & K. Seashore-Louis (Eds.), *Handbook of research on educational administration* (2nd ed., pp. 251–276). San Francisco: Jossey-Bass.

Simon, H. (1945). *Administrative behavior.* New York: Macmillan.

Slater, R. O., & Boyd, W. L. (1999). Schools as polities. In J. Murphy & K. Seashore-Louis (Eds.), *Handbook of research on educational administration* (2nd ed., pp. 323–335). San Francisco: Jossey-Bass.

Smyth, J. (1996). The socially just alternative to the "self-managing school." In K. Leithwood, J. Chapman, D. Corson, P. Hallinger, & A. Hart (Eds.), *International handbook of educational leadership and administration* (pp. 1097–1132). Dordrecht, The Netherlands: Kluwer Academic.

Tatsuoka, M., & Silver, P. (1988). Quantitative research methods in educational administration. In N. Boyan (Ed.), *Handbook of research on educational administration* (pp. 729–747). New York: Longman.

Taylor, F. W. (1895). A piece-rate system, being a step toward a partial solution of the labor problem. *Transactions of the American Society of Mechanical Engineers, 16,* 856–892.

Tyack, D. B., & Cuban, L. (1995). *Tinkering toward utopia: A century of public school reform.* Cambridge, MA: Harvard University Press.

Willower, D. J. (1988). Synthesis and projection. In N. Boyan (Ed.), *Handbook of research on educational administration* (pp. 729–749). New York: Longman.

Willower, D. J., & Forsyth, P. B. (1999). A brief history of scholarship in educational administration. In J. Murphy & K. Seashore-Louis (Eds.), *Handbook of research on educational administration* (2nd ed., pp. 1–23). San Francisco: Jossey-Bass.

Woodhead, C. (2000, January 7). Old values for the new age. *Times Educational Supplement*, p. 13.

Chapter 6

"Scientific" Research and Moral Leadership in Schools

Gail C. Furman
Washington State University

> *The function of science . . . is to establish general laws covering the behaviors of the empirical events or objects with which the science in question is concerned, and thereby to enable us to connect together our knowledge of the separately known events, and to make reliable predictions of events as yet unknown.*
> —Braithwaite (1955, p. 1)

People are natural scientists. From before we are born, we begin to learn from our sensory or empirical experiences about the world and other people. As we grow and develop language and cognition, we organize our sensory experiences to try to understand why and how things happen; in other words, we try to explain the world so we can know what to expect. We test our emerging explanations time and again, and compare them with others' ideas, until we develop our own "science" of life—our (admittedly solipsistic) accumulated theories of how the world works and our place in it. Thus, in our idiosyncratic ways, we "establish general laws covering the behaviors of the empirical events or objects" in our lives (Braithwaite, 1955, p. 1). It seems that we are hard-wired to do this—to explain the world based on empirical experience—to the extent that doing "science" can be not only productive but also extremely enjoyable. As Kerlinger (1986) stated, "Some activities command more interest, devotion, and enthusiasm than do others. So it seems to be with science and with art . . . once we become immersed in scientific research or artistic expression we . . . make passionate commitments to them" (p. vii).

Furthermore, scientific inquiry has made enormous contributions to understanding and predicting phenomena in the physical world and to the development of technology based on these understandings. Indeed, so much progress has been made that many scientists believe science is coming to an "end"; that is, they believe that the most significant discoveries have already been made (e.g., determining that all chemical reactions can be understood in terms of quantum mechanics) or that, in some fields (e.g., theoretical physics), scientific discovery has reached the limits of human understanding (Horgan, 1996).

Given these contributions, the status they have conferred on scientists in Western culture, and the human inclination to enjoy scientific inquiry, it is only natural that scholars involved in studying the social world are attracted to doing "science," and that the principles of scientific investigation have been imported into the social sciences and fields of practice like education. However, the extent to which the idea of "a science" and the principles of scientific investigation as practiced in the natural sciences can be appropriately applied to human behavior and social phenomena has always been in dispute (Griffiths, 1998; Phillips, 1987). Polkinghorne (1983) stated:

> The sciences concerned with the study of the human realm have continuously struggled with the question of appropriate methods. . . . The question has invariably been framed in some kind of relationship to the methods developed by the physical sciences. . . . The traditional debate remains essentially this: Should the human sciences emulate the methods of the natural sciences or should they develop their own methods? The advocates of special methods base their argument on the premise that human beings are different in kind from the objects of study in the physical world and that they therefore require different methods. (p. 15)

A more contemporary take on this position is that human consciousness and subjective experience—the bases for human behavior, learning, and social life—will never be fully understood through scientific investigation. Gunther Stent, a pioneer in the field of molecular biology, argued that "a purely physiological explanation of consciousness would not be as comprehensible or as meaningful as most people would like, nor would it help us to solve moral and ethical questions" (cited in Horgan, 1996, p. 14). Horgan called this the "mysterian" position in regard to human consciousness, which holds that "science cannot penetrate the realm of subjective experience" (p. 178).

Notwithstanding these debates regarding the applicability of a scientific approach to the study of human social life, educational researchers, like other social scientists, have been consistently attracted to and awed by the perspectives and methods of the natural sciences and have attempted to apply them to educational issues. Many methodological debates have been generated over the years, and the credibility of a "scientific" approach to studying problems in education has waxed and waned (Lagemann, 2000). However, current federal policy as embodied in the No Child Left Behind Act (NCLB) of 2001 once again "exalts scientific evidence as the key driver of education policy and practice" (Feuer, Towne, & Shavelson, 2002, p. 4), expressing a preference for a narrow construction of scientific inquiry (e.g., randomized, experimental designs) with the goal of determining causal relationships among educational variables. This neopositivist federal stance on research has generated a new round of methodological debates (e.g., the *Educational Researcher* "Theme Issue on Scientific Research in Education," Jacob & White, 2002), clarification and critique by the National Research Council (Shavelson & Towne, 2002), and position statements by various professional organizations (e.g., the American Educational Research Association's [AERA] "Resolution on the Essential Elements of Scientifically-Based Research," 2003), with the truncated NCLB version of scientific research an easy target for savvy critics.

Specific to the field of educational administration, the call to "scientize" research was made explicit in the 1960s by Daniel Griffiths and his colleagues (Griffiths, 1964) in their argument for an "administrative science" in education. Griffiths based his argument on three basic assumptions about administrative work in schools:

1. That administration is "susceptible to empirical research," meaning the application of "the tools of the behavioral scientist," including "operationalizing concepts, testing propositions, and developing theories based upon evidence" (pp. 2–3).

2. That educational administration is not a unique activity; rather that "administrators in all organizations are confronted with a common set of tasks" (p. 3), which are to "fulfill the goals of the organization" (p. 3), make use of other people in doing so, attend to worker morale, and provide for innovation and change.

3. That human beings in organizations should be viewed more fully in all their complexity, including their personal values; however, these values are to be seen as variables that affect organizational processes: "The values man holds are considered as variables which condition his organizational behavior" (p. 5).

Thus, according to Griffiths, the field could and should develop a "science" of educational administration. Though human values and worker morale should be acknowledged, they enter the research picture as variables to be considered in developing theories that are useful to administrators in their pursuit of organizational goals. Reflecting Braithwaite's (1955) words in the quote opening this chapter, Griffiths' notion of science meant the translation of concepts into measurable variables, the testing of hypotheses related to these variables, and based on such tests, the development of empirically supported theories to be used as the basis for prediction and control, in order to accomplish the (tacit) goals of the educational organization.

Griffiths' (1964) stance reflected the mood of the times—the striving of scholars in education and related fields to be as scientifically rigorous (and to achieve the same status) as researchers in the natural sciences (Culbertson, 1964)—and many educational administration scholars followed his lead in the ensuing decades of the 20th century. However, hopes for the development of a "science" of educational administration have not been realized. Although empirical research in the field has expanded and become ever more sophisticated, it has not stuck to the "scientific" model as represented in Griffiths' work and has not produced a "science" of educational administration. Instead, research methodology has evolved into a multiparadigmatic landscape that includes various interpretive, critical, feminist, postmodernist, and interventionist approaches, which would not meet Griffiths' or the NCLB (2001) criteria for scientific research; and a scientifically informed knowledge base—the sine qua non of a normal science, according to Kuhn (1970)—is not in evidence. Indeed, an analysis of the various efforts over the years to capture the knowledge base in educational administration[1] makes it clear that what counts as knowledge in our field shifts and evolves continually and relatively rapidly, and is a mix of fragmented empirically based findings, theoretical perspectives, and normative or advocacy stances. Bridges' (1982) words are still accurate today: "There is no compelling evidence to suggest that a major theoretical issue or practical problem related to school administrators has been removed by those toiling in the intellectual vineyards since 1967" (p. 25). In a more contemporary critique, English (1994) added that "scientific" approaches have not "provided the explanatory or predictive power of either understanding or advancing the field . . . to solve the myriad of political, moral, and technological dilemmas the schools face in late twentieth-century America" (pp. 230–231). Heck (chap. 5, this volume) points out similar issues in regard to policy research in education.

Scholars and policymakers offer various reasons for the failure to develop a scientific knowledge base in educational administration. One reason, embedded in the current federal critique of educational research in general, is that past research has been badly done; it simply has not been

---

[1]Recent efforts include the University Council for Educational Administration document base project from the 1990s; the two editions of the AERA-sponsored *Handbook of Research on Educational Administration* (Boyan, 1988; Murphy & Seashore Louis, 1999); and the two editions of the *International Handbook of Educational Leadership and Administration* (Leithwood, Chapman, Corson, Hallinger, & Hart, 1996; Leithwood et al., 2002).

scientifically rigorous enough (Shavelson & Towne, 2002). In sharp contrast, other scholars argued that educational administration is simply not a proper subject for scientific investigation, and increased scientific rigor is unlikely to lead to more useful results. English (2004) stated, for example, that "real leadership in context is as much an art as a science . . . is highly situational and involves performance and drama . . . as opposed to results obtained in the usual input-output model commonly used in [scientific] studies" (p. 2). Murphy (1999) offered another view—that traditional research in the field has focused too much on the supposedly value-neutral practices of administration rather than the "valued outcomes" or *purposes* of that practice (p. 53). Related to both English's and Murphy's arguments is yet another possibility, which has been insufficiently explored to date: that educational leadership is fundamentally a moral endeavor and, as various philosophers of science have posited, moral issues are beyond the scope of scientific investigation (Horgan, 1996).

This chapter considers several issues related to the usefulness of "scientific" research in the field of educational administration. In particular, given the increased emphasis in the field on moral leadership (Furman, 2003; Greenfield, 2004), this chapter explores the fit between scientific research and moral leadership in schools by addressing three topics. First, some of the assumptions underlying scientific research in general are explored and problematized in regard to the field of education. Second, the topic of moral leadership is briefly reviewed and the applicability of scientific research—given its ideology, assumptions, and methods—to the study of moral leadership is examined. Third, an alternative methodology is proposed for the study of moral leadership in schools. The central argument of this chapter is, if schooling is fundamentally a moral enterprise, then school leadership is fundamentally a moral endeavor, and research intended to inform leadership practice must itself embody the morality it is intended to empower.

Before proceeding, it is important to be clear about the use of the term *scientific research* in this discussion, because there are varied understandings of the term *science* in education. For some, science means any activity in which empirical data are collected and analyzed for the purpose of adding to the knowledge base in education; that is, science can be a "big tent" term that takes in a wide range of methodologies and research purposes. Others use the term *science* in a much narrower sense to mean the adherence to objective scientific methods adapted from the natural sciences, for example, the experimental testing of hypotheses aimed at discovery of cause-effect relationships with the goal of developing generalizable explanatory theory. In this chapter, the critique focuses on this narrower conception of science, because it is this narrow conception that has dominated the administrative science perspective in educational administration and is embedded in current federal policy, thereby continuing to influence the research agenda of many educational scholars; this narrow view of science has not yet been adequately critiqued in regard to the growing emphasis on moral leadership in schools.

REFLECTIONS ON THE IDEOLOGY AND ASSUMPTIONS OF "SCIENTIFIC" RESEARCH

The hallmark of science is the pursuit of objective knowledge, and scientific research is often assumed to be value neutral in its findings and methods. Although these assumptions have been questioned and often rejected by contemporary philosophers of science (e.g., Polanyi, 1969), they are still the commonsense understanding of researchers in various fields including education, and are reflected in current federal policy on scientific research (Shavelson & Towne, 2002). This assumption of objectivity obscures the fact that Western scientific traditions are embedded in the specific ideological and epistemological assumptions of a larger narrative—the "deep, culturally specific assumptions that are part of the legacy of the Western Enlightenment" (Bowers, 2001, p. 33). Smith (1999) stated, "Western research is more than just research that is located in a positivist tradition . . . it draws from an 'archive' of knowledge and systems, rules and values which stretch beyond the boundaries of Western science to the system now referred as the West" (p. 42). This "archive" of Western knowledge, rules, and values not only shapes the philosophy and practices of Western science, but, when this science is applied to a field like education, the research approach itself reciprocally influences the expectations, policies, and practices of the field (English, 2003). Thus, it is important to identify and critique the ideologies and assumptions associated with the Western scientific tradition in order to explore its fit with education and its influence on the purposes and practices of schooling. This is seldom done. In discussing this lack of deeper analysis in regard to the current federal stance on research, as reflected in the National Research Council (NRC) report (Shavelson & Towne), St. Pierre (2002) stated:

> Much educational research . . . does not even acknowledge its epistemological grounding, much less take into account the limits of that epistemology, and its methodology, in the production of knowledge. The NRC report is shockingly silent about its epistemological allegiance. (p. 26)

The discussion here of these assumptions and methodological issues is necessarily brief and serves only to illustrate the potential for this kind of analysis. Three issues discussed here are the belief in linear progress and the accumulation of knowledge (linear progressivism), the assumption that all of nature (including human social life) is the product of lawful relationships among variables, and the methodological problem of reductionism.

Linear progressivism is the assumption that human society progresses steadily from ignorance to knowledge, toward greater technological control of the natural environment, and toward greater economic prosperity, social welfare, and happiness; this assumption leads directly to the reverence for science as the tool for accumulation of knowledge in the service of humankind's progress. The technological advances achieved through the natural sciences certainly support this progressivist assumption; however, these advances were achieved through the discovery of laws of nature that lead to prediction and control of the natural environment. When applied to human social life and the field of education, the assumption of linear progress through science becomes problematic and creates unrealistic expectations.[2] It is questionable whether lawful relationships of the type found in nature (an issue discussed later) apply to social life and educational processes and whether prediction and control are appropriate goals. Yet, many policymakers and researchers continue to be driven by the expectation of fast and steady progress through scientific research. It is no wonder, then, that federal policymakers blame the educational research community for shoddy practices because expectations of linear progress have not been met.

Another assumption embedded in the Western scientific tradition is that all of nature is governed by lawful relationships that can be captured in generalizable theory. As with linear progressivism, achievements in the natural sciences reinforce this assumption; with the exception of a few remaining puzzles (e.g., the origins of life, the reconciliation between general relativity and quantum mechanics, and the phenomenon of consciousness), the natural sciences have determined lawful relationships that explain most of the natural phenomena available to human perception, according to some analysts (Horgan, 1996). However, this has been accomplished because the rules underlying nature's patterns are static and universal. The laws of physical nature do not change, and they apply everywhere in the known universe (except at "singularities"—the moment of the big bang and within black holes). Furthermore, these laws ultimately boil down to the behavior of particles and wave functions (Barbour, 2001), which, it is assumed, have no experience analogous to human consciousness, volition, desire, and intention. In contrast, the human social world is not static or universal, and is continually subject to the exercise of moral choice and in-

---

[2]Even in the natural sciences, the belief in continual progress is eroding as science reaches the limits of human understanding. Horgan (1996) stated, "Belief in the eternality of progress . . . is the dominant delusion of our culture" (p. 268).

tention. As Olson (2004) stated, "The more simple cause-effect relations so important to the physical and biological sciences are largely inappropriate to the human sciences, which trade on the beliefs, hopes, and reasons of intentional beings" (p. 25). The whole complex structure of social life—culture, language, systems of communication, organizational structures, the nature of social relationships, and so on—is not only context bound, but is continually evolving, changing, and being recreated through social interactions and cultural forces. Likewise, every aspect of education—schools as organizations, the communities served by schools, and the teaching and learning that goes on in classrooms, just to name a few—are embedded in this dynamic, ever-changing, and context-bound social world. Although the influence of local context in education is widely recognized, even among proponents of the neopositivist approach to scientific research (e.g., Feuer et al., 2002), and the instability of educational research findings over time has been established (Berliner, 2002; Kennedy, 1997), calls for scientific research in education continue to reflect the assumption that generalizable, stable explanatory theory is not only possible but is the most important goal of educational research.

In addition to these issues, the problem of reductionism is inherent in Western scientific methodology.[3] This reductionism has two aspects. First, in order to test hypotheses statistically, complex social (and educational) phenomena are fractured into parts or variables that can be counted and measured. Because not all aspects of complex social situations can be reduced to measurable variables, only some can be examined; the social situation is thus inescapably reduced to some of its parts. Similarly, a choice must be made as to how to measure the chosen variables or parts; the phenomena are thus reduced again, or operationalized into various measurements. The problem with this reductionistic approach in complex social settings like schools is that much is ignored in the push to identify measurable variables so that cause-effect relationships can presumably be determined. Teaching, for example, must be reduced to replicable treatments and learning to measurable proxies, like achievement test scores. The great sociologist C. Wright Mills (1959) long ago pointed out the dangers of "abstracted empiricism," that is, the reducing of social theory to statistically significant relationships among sets of measurable variables. If something cannot be operationalized, measured, and included as a variable in testable hypotheses, it does not exist in regard to theory development; it becomes invisible. Relatedly, Maxwell (2004) warned that the reductionistic experi-

---

[3]*Reductionism* is used here to mean the reducing of complex social phenomena and constructs to discrete measurable variables. Philosophers of science often use the term in a different sense to mean "the belief that a branch of science can be explained in terms of (i.e., reduced to) the propositions of another" (e.g., biology explained in terms of quantum mechanics; Phillips, 1987, p. 206).

mental approach of the type privileged in current federal policy is not the most useful or meaningful way to explore causal relationships and develop social theory. According to Maxwell, these methods privilege a "variable-oriented approach to research over a process-oriented approach" (p. 3); he contended that qualitative research is better able to explore how processes work in context (i.e., the actual causes of causal relationships), whereas experimental studies only determine statistical relationships between measurable variables.

In summary, a deeper analysis of the assumptions underlying scientific research is useful in surfacing numerous issues related to the scientizing of fields of practice like education. For example, these assumptions can create unrealistic expectations for the outcomes of research, including the hope for fast and steady progress in solving problems through the application of scientific findings, and can focus the attention of researchers, policymakers, and educators on the relationships among variables (including measurable achievement as a proxy for learning) rather than deeper theory (Olson, 2004) about schooling, teaching, and learning in a democratic society. In addition, the privileging of scientific research as the best method marginalizes other modes of inquiry that might be more useful in understanding schooling more fully (Maxwell, 2004; St. Pierre, 2002). These issues form the background for a more specific examination of the fit between scientific research and the concept of moral leadership in schools. In the next sections, background on the concept of moral leadership is first presented; then the implications of this concept for research are discussed.

MORAL LEADERSHIP IN SCHOOLS

Almost since its inception, the field of educational administration has been dominated by Taylorist notions of administrative work and productivity. Originating in the work of Frederick Winslow Taylor early in the 20th century, Taylorism focuses on efficiency, productivity, and scientific management in organizations.[4] Taylorism's influence spread throughout the Western industrial world of the 20th century and continues to hold sway in today's postindustrial, global corporate society, though it has morphed over time into various neo-Taylorist perspectives. Indeed, as Shipps (chap. 8, this volume) states, Taylorism has become a "worldwide narrative of compelling detail."

In the development of the field of educational administration during the 20th century, the Taylorist narrative shaped understandings of school effi-

---

[4]Shipps (chap. 8, this volume) provides a detailed and informative review of Taylorism and its influence on the American educational system. See also English (1994).

ciency as well as the administrator's role in efficient management. The Taylorist administrator would be able to "produce the greatest learning with the least effort" (Shipps, chap. 8, this volume) through detailed management and coordination of the staff, physical plant, resources, and students. Although Taylorism and the "cult of efficiency" it spawned in education were roundly criticized by many scholars (e.g., Callahan, 1962; English, 1994, 2003; Gamson, 2004), its continued influence is evident. For example, in the current educational policy environment, various accountability mechanisms hold educators—teachers and administrators—accountable for student learning outcomes. For administrators, the implication is that, through ever more efficient and effective management (e.g., data-based decision making), they can produce results in the form of ever higher student achievement scores (e.g., Schmoker, 1999).

Notwithstanding the continued influence of Taylorism in education, there is also compelling evidence that a new, competing narrative has been emerging in the field of educational administration over the last several decades. In general, the scientific management-administrative perspective is being edged out by an increased focus on leadership and, in particular, on moral leadership, "one of the fastest growing areas of study" (Leithwood & Duke, 1998, p. 36). In contrast to the administrative science perspective, which holds that school administration is not a unique activity but is similar to administrative work in other organizations (Griffiths, 1964, p. 3), the rationale for the focus on moral leadership is that the "moral dimensions of educational leadership and administration" constitute one of the special conditions that make administering schools "different from such work in other contexts" (Goldring & Greenfield, 2002, pp. 2–3). For example, Sergiovanni (1996) argued that schools are "moral communities" requiring a new type of leadership based in "moral authority" (p. 57); Lees (1995) added that school leadership is based in a "moral imperative to promote democracy, empowerment, and social justice" (p. 225); and, using more playful language, Hodgkinson (1991) stated that educators are "secular priests working in an arena of ethical excitement" (p. 7). In a nice summary of this view, Fullan (2003) stated that "the only goal worth talking about" in schools is the "*moral purpose* of the highest order . . . having a system where all students learn" (p. 29). Perhaps the key drivers of this growing interest in moral leadership are the "new realities" of the social context of schooling (Cunningham & Mitchell, 1990) and the related sense that school leaders should direct more attention to critical social needs, such as social justice and educating children for participation in a culturally diverse, democratic society (Furman & Shields, 2005).

Although much of the moral leadership literature is normative, some empirical studies have explored moral leadership in action in the practice of school administrators. Greenfield's (2004) recent review provides a good summary of several studies conducted between 1979 and 2003 (including Blumberg & Greenfield, 1980, 1986; Dillard, 1995; Kasten & Ashbaugh, 1991; Kelly & Bredeson, 1991; Marshall, 1992; Marshall, Patterson, Rogers, & Steele, 1996; Reitzug & Reeves, 1992). Across these and other studies (e.g., Enomoto, 1997; Keyes, Hanley-Maxwell, & Capper, 1999), some common findings are that "the personal qualities of school administrators [including their core values] have a big impact on what they do" (Greenfield, p. 190), administrators are very much aware of the moral aspects of their work, and administrators do practice moral leadership by relying on their core values and their commitments to particular "ends-in-view" in their daily life and work in schools.

Social Justice as Moral Purpose

One of these "ends-in-view" or moral purposes of leadership receiving much attention recently is the need to work for social justice in schools (Griffiths, 1998; Grogan, 2002a; Larson & Murtadha, 2002; Marshall, 2004). Reflecting the growing attention to this topic, Murphy (1999), in his review of major trends in the field of educational administration, identified social justice as one of "three powerful synthesizing paradigms" embedded in the "shifting landscape" of the field (p. 54). (The other two are school improvement and democratic community.) Although social justice is certainly not the only moral good that plays out in schools,[5] it appears to Murphy and others to be a critically important dimension of schooling in an increasingly diverse, democratic society. Though there is no set definition of social justice in education (Bogotch, 2002), some shared meanings have emerged, including: (a) The social justice discourse critiques current educational arrangements that are "rife with inequity . . . and lead to inequitable outcomes" for children (Pounder, Reitzug, & Young, 2002, p. 270); (b) the social justice discourse calls for radical change to address these inequities, for example, Bogotch stated that social justice is "a deliberate intervention that requires the moral use of power" (p. 140); and (c) the primary goal of social justice intervention is the improvement of the "education and life chances of poor and minority children" (Larson & Murtadha, p. 150) through these radical changes in schooling.

Regarding leadership for social justice in schools, the literature is overwhelmingly normative (e.g., Starratt, 2003; special issues of *Journal of School Leadership*, 2002; and *Educational Administration Quarterly*, 2004), leading Larson and Murtadha (2002) to conclude that there is "a vagueness as to

---

[5]In discussing the moral pluralism that plays out in education, Strike (1999) warned that "we need to be very careful in our reflections on education that we not substitute part of the moral life for the whole" (p. 35).

what all of this means to researchers and practitioners" and a "need for a leadership theory and practice that is robust enough to enhance social justice in education" (p. 157). However, many scholars are working on these issues and have recently offered some empirically based guidelines (e.g., Scheurich & Skrla, 2003; Shields, 2003) as well as some deeper theoretical analyses regarding leadership for social justice (e.g., Furman & Shields, 2005). Because these guidelines and analyses have major implications for the type of research that might be productive in furthering understandings of moral leadership, a few examples are summarized here.

Scheurich and Skrla (2003), based on their research in Texas schools, suggested that "leadership for equity and excellence" is shared or "distributed" across all educators in a school and is characterized by an ethical core, a belief that equitable schools are possible, and a commitment to "never quit" (p. 110). Similarly, Shields (2003) found that "numerous people are bound together in a moral commitment, a sort of covenant" to work for social justice in schools (p. xxii). Based on multiple studies conducted cross-nationally, she offered a framework for "transformative, cross-cultural" (p. 3) leadership that includes attention to cultural differences, parent involvement and power relationships, and facilitation of "moral dialogue" among all school stakeholders around social justice issues. Echoing Shields' findings about moral dialogue, Goldfarb and Grinberg (2002) found in a case study of an urban school in Venezuela that "an important role of leadership for social justice is providing opportunities for authentic participation" (p. 170). They argued that school leaders should "foster an organizational structure that is flexible and democratic" and "create a safe (trusting) environment where the local community is engaged in authentic participation" (p. 171). Similarly, Rusch (1998) found that school principals engaged in "democratic" leadership focused more on "mutual influence" among school staff members than on power and control and worked to teach and reinforce group process skills.

Based on an analysis of this emerging literature, Furman and Shields (2005) identified five common dimensions of leadership for social justice in schools: (a) ethical and moral, (b) communal and contextual, (c) processual, (d) transformative, and (e) pedagogical. The ethical and moral dimension reflects a common theme in the literature that leaders for social justice need to operate from a deeply held ethical core and have a sense of commitment to working for social justice in schools. The communal and contextual dimension reflects the distributed or shared nature of leadership and how this shared leadership evolves from and is unique to the local context of a school. Relatedly, the processual dimension captures the dialogic nature of leadership and the need for continual striving toward the ideal of social justice through the processes of authentic participation. The transformative dimension reflects the call in the literature for critique, "deliberate intervention" (Bogotch, 2002, p. 140), and radical change to address social justice issues. Finally, the pedagogical dimension explicitly recognizes the importance of the core work of schools—curriculum and instruction—in working for social justice. This dimension is often neglected in discussions of social justice, yet what is taught and how it is taught are critical influences on the nature of justice in schools, according to Furman and Shields.

In summary, scholars of educational administration have been developing a new "narrative" for the field, shifting away from the scientific management perspective and focusing more on moral leadership and social justice, and reconceptualized leadership practice "as a democratic and dialogical process" (Larson & Murtadha, 2002, p. 147) that is driven by moral purpose. Marshall (2004) stated, "The knowledge base for educational administration has traditionally emphasized management and a narrow view of leadership theory. That knowledge base is being challenged by research and policy demands for leading and structuring schools that create more socially just societal outcomes" (p. 8). This growing emphasis on moral leadership does not mean that technical competence is not important for school leaders. Indeed, without technical competence, school leaders can accomplish little in the way of achieving their moral purposes. What the new narrative does suggest, however, is that the practice of educational leadership, including the application of technical competence, is fundamentally grounded in moral purpose and action and that this moral grounding shapes the practice of moral leadership. What is the role of research in this new narrative for educational leadership? How can research findings help to inform moral leadership practice and support working for social justice in schools? What kind of research is most appropriate? Is "scientific" research useful in supporting this new narrative, or are there more promising alternative methodologies? The next section turns to these questions.

RESEARCH AND MORAL LEADERSHIP

In a recent review of research on moral leadership in schools, Greenfield (2004) concluded, "To understand moral leadership requires that one gain an understanding of the perspectives, the lived experiences and the subjective meanings, of the participants in the leadership relationship. To do this requires that they be studied '*in situ*' " (p. 191). Greenfield's statement suggests three things: the need to better understand the concept of moral leadership through studies of leaders engaged in it; the importance of context in understanding how moral leadership plays out in individual school settings; and the importance of exploring both individuals' perspectives and leadership as a relationship among participants. Reflecting these points,

Greenfield made several recommendations for research, including that
studies focus on "the social relations among school leaders and others, . . .
the meanings and perspectives underlying what school leaders are doing
. . . the nature of the espoused purposes of school leaders' actions . . . [and]
the emotional dimensions of being a school leader" (p. 191). Although
Greenfield avoided specific methodological suggestions, he cited numerous studies that use qualitative field methods to explore moral leadership,
and his recommendations strongly suggest a phenomenological approach
to exploring moral leadership as it is understood by individuals.

Complementing and expanding Greenfield's (2004) suggestions for research, Furman and Shields (2005) focused more specifically on moral
leadership aimed at the specific purpose of enhancing social justice in
schools, and placed more emphasis on exploring the communal and processual aspects of this leadership. For example, they suggested that research
should explore not only the perceptions and experiences of individuals in
leadership positions and their relationships with others, but also the communal leadership processes engaged in by all participants at a particular
site, and how these processes lead to transformative action in the interest of
social justice. In addition, Furman and Shields noted that research focused
on leadership practice for social justice can be described as fundamentally
interventionist and advocacy oriented; as such, it must strive to be "in and
of itself, just and deeply democratic" or it is hypocritical (p. 28). Reflecting
this latter point, Griffiths (1998)[6] argued that research for social justice is
"research in which the methodology or epistemology of the research is itself a reason for claiming it to be research for social justice" (p. 26). In
other words, the design of the study, including the methods used as well as
the researcher's conduct in the field, needs to be just and respectful, and
the products of the study need to be beneficial to the participants as well as
to the researcher.

Taken together, these points suggest that research on moral leadership
in schools might involve in-depth exploration in specific school contexts of:
(a) the phenomenology of moral leadership, that is, the values, motiva-
tions, and experiences of individuals involved in or striving toward moral
leadership practice; (b) the observable practices of moral leadership, for
example, leaders' ethical decisions and how they conduct their relationships with others; (c) the communal nature of moral leadership, including
how communal or dialogic processes are facilitated by those in leadership
positions, the nature of these processes, and how leadership becomes distributed through them; (d) how transformative actions aimed at specific
moral purposes (e.g., enhancing social justice) emerge from these commu-

---

[6]There is no relationship between the Griffiths (1998) cited here and Daniel Griffiths
(1964), cited earlier.

nal processes and the nature of these actions; and (e) how these transformative actions or communal processes relate to and address the nature of pedagogy in the specific school context. Finally, in addressing these research foci, the methodology employed should be in and of itself just and democratic.

These implications for research suggest that the "scientific" approach, as advocated by Griffiths (1964) and mandated in current federal policy, is not particularly relevant or useful in addressing the topics of moral leadership and social justice in schools. The central point here is that, if schooling is fundamentally a moral endeavor, educational administration is not primarily about efficient, scientific management based in scientifically established cause-effect relationships and aimed at measurable outcomes; rather, educational administration is primarily a matter of moral leadership that is deeply engaged with relationships, moral dilemmas, and the moral purposes for schooling. As many philosophers of science have noted, moral issues such as these are considered to be outside the scope of "scientific" investigation and explanation (Horgan, 1996). Ironically, Griffiths' colleague Culbertson (1964) recognized this problem in his chapter in Griffiths' 1964 book:

> A limitation of the new science, strictly defined, is its neutral posture on moral issues. For example, social science potentially has the capacity to describe and explain community power structure and how administrators actually cope with it; however, it cannot define what administrators *should* seek to achieve as they work with those in positions of power or how they *should* resolve moral dilemmas which they confront in the process. It seems clear, then, that even though the products of basic research are fundamental to sound preparatory programs, they are not, in and of themselves, sufficient, because administration is in part an idealistic venture performed in a setting where there are many conflicting issues and views. (p. 311)

More specifically, the reductionism of scientific research and its focus on cause-effect relationships make it largely irrelevant to the study of moral leadership in schools. For example, the moral purpose that drives moral leadership practice, such as working for social justice in schools, cannot be reduced to an effort to achieve specific measurable targets, that is, discrete outcome variables; in other words, operationalizing social justice and other moral purposes as dependent variables is meaningless, because these are ideals to work toward, and how they are understood and addressed depends on "authentic participation" (Goldfarb & Grinberg, 2002) at the local level. Relatedly, the practice of moral leadership, which is shaped by dynamic relationships and communal processes, cannot be operationalized as a set of independent, replicable variables representing "treatments" or discrete administration actions. Indeed, as the sources cited previously indicate, moral leadership for social justice involves continual striving in a complex environment, rather than discrete actions that lead to discrete outcomes. Schon's (2001) description of professional practice in a complex environment like schools is relevant; such practice confronts "messy, indeterminate, problematic situations" characterized by "complexity and uncertainty, unique cases that require artistry—the elusive task of problem setting, the multiplicity of professional identities" (p. 186). Research on moral leadership seeks to understand the lived experiences of individuals in these complex environments as they engage in this messy, processual striving, not how specific measurable outcomes can be achieved through specific replicable practices.

Related issues pertain to the scientific research assumptions about the possibility of lawful, generalizable theory and steady, linear progress in developing and applying this theory. From the background presented earlier, moral leadership aimed at social justice is seen to be dynamic, contextual, and communal. In other words, it is leadership that responds to the social justice situation in a unique local context; both the meanings of social justice as well as the processual striving to achieve it are constructed locally through communal participation. Furthermore, the local context continually changes, as do actions in response to this context. Thus, it is inappropriate to assume that research on moral leadership can produce scientifically based replicable practices that can be generalized across settings. Although findings from one specific setting might generate understandings that can be effectively disseminated and might be useful to educators in other sites, as they strive to understand their own social justice issues and how to respond to them (Smith, 1999), progress in developing lawful, generalizable theory related to moral leadership practice would be a specious goal.

A final point relates to the claim that research on moral leadership for social justice must be in and of itself just and democratic. Many critics of traditionally conducted scientific research have argued that such research is inherently unjust and undemocratic because it reflects the patriarchal system of power, privilege, and status conferred on researchers as intellectuals in Western society (Lather, 1991; Smith, 1999). For example, Lee, Spencer, and Harpalani (2003) claimed that research involving racial and ethnic minority youth "has suffered from many stereotypes and misconceptions" (p. 6), whereas Orellana and Bowman (2003) argued that researchers treat "race, ethnicity, culture, and social class as fixed and often essentialized categories rather than as multifaceted, situated, and socially constructed processes" (p. 26). This objectification of the "other" is damaging because it is "dehumanizing" (Smith, p. 39). Furthermore, the dark side of traditional educational research is that it often benefits the researcher, but not the subjects of the research (Wolcott, 2001). Smith summarized these issues of power, misrepresentation, and self-interest:

Research in itself is a powerful intervention . . . which has traditionally benefited the researcher, and the knowledge base of the dominant group in society. When undertaking research, either across cultures or within a minority
culture, it is critical that researchers recognize the power dynamic which is
embedded in the relationship with their subjects. . . . They have the power to
distort, to make invisible, to overlook, to exaggerate and to draw conclusions,
based not on factual data, but on assumptions, hidden value judgments, and
often downright misunderstandings. (p. 176)

In summary, these arguments suggest that traditionally conducted "scientific" research does not meet the criterion for just and democratic research.

If, for all these reasons, "scientific" research is a poor fit with moral leadership in schools, what research approaches and methodologies might be
more appropriate? The next section explores some possibilities.

RESEARCH FOR MORAL LEADERSHIP
AND SOCIAL JUSTICE IN SCHOOLS

What kind of knowledge can create moral action? It is immediately clear that
it cannot be the detached knowledge of prescientific or scientific inquiry, nor
can it be the practical knowledge of the day-to-day handling of things and
people, even if such knowledge is elevated to the level of technical expertise
or psychological skill, for any of this can be used for the performance of the
most anti-moral actions. (Tillich, 1963, p. 57)

The quote from Tillich supports the argument in the previous section that
knowledge that can inform moral leadership practice is unlikely to be
gained from the value-detached, "scientific" research critiqued in this chapter. Rather, it is knowledge that arises from the recognition and exploration of the deeply moral nature and purposes of educational leadership
practice. Specifically, educators seeking to practice moral leadership in
schools might benefit from the types of knowledge generated through studies that focus on the topics mentioned earlier—the phenomenology of
moral leadership, its observable practices in response to local context, its
communal or dialogic nature, the transformative actions it generates, and
its relationship to pedagogy. In addition, knowledge of broader social and
educational issues that interface with moral issues in schools would be essential.

Clearly, a wide range of research approaches can contribute to the development of this knowledge. Phenomenological studies of the type suggested
by Greenfield (2004) can help individuals understand their own moral
stances and responsibilities as well as how others in similar settings experience and interpret these issues. Similarly, self-study approaches (Bullough

& Pinnegar, 2001; Feldman, 2003), in which individuals reflect on who they are as educators, the decisions and actions they take, and the impact of these actions on others, can help individuals understand and improve the moral dimensions of their leadership work. In addition, quantitative studies can provide wide-ranging data on broad social and educational issues, for example, the disaggregating of school achievement data can reveal the differences across racial, gender, and economic groups as an indicator of inequities in the school system. However, the core knowledge related to moral leadership practice—knowledge that creates greater understanding of the nature of moral issues in today's schools and the role of leadership in addressing them—requires in-depth field studies conducted in situ, studies that explore the communal, processual, and transformative dimensions of such leadership and that are just and democratic in terms of their methodologies and purposes (Furman & Shields, 2005).

The qualitative methods relevant to such in-depth field studies are no mystery; most educators today are well versed in the appropriate qualitative perspectives and methods, and a plethora of methodological writings is available to guide them. However, the point that research should be in and of itself just and democratic is not always addressed in this literature and deserves some brief development here. Perspectives that inform a just and democratic approach to inquiry include critical theory, feminist theory, and postmodernist perspectives. Briefly, critical theory suggests that research itself is an "ethical and political act" (Roman & Apple, 1990, p. 41) that always benefits a certain group. Given this stance, critical theorists would rather benefit the marginalized or less powerful to help transform "existing social inequalities and injustices" (McLaren, 1994, p. 168). Hence, researchers who take a critical theory perspective are very interested in the voices of the marginalized and in exposing power inequities in institutions such as schools. Feminist theory takes this concern with power into the relationship between researcher and subjects. Feminist researchers seek to balance this power or one-up relationship by, for example, including subjects as full participants in research studies (Oakley, 1981) and striving to conduct their research in a way that benefits the subjects as well as the researcher. Postmodernists add a third dimension through standpoint theory—the notion that you can know something only from a certain position. In other words, "People do not reason or conceptualize outside of the self's location in a specific historical time and body" (Bogdan & Biklen, 2003, p. 20). Thus, researchers should seek to understand and disclose their own position and standpoint and their role as interpreters of social phenomena.

Taken together, these perspectives suggest that researchers interested in moral leadership and social justice in schools should recognize that their role is not neutral; they have an impact on their research sites and should strive to ensure that the research process itself, as well as its formal products, are beneficial to participants and to themselves. To do this, researchers should seek to understand the research context, not from the point of view of their own theoretical perspectives and assumptions, but from exploring the lived experiences and perceptions of individuals within that context, especially the less powerful. Furthermore, researchers might address the inherent power imbalance between researcher and "subject" by allowing participants to help shape the research process by participating in research decisions. Finally, these perspectives suggest that the products of this research should be offered as interpretations rather than as nomothetic truths.

Several methodologies that reflect these perspectives have emerged in recent literature. "Culturally sensitive research approaches" that "recognize ethnicity and position culture as central to the research process" (Tillman, 2002, p. 3) have been developed in regard to research with African Americans (Collins, 2000; Dillard, 2000; Kershaw, 1992; Tillman). Methodologically, culturally sensitive research honors the "cultural standpoint" of participants by using "culturally congruent research methods," which may include life histories and other qualitative methods that seek to "capture holistic contextualized pictures of the social, political, economic, and educational factors that affect the everyday existence" of participants (Tillman, p. 6). In addition, culturally sensitive research avoids theoretical dominance, or the imposition of theoretical frames that marginalize the cultural standpoints of participants. Similarly, in discussing and critiquing research with indigenous peoples, Smith (1999) argued for "decolonizing methodologies" that are "more respectful, ethical, sympathetic, and useful" (p. 9) than the traditional studies conducted with these peoples. She suggested that critical questions to ask about any research project are: "Whose research is it? Who owns it? Whose interests does it serve? Who will benefit from it? Who has designed its questions and framed its scope? Who will carry it out? Who will write it up?" (p. 10).

Kaomea (2003) developed the related idea of "defamiliarizing interpretive methods" (p. 24) that intentionally seek to make the familiar strange in order to unveil the "silences and erasures" (p. 16) in taken-for-granted school situations. Based on techniques drawn from literary and critical theory, defamiliarizing research methods seek to "peel away surface layers" (p. 23) by, for example, using art media to probe the previously unexpressed feelings and opinions of children and other typically silenced participants. Specific to research for social justice in schools, Griffiths (1998) added that researchers interested in social justice must "get off the fence" and acknowledge their ethical position in using research to work toward "justice, fairness, and equity in education" (p. 3).

Another recently developed methodology that is consistent with these perspectives was offered by Thompson and Gitlin (1995). Drawing from postmodernist standpoint theory and postfeminist orientations, Thompson and Gitlin noted that sometimes educators working from a critical theory perspective call for change yet reproduce "existing power relations in seeking to impose a direction on educational inquiry" (p. 2). Thus, when researchers engage in research for social justice, they must be aware of the pitfall of focusing on them—that is, those whom we hope to liberate or for whom we are advocating a more just and democratic learning community. In contrast, Thompson and Gitlin advocated what they called "reconstructed knowledge"—a form of knowledge that "looks to create spaces in which relationships among the [research] participants are realigned, shifting the balance and authority and thereby challenging the ways in which institutional relations and local actions construct what is important in these relationships" (p. 7). They acknowledged the important contributions of standpoint theory in reminding us that "knowledge is always referenced to some standpoint, and that such standpoints may represent significant political investments in the claims and characterizations offered" (p. 13). They called for a method that does not focus so much on hearing from oppressed or marginalized groups, but on what they called "conversation as method"—a focus "on relations with members of groups *other* than one's own" (p. 15).

Conversation as method seems to offer considerable promise in terms of conducting research into moral leadership for social justice in schools. It calls for researchers to acknowledge their standpoint. It includes the recognition that roles (e.g., researcher, principal, teacher, student) are "taken up as both institutional and embodied, but in ways that allow for significant reconstruction" (Thompson & Gitlin, 1995, p. 20). Moreover, although the standing forms of power may remain in place, "a space is created in which the roles and relationships involved may be problematized so as to effect new possibilities" (p. 21). In other words, conversation as method is a dialogic process through which both researchers and researched can be transformed in certain ways and engage in action toward new possibilities.

Proceeding from these ideas, research that is in and of itself just and democratic would be fundamentally dialogic, relational, and interventionist; it would involve learning with and from those in schools who share an interest in these moral goods. Methodologically, it would necessarily entail in-depth participation in school sites with data collected through open-ended, conversational interviews and participant observation. The agenda for such research cannot be predetermined but emerges through the dialogic process as research participants help determine the course of the inquiry. Nevertheless, an entry point for such research in schools is required; this entry point may consist of a set of preliminary guiding questions to be considered by the research participants as they problematize and explore the concepts of moral leadership and social justice in their school site. For example, if the starting point of the inquiry is the moral dimension of educational leadership (Furman & Shields, 2005), researchers may initiate conversations with participants by posing questions such as these:

- What values (explicit or implicit) influence the practices and behaviors in this school?
- Where do these values come from?
- Do school leaders espouse or model these values?
- Whose values are included and whose are excluded?
- What are the opportunities for inquiry, critique, and dialogue around these values?
- How can dialogue about educational values be generated and maintained in this site?

In summary, to produce knowledge that informs the new narrative of moral leadership in schools and is useful to educators, researchers should "get off the fence" (Griffiths, 1998) and acknowledge the interventionist and advocacy potential of their work. They should take advantage of many new research perspectives and methods that can lead to more just and democratic studies. And they should focus primarily on in-depth field studies that help participants explore and problematize moral leadership issues in their unique, local school contexts.

CONCLUSION

Given its mechanistic, efficiency-productivity orientation to school administration, the "old" narrative of Taylorism goes hand in glove with the hope for a "science" of educational administration and the use of scientific research methods. If it is assumed that administrators can, through their leadership practices, create more efficient and productive schools, and that this is the most important goal of leadership, then it makes sense to seek out the underlying cause-effect relationships through hypothesis-testing scientific research studies: What actions, decisions, and behaviors can administrators engage in (independent variables) that will produce the desired outcomes (dependent variables)? Looking at leadership practice and research in this way, both Griffiths' (1964) original call for an administrative science and the current federal guidelines and mandates about scientific research make sense.

However, if school leadership is not primarily about efficiency and productivity, if schooling is fundamentally a moral enterprise, and if educational leadership is fundamentally a moral endeavor, then morally serious inquiry is needed to inform leadership practice in schools. The truncated version of scientific inquiry proposed by Griffiths (1964) for the field and reborn in current federal policy cannot be the primary basis for this inquiry. Though scientific research can be useful in limited ways (e.g., generating statistics regarding differential achievement across demographic groups) and can support a school leader's technical competence, its value-neutral stance regarding the moral purposes and dilemmas of educational leadership, its reductionistic focus on treatments and measurable outcomes, and its failure to account for the dynamic, unique, and messy contexts in which leadership is practiced make it a poor fit with the concept of moral leadership in schools. A morally serious inquiry for leadership in schools must help educators understand the moral challenges they face in today's schools and the possibilities for transformative action to address these challenges, and it must produce results that are beneficial to participants as well as researchers. The various alternative methodologies reviewed here offer a promising direction for this inquiry.

REFERENCES

Barbour, J. B. (2001). *The end of time: The next revolution in physics.* New York: Oxford University Press.

Berliner, D. C. (2002). Educational research: The hardest science of all. *Educational Researcher, 31*(8), 18–20.

Blumberg, A., & Greenfield, W. D. (1980). *The effective principal: Perspectives on school leadership.* Boston: Allyn & Bacon.

Blumberg, A., & Greenfield, W. D. (1986). *The effective principal: Perspectives on school leadership* (2nd ed.). Boston: Allyn & Bacon.

Bogdan, R. C., & Biklen, S. K. (2003). *Qualitative research for education: An introduction to theories and methods* (4th ed.). Boston: Allyn & Bacon.

Bogotch, I. E. (2002). Educational leadership and social justice: Practice into theory. *Journal of School Leadership, 12,* 138–156.

Bowers, C. A. (2001). *Educating for eco-justice and community.* Athens: University of Georgia Press.

Boyan, N. J. (1988). *Handbook of research on educational administration.* New York: Longman.

Braithwaite, R. B. (1955). *Scientific explanation: A study of the function of theory, probability and law in science.* Cambridge, England: Cambridge University Press.

Bridges, E. (1982). Research on the school administrator: The state of the art, 1967–1980. *Educational Administration Quarterly, 18,* 12–23.

Bullough, R. V., & Pinnegar, S. (2001). Guidelines for quality in autobiographical forms of self-study research. *Educational Researcher, 30*(3), 13–21.

Callahan, R. E. (1962). *Education and the cult of efficiency: A study of the social forces that have shaped the administration of the public schools.* Chicago: University of Chicago Press.

Collins, P. H. (2000). *Black feminist thought: Knowledge, consciousness, and the politics of empowerment.* New York: Routledge.

Culbertson, J. (1964). The preparation of administrators. In D. E. Griffiths (Ed.), *Behavioral science and educational administration: The sixty-third yearbook of the National Society for the Study of Education* (pp. 303–330). Chicago: National Society for the Study of Education.

Cunningham, L. L., & Mitchell, B. (Eds.). (1990). *Educational leadership and changing contexts in families, communities, and schools: Eighty-ninth yearbook of the National Society for the Study of Education.* Chicago: National Society for the Study of Education.

Dillard, C. B. (1995). Leading with her life: An African American feminist (re)interpretation of leadership for an urban high school principal. *Educational Administration Quarterly, 31,* 539–563.

Dillard, C. B. (2000). The substance of things hoped for, the evidence of things not seen: Examining an endarkened feminist epistemology in educational research and leadership. *International Journal of Qualitative Studies in Education, 13,* 661–681.

English, F. W. (1994). *Theory in educational administration.* New York: HarperCollins.

English, F. W. (2003). *The postmodern challenge to the theory and practice of educational administration.* Springfield, IL: Charles C. Thomas.

English, F. W. (2004, April). *"Scientific research in education": The institutionalization of "correct science" and the triumph of verification over discovery: Some implications for the study of educational leadership.* Paper presented at the meeting of the American Educational Research Association, San Diego, CA.

Enomoto, E. K. (1997). Negotiating the ethics of care and justice. *Educational Administration Quarterly, 33,* 351–370.

Feldman, A. (2003). Validity and quality in self-study. *Educational Researcher, 32*(3), 26–28.

Feuer, M. J., Towne, L., & Shavelson, R. J. (2002). Reply to commentators on "Scientific Culture and Educational Research." *Educational Researcher, 31*(8), 28–29.

Fullan, M. (2003). *The moral imperative of school leadership.* Thousand Oaks, CA: Corwin Press.

Furman, G. (2003). The 2002 UCEA presidential address: Toward a new scholarship of educational leadership. *UCEA Review, 45*(1), 1–6.

Furman, G. C., & Shields, C. M. (2005). How can educational leaders promote and support social justice and democratic community in schools? In W. A. Firestone & C. Riehl (Eds.), *A new agenda for research in educational leadership* (pp. 119–137). New York: Teachers College Press.

Gamson, D. A. (2004). The infusion of corporate values into progressive education: Professional vulnerability or complicity? *Journal of Educational Administration, 42,* 137–159.

Goldfarb, K. P., & Grinberg, J. (2002). Leadership for social justice: Authentic participation in the case of a community center in Caracas, Venezuela. *Journal of School Leadership, 12,* 157–173.

Goldring, E., & Greenfield, W. (2002). Understanding the evolving concept of leadership in education: Roles, expectations, and dilemmas. In J. Murphy (Ed.), *The educational leadership challenge: Redefining leadership for the 21st century. One-hundred-first yearbook of the National Society for the Study of Education* (pp. 1–19). Chicago: National Society for the Study of Education.

Greenfield, W. D. (2004). Moral leadership in schools. *Journal of Educational Administration, 42,* 174–196.

Griffiths, D. E. (1964). *Behavioral science and educational administration: The sixty-third yearbook of the National Society for the Study of Education.* Chicago: National Society for the Study of Education.

Griffiths, M. (1998). *Educational research for social justice.* Buckingham, England: Open University Press.

Grogan, M. (2002a). Guest editor's introduction: Leadership for social justice. *Journal of School Leadership, 12,* 112–115.

Grogan, M. (Ed.). (2002b). Leadership for social justice [Special issue]. *Journal of School Leadership, 12.*

Hodgkinson, C. (1991). *Educational leadership: The moral art.* Albany: State University of New York Press.

Horgan, J. (1996). *The end of science: Facing the limits of knowledge in the twilight of the scientific age.* London: Little, Brown.

Jacob, E., & White, E. (Eds.). (2002). Theme issue on scientific research in education. *Educational Research, 31*(8).

Kaomea, J. (2003). Reading erasures and making the familiar strange: Defamiliarizing methods for research in formerly colonized and historically oppressed communities. *Educational Researcher, 32*(2), 14–25.

Kasten, K. L., & Ashbaugh, C. R. (1991). The place of values in superintendents' work. *Journal of Educational Administration, 29*(3), 54–66.

Kelly, G. E., & Bredeson, P. V. (1991). Measures of meaning in a public and in a parochial school: Principals as symbol managers. *Journal of Educational Administration, 29*(3), 6–22.

Kennedy, M. M. (1997). The connection between research and practice. *Educational Researcher, 26*(7), 4–12.

Kerlinger, F. N. (1986). *Foundations of behavioral research* (3rd ed.). New York: Holt, Rinehart, and Winston.

Kershaw, T. (1992). Afrocentrism and the Afrocentric method. *Western Journal of Black Studies, 16*(2), 160–168.

Keyes, M. W., Hanley-Maxwell, C., & Capper, C. A. (1999). "Spirituality? It's the core of my leadership": Empowering leadership in an inclusive elementary school. *Educational Administration Quarterly, 35,* 203–237.

Kuhn, T. S. (1970). *The structure of scientific revolutions* (2nd ed.). Chicago: University of Chicago Press.

Lagemann, E. C. (2000). *An elusive science: The troubling history of education research.* Chicago: University of Chicago Press.

Larson, C. L., & Murtadha, K. (2002). Leadership for social justice. In J. Murphy (Ed.), *The educational leadership challenge: Redefining leadership for the 21st century. One-hundred-first yearbook of the National Society for the Study of Education* (pp. 134–161). Chicago: National Society for the Study of Education.

Lather, P. (1991). *Getting smart: Feminist research and pedagogy with/in the postmodern.* New York: Routledge.

Lee, C. D., Spencer, M. B., & Harpalani, V. (2003). "Every shut eye ain't sleep": Studying how people live culturally. *Educational Researcher, 32*(5), 6–13.

Lees, K. A. (1995). Advancing democratic leadership through critical theory. *Journal of School Leadership, 5,* 220–230.

Leithwood, K., Chapman, J., Corson, D., Hallinger, P., & Hart, A. (Eds.). (1996). *International handbook of educational leadership and administration.* Boston: Kluwer.

Leithwood, K., & Duke, D. L. (1998). Mapping the conceptual terrain of leadership: A critical point of departure for cross-cultural studies. *Peabody Journal of Education, 73*(2), 31–50.

Leithwood, K., Hallinger, P., Furman, G. C., Riley, K., MacBeath, J., Gronn, P., et al. (Eds.). (2002). *Second international handbook of educational leadership and administration.* Boston: Kluwer.

Marshall, C. (1992). School administrator's values: A focus on "atypicals." *Educational Administration Quarterly, 28,* 368–386.

Marshall, C. (2004). Social justice challenges to educational administration: Introduction to a special issue. *Educational Administration Quarterly, 40,* 5–15.

Marshall, C., Patterson, J. A., Rogers, D. L., & Steele, J. R. (1996). Caring as career: An alternative perspective for educational administration. *Educational Administration Quarterly, 32,* 271–295.

Maxwell, J. A. (2004). Causal explanation, qualitative research, and scientific inquiry in education. *Educational Researcher, 33*(2), 3–11.

McLaren, P. (1994). *Life in schools* (2nd ed.). New York: Longman.

Mills, C. W. (1959). *The sociological imagination.* Oxford, England: Oxford University Press.

Murphy, J. (1999). *The quest for a center: Notes on the state of the profession of educational leadership.* Columbia, MO: University Council for Educational Administration.

Murphy, J., & Seashore Louis, K. (1999). *Handbook of research on educational administration* (2nd ed.). San Francisco: Jossey-Bass.

No Child Left Behind Act of 2001, Pub. L. No. 107-110 (2001). Retrieved March 15, 2004, from http://www.ed.gov/legislation/ESEA02/

Oakley, A. (1981). Interviewing women: A contradiction in terms. In H. Roberts (Ed.), *Doing feminist research* (pp. 30–61). London: Routledge and Kegan Paul.

Olson, D. R. (2004). The triumph of hope over experience in the search for "what works": A response to Slavin. *Educational Researcher, 33*(1), 24–26.

Orellana, M. F., & Bowman, P. (2003). Cultural diversity research on learning and development: Conceptual, methodological, and strategic considerations. *Educational Researcher, 32*(5), 26–32.

Phillips, D. C. (1987). *Philosophy, science, and social inquiry: Contemporary methodological controversies in social science and related applied fields of research.* New York: Pergamon Press.

Polanyi, M. (1969). *Knowing and being: Essays by Michael Polanyi.* Chicago: University of Chicago Press.

Polkinghorne, D. (1983). *Methodology for the human sciences: Systems of inquiry.* Albany: State University of New York Press.

Pounder, D., Reitzug, U., & Young, M. D. (2002). Preparing school leaders for school improvement, social justice, and community. In J. Murphy (Ed.), *The educational leadership challenge: Redefining leadership for the 21st century. One-hundred-first yearbook of the National Society for the Study of Education* (pp. 261–288). Chicago: National Society for the Study of Education.

Reitzug, U. C., & Reeves, J. E. (1992). "Miss Lincoln doesn't teach here": A descriptive narrative and conceptual analysis of a principal's symbolic leadership behavior. *Educational Administration Quarterly, 28,* 185–219.

Roman, L., & Apple, M. (1990). Is naturalism a move away from positivism? Materialist and feminist approaches to subjectivity in ethnographic research. In E. Eisner & A. Peshkin (Eds.), *Qualitative inquiry in education: The continuing debate* (pp. 38–73). New York: Teachers College Press.

Rusch, E. A. (1998). Leadership in evolving democratic school communities. *Journal of School Leadership, 8,* 214–250.

Scheurich, J. J., & Skrla, L. (2003). *Leadership for equity and excellence.* Thousand Oaks, CA: Corwin Press.

Schmoker, M. (1999). *Results: The key to continuous school improvement.* Alexandria, VA: Association for Supervision and Curriculum Development.

Schon, D. (2001). The crisis in professional knowledge and the pursuit of an epistemology of practice. In J. Raven & J. Stephenson (Eds.), *Competence in the learning society* (pp. 183–207). Washington, DC: Peter Lang.

Sergiovanni, T. J. (1996). *Leadership for the schoolhouse: How is it different? Why is it important?* San Francisco: Jossey-Bass.

Shavelson, R. J., & Towne, L. (Eds.). (2002). *Scientific research in education.* Washington, DC: National Academy Press.

Shields, C. M. (2003). *Good intentions are not enough: Transformative leadership for communities of difference.* Lanham, MD: Scarecrow Press.

Smith, L. T. (1999). *Decolonizing methodologies: Research and indigenous peoples.* New York: Zed Books.

St. Pierre, E. A. (2002). "Science" rejects postmodernism. *Educational Researcher, 31*(8), 25–27.

Starratt, R. J. (2003). *Centering educational administration: Cultivating meaning, community, responsibility.* Mahwah, NJ: Lawrence Erlbaum Associates.

Strike, K. A. (1999). Justice, caring, and universality: In defense of moral pluralism. In M. S. Katz, N. Noddings, & K. A. Strike (Eds.), *Justice and caring: The search for common ground in education* (pp. 21–36). New York: Teachers College Press.

Thompson, A., & Gitlin, A. (1995). Creating spaces for reconstructing knowledge in feminist pedagogy. *Educational Theory on the Web, 45*(2), 1–28.

Tillich, P. (1963). *Morality and beyond.* New York: Harper & Row.

Tillman, L. C. (2002). Culturally sensitive research approaches: An African-American perspective. *Educational Researcher, 31*(9), 3–12.

Wolcott, H. F. (2001). *The art of fieldwork.* Walnut Creek, CA: AltaMira Press.

NEW DIRECTIONS IN EDUCATION POLITICS AND POLICY RESEARCH

The two chapters in Part III of this book do for the study of education politics and political policy formation what Part II does for school administration and organizational policy.

In chapter 7, Kenneth Wong addresses two broad issues. First, he develops a framework for analyzing key elements in the most sweeping school governance alternatives currently being politically debated and scientifically analyzed. The goal of this part of his chapter is to show how political purposes shape policy decision making and to argue that political science contributes to policy formation and implementation by delineating and analyzing alternative policy models. Like Brian Rowan (chap. 3), he endorses in broad outline the theory movement commitment to developing theoretical models capable of summarizing and interpreting carefully analyzed empirical data. Reminiscent of Max Weber's utilization of "ideal types" to summarize the essential features of alternative policy schemes, Wong creates a table of the critical properties of current efforts to reform urban school systems. He then uses these ideal type models to sketch out a vision of where school governance reform is likely to be moving in the near future.

Wong's second purpose is to delineate his conception of how social research can and should produce reliable knowledge of education governance and politics. His view corresponds quite well to the model embraced by the Institute for Education Science—carefully defined and operationalized variables, randomized field trials whenever possible, theory-based research designs, and repeated studies in differing contexts.

In chapter 8, Dorothy Shipps offers a very different view of the politics of education. First, she argues that political research and political theory need to move beyond schools and schooling policies to address broader issues of civic capacity and civil governance. She insists that school policies and politics can only be understood from this broader perspective. Second, Shipps proposes that politics is best understood in terms of competing interpretative narratives rather than in terms of the analysis of isolated variables. By political narratives she means a story-line-based framework that purports to explain the global structure of action within the policy system—a story line that reaches well beyond proven causal relationships to provide guidelines for practical action. Historically, the public school narrative has been dominated by the scientific management narrative originated by Frederick Taylor near the beginning of the 20th century. This narrative, she argues, has been responsible for an inward and narrow focus for educational policy and professional practice. Although many scholars interested in the politics of education have been critical of this narrative, the criticisms have generally had the perverse effect of encouraging elaboration and revitalization of the Taylorist narrative. What is needed, Shipps argues, is a fully developed political narrative. The body of her chapter is devoted to developing just such an interpretation of educational politics and policymaking.

The Changing Landscape in School Governance: Implications for Establishing Knowledge Claims

Kenneth K. Wong
Brown University

Political scientists are keenly interested in the balance of power among all levels of government in our federal system. Drawing on a variety of data sources, political analysts have written extensively on the implementation of federal educational programs, the local-state tension in meeting standards-based reform, and the challenge of building sustainable civic capacity (Cibulka & Boyd, 2003; Stone, Henig, Jones, & Pierannunzi, 2001; Wong, 2003). Although an ongoing search for the proper balance between centralization and decentralization remains highly relevant, recent moves to enhance school choice, allow mayoral or state takeover of local schools, and outsource school management responsibilities are providing a new empirical basis for conceptualizing school governance. Hybrid forms of school governance with divergent mechanisms for accountability have emerged. These new institutional forms are able to accommodate a wider range of governance practices and are giving birth to both centralized and decentralized authority structures in both public and nonpublic service delivery systems.

Reflecting on this changing landscape in educational governance, this chapter pursues two interrelated objectives, namely, the what and the how of educational policy research. First, I identify substantive areas where educational policy researchers can establish their claim to knowledge contribution. These areas address the changing needs of the broad community and policymakers. More specifically, I try to synthesize several competing governance models that have emerged in the context of rising public expectations on school performance. This synthesis pays attention to issues of design and implementation by asking the following questions: What are the mechanisms that drive different models of school reform? What are the enabling and constraining conditions that shape the implementation of the reform? and How much do we know about evidence-based consequences of these reform initiatives? These questions provide a substantive understanding of the changing landscape in school governance.

The second objective of this chapter addresses a central concern of this book: Given the emerging governance models, how can we develop greater confidence in our knowledge claims? This is a timely question as policymakers, parents, and the general public pay close attention to whether educational reform improves student performance in the context of the No Child Left Behind Act of 2001. Indeed, underlying the new governance arrangements is a paradigmatic shift in how research in educational policy is conducted. In the current climate of outcomes-based accountability, the federal government, including the newly created Institute of Education Sciences (IES), has challenged the research community to take a more active role in identifying reform strategies that can raise student performance (see National Research Council, 2002; Sroufe, 2003). To improve our confidence in causal inferences about reform programs, the IES has prioritized its funding to support experimental studies on student achievement. Clearly, the changing federal agenda in educational research and development will have far-reaching implications on training and research in the academy.

CHANGING GOVERNANCE, NEW UNDERSTANDING

As policymakers formulate new strategies to improve public schools, policy researchers have contributed to a growing knowledge base on reform design and implementation. When the *what* of educational policy research is closely related to current problems, policy analysts can maintain a strong knowledge claim. For analytical purposes, the new school governance models can be incorporated into the conceptual scheme presented in Table 7.1. Be advised that this scheme is not comprehensive and does not include all the prominent efforts to reform the public schools, especially not those involving professional efforts to gain greater autonomy at the school-building level within existing governance arrangements. The proposed framework has two key dimensions. First, it differentiates governance models on the basis of the degree to which they rely on consumer choices or on management-led initiatives. Although these two mechanisms are not necessarily mutually exclusive, as suggested in Fiske and Ladd's (2000) study of New Zealand, the distinction illuminates fundamental differences in reform models. On a second dimension, school governance models differ in terms of their relative autonomy from state-designated accountability require-

TABLE 7.1
Proposing a Framework in Understanding
School Governance Arrangements

	Sources of Accountability	
Mechanisms that drive management and operation	State-enabling legislation and system-wide academic standards	A hybrid of public and nonpublic interests
Consumer preferences of schooling services	I. State-funded choice initiatives (charter, vouchers)	II. Privately funded choice initiatives
Management-led reform	III. State or city takeover of districts and schools	IV. Contracted service providers (EMOs)

ments. At the risk of oversimplifying, on the one end of the accountability continuum are state legislative mandates setting the parameters of support and sanctions; at the other end are hybrids of public and nonpublic agencies with substantial discretionary authority.

As Table 7.1 suggests, the two dimensions together distinguish four new models of school governance. First, state-led initiatives supporting school choice have gained prominence in the last decade. About 80% of the states have charter school legislation, and state-funded voucher programs are currently implemented in Milwaukee, Cleveland, and Florida. These state-funded choice programs typify consumer-based reforms governed by state-wide accountability standards. Second, privately funded vouchers are bounded neither by statewide accountability requirements nor by state funds. These private voucher programs, found in several large districts, are consumer driven and are supported primarily by corporate sources. Third, takeover of school districts by city mayors or state agencies is an example of management-oriented reform that operates within the state accountability framework. Fourth, an emerging number of districts have contracted out some of their lowest performing schools to private companies and nonprofit organizations (such as universities). These Educational Management Organizations (EMOs) often operate side by side with schools that are managed by the district. Nonetheless, these EMOs constitute a hybrid of alternative service delivery in public education. In the following sections, I highlight the main features of these models and what we know about their effectiveness.

Model I: State Initiatives to Promote Consumer Choice

Dissatisfied with low performance in public schools, an increasing number of states are focusing on marketlike competition as the driving force to raise student performance (Hirschman, 1971). Four specific mechanisms were weighted equally by Jay Greene (2002) to develop an Education Freedom Index for each of the 50 states. The four components are: charter schools, subsidized private schools, home schooling, and public school choice. According to Greene, Arizona provides the highest degree of school choice to families, whereas Hawaii maintains the least choice. During 2000 and 2001, Florida showed the greatest gain in school choice, whereas Utah seemed to regress.

Home schooling is widespread, allowed by all but two states and involving more than a million school-age children, but authorization of charter schools is the most substantial state effort to promote choice. With over 40 states and the District of Columbia operating a total of about 3,000 charter schools, charter school reform has taken on a national character as an alternative to failing public schools. Although charter schools are labeled as public schools, they are distinctive in several major aspects. The school's charter or contract explicitly states the conditions and expectations for outcome-based performance that are consistent with the state framework (Bierlein, 1997; Hill, 1997). The authorizing agency can be the local school board or other legal entities such as universities. Once established, charter schools enjoy substantial autonomy in setting teachers' salaries and work conditions, although they are governed by state regulations regarding safety, health, dismissal, and civil rights. School funding follows students to the charter schools, which are operated on a multiyear renewable contract. At least one district in California has converted to a system of charter schools. Enrollment in charter schools increased to about 2.5% of the nation's public school student population in 2000. In Arizona, California, and Michigan, charter enrollment figures are much higher.

Do charter schools create a competitive environment that causes regular public schools to make greater efforts to raise their performance? The rationale of competition has been widely cited, but there is a need to determine whether evidence exists to support such a claim. The literature, not surprisingly, is split on this issue (Wong & Shen, 2001, 2004).

Competitive effects of charter schools are constrained by legislative compromise. Based on interviews and policy and legal analysis in four states, Bryan Hassel (1999) found that legislative compromise has played a significant role in reducing the competitive impact of charter schools. Laws that cap the number of charter schools, cushion the financial blow to traditional district schools, or reduce the autonomy of charter schools all contribute to reducing the impact a charter school can make. In a study of five urban districts, Teske, Schneider, Buckley, and Clark (2001) attributed the modest effects of competition to several factors. The effects of charter school competition are lessened by financial cushioning and by a lack of school-level penalties for losing students to charter schools. Growing student populations may also reduce the competitive effects; even though traditional public schools are losing relative market share, the absolute number of their students remains constant. In districts where charter schools did have an impact, piecemeal rather than systemwide changes were made, mostly concerned with expanding the school day by offering new add-on programs.

Charter schools also vary in their effects on racial segregation or stratification, a concern widely shared by skeptics of school choice initiatives. Wong and Shen (2000), for example, found that California and Michigan have quite different charter school landscapes. Although each state has relatively strong charter legislation and a large number of charter schools, the two states differ in terms of innovation and stratification effects. In California, for example, there is a clustering of high-achieving students by race. In Michigan, there seems to be less of a stratification effect. Other differences between the two states include the extensive involvement of higher education institutions in Michigan and the large number of home-school-focused charter schools in California. These and other differences may account for the varying degree of stratification in the two states.

Voucher experiments, like those implemented in Florida, Milwaukee, and Cleveland, represent a second important state-initiated marketlike reform effort. These experiments are signaling an unusual kind of political alliance that has emerged to address growing concerns about failing public schools in the inner city. This new alliance consists of two core segments of the Republican and Democratic parties. Frustrated with the low quality of schooling opportunities for their constituencies, lawmakers and religious and community leaders in African American neighborhoods (a traditional core of the Democratic party) have parted company with the teachers' union (another Democratic core) and supported a more radical solution to the crisis in urban education. In the Republican party, some governors and lawmakers have joined this search for alternative strategies to improve failing schools in the urban neighborhoods In Milwaukee, Polly Williams, a Black state lawmaker, and Howard Fuller, a Black activist and former superintendent, became the most outspoken supporters of the state-funded voucher program, which began in 1990. In Cleveland, Fannie Lewis, a Democratic member of the city council, spearheaded the 1994 passage of the choice program in the Ohio legislature. Joining the Democratic core were Republican governors and their business allies, who saw choice as a mechanism not only to improve school performance and market efficiency but also to weaken the influence of the teachers' union. In both Milwaukee and Cleveland, this unique alliance was gradually broadened to include the Catholic Church and a wide range of business interest groups. Seeing a broadening of support, key proponents of choice have attempted to increase the demand and supply of choice programs. For example, Milwaukee Mayor John Norquist favored raising the income ceiling on eligibility. Prochoice advocacy groups, such as the

Heartland Institute in Chicago, continue to play an active role in organizing lobbying efforts in state capitals.

The Cleveland voucher program has gained national attention. Started in the fall of 1996, it immediately faced a court challenge for violating the "establishment clause," as students were allowed to choose religious schools. Initially restricted to lower elementary grades, about two thirds of the nearly 2,000 first-year participants were in kindergarten or first grade; about 25% had previously attended private schools. Over 90% of the voucher students chose sectarian schools. In December of 2000, the federal appeals court in Cincinnati ruled that the enrollment pattern did have the "impermissible effect of promoting sectarian schools" (New York Times, p. 1). However, in June 2002, the U.S. Supreme Court (*Zelman v. Simmons-Harris*) by a narrow five-to-four margin found that the Cleveland voucher program did not violate the First Amendment's establishment clause. *The New York Times* headline read, "Majority Says Cleveland Program Offers 'True Private Choice' " (cited in Greenhouse, 2002, p. 1).

The *Zelman v. Simmons-Harris* (2002) decision is likely to encourage the spread of voucher experiments to a growing number of states. Moreover, with state funding support, parental demand for school choice will probably grow. In response to these initiatives, diverse suppliers of schooling services will emerge. No doubt, faith-based organizations, discontented parents and teachers, and nonprofit and community-based organizations will be involved. If the voucher movement grows as fast as charter school reform, the supply of public schooling in the next 10 years will be significantly different from the existing system. However, the voucher movement, like charter school reform, may also necessitate a more active state monitoring and support role (Fiske & Ladd, 2000). As parents exercise school selection, the information needed for accountability and school performance will not subside.

As described in more detail later, findings from the research on both charter schools and vouchers have become more and more controversial as level of resources and relationship to core public values have become more obvious.

Model II: Privately Funded Vouchers Not Subject to State Accountability

Although published research has focused primarily on state-funded vouchers, privately funded vouchers have also been implemented since the early 1990s. The first private program was started by the CEO of the Golden Rule Insurance Company in Indianapolis, providing scholarships to 746 inner-city children. By 1998 and 1999, over 13,000 students had used private scholarships to attend schools of their choice in over 30 cities. These programs were shaped by the first Golden Rule initiative—private funds to provide scholarship to low-income children on a first-come, first-served basis for whatever private or religious schools they select. In a review of the privately funded vouchers across the nation as of the late 1990s, Moe (2001a) highlighted the policy significance of this initiative. He pointed out, "But by comparison to the public programs, private voucher programs give us a much simpler, more direct indication of how choice and markets actually operate when the most burdensome trappings of bureaucracy and political control are removed" (p. 100).

The design of privately funded vouchers has changed from first-come, first-served to a lottery in recent years (Godwin & Kemerer, 2002; Howell & Peterson, 2002). This shift resulted in part from negotiation between the corporate funders of the programs and the Harvard-led research team that argued for a more scientific design in gathering data on program effects on student achievement. The study team was directed by Paul Peterson, whose early concerns about self-selection bias led him to compare voucher participants with those who applied but did not receive the voucher in the state-funded pilot programs in Milwaukee and Cleveland. In light of these concerns on the quality of evaluation, designers of privately funded voucher programs have adopted the practice of random assignment.

Implementation of privately funded voucher programs clearly involves significant trade-offs among societal and educational values. Godwin and Kemerer (2002) examined advantages and risks in school choice from a liberal democratic framework. Their synthesis of competing philosophical, constitutional, and economic perspectives identified four normative aims of education in a liberal democracy (p. 234). The four major aims are to provide students with: the skills to become economically independent, the political knowledge and skills to participate in democratic government, the moral reasoning to guide ethical behavior, and an equality of educational opportunity. These educational goals are proposed as the basis for the standards to be used in designing school choice policy (see their proposal to expand school choice, p. 235). They saw a state system expanded to include nonpublic schools. With 20% of the students identified as low income, schools admitting state-supported students are required to have at least 20% of their students from low-income families. Both private and public schools are to be exempt from collective bargaining laws, except when a majority of the teachers in public schools decide otherwise. To some extent, Godwin and Kemerer's proposal resembles the school policy systems in the United Kingdom (Wong, 2001) and New Zealand (Fiske & Ladd, 2000), where choice is among several key policy levers to improve accountability and service quality. Unlike these systems, the Godwin and Kemerer proposal does not challenge the tradition of state control by calling for a national graduation examination system for the purpose of accountability (see also Moe, 2001b).

As with the public-funded vouchers and charter schools, the question of whether research can validate the efficacy of such a system remains tenuous. Political and ideological arguments are strong and can easily lead policymakers, and even researchers themselves, to press the most accommodating interpretations on to available data.

Model III: State and District Takeover of Failing Schools

Where concerns regarding accountability outweigh those related to choice, states have begun to allow for takeover of school district operations, by either a state authority or city mayors. Most states have long had provisions for emergency state takeover of local school districts, but states rarely invoked them, except in cases of clear financial mismanagement or illegal activity (Cibulka, 1999). More recent state takeover laws have shifted focus toward breaches of academic accountability. Twenty-four states allow state takeover of local school districts, permitting state officials to exert authority over a district in the case of "academic bankruptcy," or woefully low-performing schools, but only 11 states have exercised the law. Most recently, on October 4, 2003, voters across Louisiana approved a referendum to amend the state constitution so that the state can have the option of taking over persistently failing schools.

School district takeover is becoming an important political and policy issue in many states. In Missouri, school districts in both St. Louis and Kansas City are facing possible takeovers by the State Board of Education. In New York, there is discussion of a takeover by state education officials of the Roosevelt school district on Long Island ("New York State Eyes District Takeover," 2001). In these and other instances, state or mayoral takeover seems to be an attractive option to turn around failing school districts.

In analyzing the facilitating factors and barriers to success in takeover reform, the most important distinction is between city or mayoral and state takeovers. This is a somewhat artificial distinction because the states must authorize any mayoral takeover. The important difference is in who gets to appoint the new school management teams—state or local officials.

A review of recent cases reveals the differences between mayoral and state takeovers (Wong & Shen, 2002). The racial makeup of the students involved is similar, but city takeovers involve much larger districts. They involve districts with an average of five times as many students and more than four times as many schools. Thus, when mayors decide to take over an educational system, they take on enormous challenges.

Mayoral takeover involves greater political risks in that unhappy parents, residents, or local interest groups can choose to vote the mayor out of office. When state-appointed officials are put in charge, however, it is more difficult to see who is accountable if the district does not improve.

Another important difference between city and state takeovers is the balance of revenue coming from city versus state sources. Mayoral takeover districts receive a significantly larger percentage of their education revenue from local sources. In the state takeover districts, state revenue makes up about 70% of total revenue, and this number increased from 1992 to 1997. In contrast, the mayoral takeover districts receive approximately 50% of their total revenue from the state. It is apparently easier for states to exercise their takeover authority when they are also shouldering more of the financial burden. Mayors can have more control where there is greater fiscal accountability to local taxpayers.

State Takeovers.   State takeovers have proven highly controversial and may be managerially unstable. In Compton, California and Lawrence, Massachusetts state takeover led to widely publicized, bitter fights between the state and local authorities. More generally, in assessing state takeovers in New Jersey and elsewhere before 1996, "Ill Will Comes With Territory" (1996) observed, "In case after case, when state administrators have tried to elbow out local officials and run a failing district themselves, improvements have come at the heavy cost of lawsuits, bitter media battles, and confused and angry teachers and parents" (p. 2). In the state takeover city of Hartford, for instance, it became clear that the public had little to say about the tenure of superintendent Tony Amato. Though the state-appointed board of trustees made the hiring decision, local cynicism was engendered when Amato was "caught applying for the superintendent's post in San Francisco even though his current contract had not expired—and in spite of his pledges to stay in Hartford for a while" ("Amato's Shooting From Hip," 2000, p. C.3). As a state appointee, Amato stirred more local anger when he "made sweeping generalizations about the inadequacy of music programs" ("Amato's Shooting From Hip," p. C.3). Amato subsequently left for the superintendent's position in New Orleans.

Mayoral Takeovers.   Mayoral takeovers may be more promising, but there are variations in the implementation of this type of takeover reform. In Chicago, Boston, and Cleveland mayoral takeover led to the creation of substantially integrated civic and educational governance structures. In each of these cities the mayor exercises fairly complete control over all district functions (Kirst & Bulkley, 2003; Wong & Shen, 2003). Governance integration in these cities has been facilitated by the following factors:

1. Mayoral vision on outcome-based accountability.

2. Broad public dissatisfaction with a crisis in school performance over several years preceding integrated governance.
3. State leadership that is dominated by Republicans who are willing to empower the mayoral office to address school problems.
4. Strong business support that has translated into adoption of corporate management practices to address complex bureaucratic problems in school districts.
5. Weakened legitimacy of traditionally powerful service provider groups (unions) and service demand groups (racial- and neighborhood-based groups).

In Cleveland, for example, when Mayor White initially took over the district in 1998, the reform did not obtain unanimous support in the Cleveland education community. Notably, the teachers' unions actually went to court in an attempt to block the takeover. Today, however, it is a different story. Mayor White's successor, Jane Campbell, enjoys the support of the unions on the issue of mayoral control. She also enjoys the support of many others, as evidenced by the vote on November 5, 2002: More than 70% of voters supported Issue 4 on the ballot, leaving the schools under mayoral control.

Mayors who maintain integrated governance have indicated a strong commitment to enhance management efficiency in their city services. These mayors are keenly aware of the ongoing challenge of retaining productive resources within the city (Tiebout, 1956). Unless city services provide the optimal level of cost-benefit ratios to the middle class, cities are likely to face a declining revenue base in the longer run. To stem the Tiebout-like dilemma, these mayors have decided to bring public schools as part of the overall city strategy to improve service quality and management. An insulated school system would mean business as usual, where the mayor lacks direct control over the use of about one third of the local property tax revenues. To the extent that schools can become an economic development strategy for the city as a whole, these mayors may be able to restore public confidence in public schools, thereby changing the marketlike dynamics of middle-class migration to the suburbs.

The takeovers in Oakland, Washington, DC, and Baltimore look rather different. The integration of civic and educational governance has not been complete. The quasi-integration in Washington, DC includes a citywide reform board that exercises some formal control over the school system, but Congress, exercising its higher legislative authority, has stripped the mayor of functional authority until Washington, DC cleans up its image of mismanagement. In Baltimore, the state legislature has not been willing to give power directly to the mayor because of partisan and territorial politics. The mayor has actually lost some of his authority, sharing it now with the governor and the Maryland State Department of Education. In Oakland, Mayor Brown tried to establish control over the school district, but was not able to avoid the political quarrels that prevented systemic change in the district. The mayor appointed only 3 of the 10 school board members and did not appoint the school superintendent. Due to a steep budgetary crisis in 2003, Mayor Brown asked the state to take over the school district in exchange for state funds to close the deficit. These three quasi-integrated governance systems are still dominated by traditional politics and are not moving toward an accountability-based policy framework.

Whether mayoral control can be widely adopted beyond these few cities remains to be seen. The political capital of the mayor is certainly a key element. Using this capital, the mayor must negotiate the political process of appointing competent administrators and board members. Moreover, the mayor's governance reforms need to be potent enough to permeate through a complex, multilayered school policy system. This is virtually impossible when, as happened in Baltimore, the mayor's initiatives are constrained by gubernatorial involvement in school board appointments.

Of course, any kind of governance reform can only succeed if it facilitates educational practices that improve student performance. On this important issue of productivity, there seems to be some promising evidence that mayoral control can make a difference. In comparing the mayoral takeover districts with similar urban districts in a nationwide database, Wong and Shen (2003) found that the former are more likely to invest in a higher level of per student spending and student support services without incurring additional debts. More importantly, mayoral control systems show promising gains in student performance not only at the aggregate level but also among the lowest performing schools. In Boston, Chicago, and Cleveland, Wong and Shen found that the lowest performing schools were able to improve their student achievement at a faster rate than the districtwide average during the years after the mayor took over the school district.

Model IV: Contracted Service Providers to Operate Low-Performing Schools

Replacing public with private management of the schools is the fourth new governance reform strategy. Nonprofit and for-profit organizations are expanding their presence and competing successfully for government contracts to run public schools that continue to be subject to district governance. These contracted schools are not charter schools, enjoying school site autonomy over personnel hiring, student recruitment, and staff compensation. Although contracted schools do exercise a certain degree of management and programmatic discretion, they are often governed by virtually all the district and state guidelines, including collective bargaining agreements between the district and the unions and academic standards and assessment that are applicable across the school district. The key feature of this reform is that the contracting agency (whether a district or the state) is willing to grant management autonomy to the contracted service providers, which, in turn, agree to meet certain measurable outcomes within a given time frame.

In this governance arrangement, the contracted service providers are expected to "do the job better, or cheaper, with no fewer positive side effects and no more negative ones than the public alternative" (Donahue, 1989, p. 221; see also Walberg & Bast, 2001). Previous small-scale attempts to contract out low-performing schools have produced mixed results (Orr, 1999). Although service providers seem to be able to raise student performance, they are less ready to address broader community concerns of school quality (Donahue, p. 219). School contexts and educators' skepticism pose major challenges to any generic approach adopted by the EMOs (Hernandez & Mahoney, 2002).

According to Arizona State University's Education Policy Research Unit, there are over 30 major for-profit companies managing almost 400 traditionally public and public charter schools in two dozen states. According to a September 2002 count in *Education Week* ("Wall Street Blues," 2002), there were 12 publicly traded companies engaging in a wide range of activities in elementary and secondary education. Among these are Edison Schools, Inc. (which is no longer publicly traded), Renaissance Learning, Inc., and Sylvan Learning Systems, Inc. In addition, many universities and community-based organizations are contracted to manage low-performing schools. For my analytical purpose, the role of the EMOs as contracted service providers in public, noncharter schools needs to be considered further.

The most extensive effort to contract out persistently low-performing schools is in the Philadelphia school district. Edison Project was commissioned by former Governor Tom Ridge to conduct an assessment of the academic and financial position of the Philadelphia school district in the fall of 2001. The report's findings provided the basis for the legislation that granted the governor appointive power of the majority of the school board. Edison Project was subsequently hired as the "lead district advisor" to manage the central administration during March and July of 2002. An initial plan of granting Edison management over a substantial number of schools was terminated when the school board hired Paul Vallas, the former CEO in Chicago, to become the district's CEO in July 2002. Instead, the Vallas administration selected seven outside managers (or EMOs) to manage 45 low-performing schools beginning in August 2002. EMOs, which included Edison Project (20 schools), University of Pennsylvania, and Temple University, among others, were given extra financial incentives that ranged from $450 to $881 per student. In April 2003, the district terminated the contract with one of the EMOs, Chancellor Beacon Academies, for lack of progress. Thus, it remains to be seen if the EMOs in the Philadelphia experiment will raise student performance. More importantly, the underlying belief that private managers, operating within the regulatory and political structures governing public schools, can significantly alter school productivity has yet to be subjected to persuasive evaluation research.

CHANGING RESEARCH AGENDA, NEW KNOWLEDGE CLAIMS

The new governance structures are not only altering the political and operational character of public schools, they are also reshaping research agendas. The knowledge base on the reform initiatives discussed previously is expanding rapidly. Take charter school reform as an example. The Center for Education Reform (2003) found more than 70 major evaluation studies addressing student achievement since 1997, and Lubienski (2003) identified 190 published studies on charter school innovations. At this point, as Hassel and Batdorff (2004) observed, "Charter authorizing has reached the point that it is possible for researchers to study charter school accountability in practice, moving past theoretical debates to determine what is actually happening in the field" (p. 39).

Given this proliferation of research on the changing governance landscape and the important differences in reported findings, it is important to address the following question: How can we develop greater confidence in policy and political knowledge claims? This is a timely question as policymakers and the general public heighten their focus on school performance. Social scientists have occasionally visited this issue of confidence in knowledge claims (Coleman, 1987; Herrington, 1998; Mitchell & Boyd, 1998; Weiss, 1983; Wilson, 1980; Wong, 1998). Particularly useful for the present purpose is the perspective developed by Gary King, Robert Keohane, and Sidney Verba (1994), three Harvard political scientists with different methodological and substantive orientations. In *Designing Social Inquiry*, King et al. argued that research in the social sciences, which includes both qualitative and quantitative studies of school politics and policy, can earn greater scientific credibility in terms of making "valid descriptive and causal inferences" (p. 3). These authors proposed five criteria for improving the design and conduct of social science research:

1. Addressing audiences and their values: First, social scientists who study governance and policy need to frame research questions to satisfy dual audiences—the broader civic community and their specialized schol-

arly peers. Clearly, the research needs to address issues that are consequential for the real world. As Mitchell and Boyd (1998) pointed out, knowledge claims in the domain of educational politics and policy are "always dependent on the value system used to frame action alternatives" (p. 127). These values can be found in institutional agendas or political ideologies and are often articulated by the mass media. The governance reform initiatives described earlier in this chapter are colored by values related to consumer preferences, confidence in management control, and attitudes toward resource allocation.

King et al. (1994) suggested various approaches to eliciting greater confidence from scholarly peer audiences (pp. 16–17). Among these are: conducting empirical assessment of widely accepted propositions that lack full empirical support (e.g., particular aspects of site-based management in public schools), providing fresh and further evidence on the validity of controversial policy positions (e.g., the school choice debate), conducting studies that illuminate the complexity of key assumptions in a prominent school of thought (e.g., the literature on how money matters), and showing the promise and limits of applying theories and methods from one policy domain to another (e.g., using cultural anthropology to understand professional culture in schools).

2. Theory or paradigm focus: King et al. (1994) urged policy researchers to see their work as organizing evidence to improve a particular theory or policy paradigm. Whereas natural scientists tend to rely on controlled experiments to isolate the effects of a single or a few variables at any given time, social scientists typically strive for more comprehensive, global theory building. Taking a middle-range perspective may be more appropriate in the domain of public policy. After assessing the balance of the evidence in testing key hypotheses, researchers with a middle-range perspective can specify the conditions under which an original theory needs revision to accommodate previously unstudied circumstances. This occurred, for example, in Barr and Dreeben's (1983) study of first-grade reading and the common practice of organizing students into ability groups. They were surprised to see that some first graders were able to learn more even when placed in lower tracks. This finding ultimately led these researchers to distinguish the structure of ability groups from instructional coverage in each ability group (see Hallinan & Dreeben, 2003). Another example is the literature on intergovernmental conflict. Whereas political scientists in the 1970s and 1980s focused on implementation problems in federal programs, Peterson, Rabe, and Wong (1986) saw a more complex pattern. Whereas redistributive programs such as low-income housing showed extensive federal-city conflict, antipoverty programs in education were much more manageable. Based on these findings, Peterson et al. developed a more differentiated theory of federalism. In these and

other instances, policy analysts have used their observations to specify boundary conditions for a dominant theoretical perspective, reinforcing but limiting its applicability.

3. Methodology: A third way of enhancing confidence is to be completely open about the way research is carried out. Regardless of whether one engages in qualitative or quantitative research, it is necessary to report on the rules, procedures, and tools employed in gathering and analyzing data. Open discussion of all the operational details of data collection, preparation, coding, and analysis not only strengthens any conclusions reached but also encourages replication of the study, enhancing the scientific credibility of the research. Equally important is the need to refrain from discouraging those peers who may hold a different view on the issue from asking questions on data quality. To be sure, publication in peer-refereed journals serves just this purpose of reinforcing scientific norms in data collection, analysis, and interpretation.

4. Data quality: Among the most obvious, but often overlooked, principles of improved credibility is improving data quality. Reliability of how the observable implications are being measured, replicability of results when one uses the same methods, and documentation of all the data sources are some of the scientific practices that all researchers are expected to follow. Clearly, an ongoing challenge is to develop a process whereby researchers can guard against data bias. A common strategy is triangulation of multiple sources of data on the same occurrences. Studies that used a mixed-methods approach, for example, have yielded more comprehensive findings on state takeover of failing districts (Wong, Langevin, & Shen, 2004). Researchers also can situate their findings in the larger context to maximize the potential for causal inference. Policymakers, for example, are often suspicious of program evaluations conducted by program designers. Consequently, independent or third-party evaluators are recruited to keep program optimism (or pessimism) from unduly influencing interpretations of program data.

5. Reporting uncertainties: Finally, King et al. (1994) emphasized the importance of reporting uncertainties associated with research results. As they put it, "Perhaps the single most serious problem with qualitative research in political science is the pervasive failure to provide reasonable estimates of the uncertainty of the investigator's inferences" (p. 32; see also King, 1989). To avoid reaching premature conclusions, social scientists often treat causal inferences with a degree of skepticism. But it is also important to propose alternative explanations for further investigation even when one is satisfied with the results at the end of a research undertaking (Yin, 1998). As I learned from the late J. David Greenstone when I was a graduate student, social science is an accumulated enterprise.

Experimental Designs and Program Effectiveness

Arguably the most extensive debate that illuminates the interplay between the substance of governance reform and the analytical quality of the research is found in the literature on school choice. At issue is the need for the most appropriate research design to study the effect of choice programs on student achievement. Evaluation studies of charter schools and voucher programs often use quasi-experimental design where the treatment group (students who enroll in choice programs) is compared with a comparison group (students who enroll in public schools but share similar socioeconomic characteristics or academic readiness). Notwithstanding their widespread use, these quasi-experimental designs do not yield reliable causal inferences. Quasi-experimental designs cannot fully distinguish the effects of the choice programs from the effects of self-selection by program participants. The latter could undermine the argument that the program (or treatment) contributes to academic performance. There are studies indicating that school choice participants come from families whose parents are more ready to seek out alternative schooling, better networked, and more likely to spend time with their children on academic tasks (Schneider et al., 2001). A study of San Antonio's first-come, first-served selection process in the privately funded Children's Educational Opportunity program found that the program benefited students who were academically prepared and whose parents were more actively involved (Godwin & Kemerer, 2002). In other words, comparisons of program participants with their public school peers, even when findings show positive effects for charter schools and voucher programs, cannot confidently claim causal efficacy for the reform programs due to the confounding factor of self-selection.

In light of these inferential validity concerns, a growing number of policy researchers have adopted Randomized Field Trial (RFT) designs for their school choice studies. RFTs minimize (or even eliminate) the biasing effect of self-selection by comparing groups of students randomly accepted into the choice programs with applicants who were not selected. The RFT design creates groups with similar levels of parental motivation and access to schooling information by dividing the charter applicants into two groups following the random assignment (or lottery) that occurs when a school is oversubscribed: a treatment group composed of those who applied and lotteried in and a control group composed of those who applied but lotteried out. Detailed student-level analyses of these two groups of students and their academic achievement enable researchers to reach reliable causal inferences on the effects of the choice program. Findings from RFT evaluation can provide more compelling evidence on a key accountability question: Does school choice reform raise student performance?

The importance of the RFT design is underscored by conflicting findings from the Milwaukee voucher program. The Peterson team at Harvard and the Witte group at Wisconsin drew substantially different conclusions about the efficacy of this program. Witte and Thorn (1996) found that voucher participants were different from nonparticipating students, and Witte (1997) saw no evidence that the students who used the vouchers to attend private schools performed better than their public school peers. However, when using the RFT design, Greene, Peterson, and Du (1998) reached a different conclusion on the effectiveness of the program. Supporting the Peterson team's approach, Hoxby and Rockoff (2004) used an RFT design to examine three oversubscribed charter schools in Chicago and found positive effects.

The most comprehensive analysis that uses RFT to study school choice in multiple cities over several years comes from the Howell and Peterson team at Harvard. In a study of several privately funded voucher programs for urban low-income children, Howell and Peterson (2002) found that African Americans benefited more from school choice than their peers. African American students who were program participants as a result of lottery in New York, Dayton, and Washington, DC, according to the authors, "gained, on average, roughly 3.9 [national percentile ranking] points after Year 1, 6.3 points after Year II, and 6.6 points after Year III" (p. 146). These findings led them to offer a "differentiated theory of choice," in that the program's marginal benefits tend to be greater for those who encounter poor educational options (such as inner-city low-income African American children). The benefits gap, as measured by statistically significant effect sizes, illuminates the consequences of shifting from public to private schools. Although parental satisfaction was persistently strong in the voucher program, student departure from public schools showed "few adverse side effects" (p. 186).

A major part of the Howell and Peterson (2002) study lies in its application of the RFTs. Although RFTs have been used in evaluation of intervention programs in health care, housing, and welfare assistance, they are rarely used in educational research. The Harvard research team collected baseline information (including student test performance) at the time of the application as well as follow-up information through the third program year. A lottery was used to randomly select voucher participants from the whole applicant pool. Those who were not selected became the control group for analytical purposes. The lottery fits the two essential criteria to aid in "an instrumental variable technique," namely, that the lottery itself is a good predictor for students attending private schools and at the same time does not highly correlate with the outcomes (including student performance). Clearly, the RFTs offered a robust scientific base for the study's internal validity.

Notwithstanding the potential of school vouchers to raise urban school performance, particularly among African American students, the proposed differentiated theory needs to take into consideration that vouchers by themselves may not be a sufficient incentive to keep the participants in the private schools. Although the initial parental demand seemed strong at the application stage, the attrition rates were fairly high during the first 3 program years (see Howell & Peterson, 2002, pp. 34–35). For example, in New York City, only 70% of those who received vouchers remained in the private schools toward the end of the third year. In Washington, DC, only 29% of the first-year cohort remained through the third year. Using these attrition rates for the three cities for the first cohort, I calculated that only about 54% of the students remained in private schools of their choice. What happened to the 46% who left would be an important research undertaking toward a more complete understanding of school choice. As Howell and Peterson briefly acknowledged (pp. 66–67), parental decisions not to use their vouchers were related to their inability to supplement their own income to pay for higher tuition, transportation costs, and the timing of getting the lottery results. In the Washington, DC program, schools tended to select higher performing applicants in grades 6 to 8 (pp. 68–70). Peers, too, can dampen what may have been a positive experience when a student switched from public to private school. As Howell and Peterson found, vouchers had "only modest effects on peer friendships and racial integration" (p. 126). In other words, although the lottery is designed to ensure equal chances among applicants, peer culture autonomy within the selected schools can exclude voucher participants from social networks, undercutting the fairness intended by the lottery selection process.

From a broader perspective, although RFT designs are likely to gain acceptance among educational policy researchers, there are several limitations. Random assignment may not be practical in situations where alternative schooling programs are already in full implementation, and educational services must remain accessible (often for legal and ethical considerations) to all those who are eligible. In these circumstances, researchers have to settle for a series of quasi-experimental studies with carefully designed control groups that would match the treatment groups, use multiple and scalable outcome measures, and focus on longitudinal growth that takes into consideration baseline performance. These studies provide useful assessment of the effects of reforms on program participants, although data are not available to compare them with their eligible peers who applied but did not receive the treatment. In other words, quasi-experimental studies do not have the benefits of randomization to draw causal inference with confidence. Nonetheless, quasi-experimental studies, when carefully designed, can provide useful tests of key hypotheses on the effectiveness of school choice and other school reform initiatives.

IMPLICATIONS FOR RESEARCH ON SCHOOL GOVERNANCE AND REFORM

Efforts to redefine the boundary among key institutions in the management of schools have broadened the level of scholarly engagement in educational policy research. In response to mayoral takeover, school choice, and outsourcing, a growing number of political scientists have taken an active role in debating the future direction of public schools. For example, an unanticipated development in the school choice controversy between the Peterson and the Witte research teams is a revival of the subfield of the politics of education (a particularly welcome trend from my perspective as the immediate past president of the Politics of Education Association). The debate also attracts greater national media attention to educational reform issues. Equally important is the growing number of panels in school politics and policy at the annual meetings of the University of Continuing Education Association, Association for Public Policy Analysis and Management, and the American Political Science Association.

Furthermore, the policy shift toward accountability is likely to sharpen the focus on scientific investigation in the field of educational policy. The debate over the effects of privately funded and state-funded vouchers on student achievement has been fueled by researchers' uses and counteruses of increasingly sophisticated research designs and data-collection methods. To be sure, the overall concern about productivity goes well beyond school choice programs. Federally funded programs, particularly the comprehensive school reform initiative, are increasingly subject to systemic scrutiny. Consequently, this current focus on useable knowledge for policymaking may strengthen the institutional agenda on productivity in public education.

Moreover, in the post *Zelman v. Simmons-Harris* (2002) era, when the constitutionality of school choice is less an issue, philosophical differences are likely to become more contentious on the aims of public education. Scholarship can play a constructive role in mediating the tension in public discourse in two areas. First, issues related to externalities of school choice must be systematically examined. What happens to those who used the scholarship or voucher in the initial year but later left the program? What were the factors that explain their decision to move back to public schools? And what happens to those students who did not choose vouchers when a high proportion of their peers left for another school? Are there differences across racial, ethnic, and cultural subgroups? Second, the politics of sustainability needs to be examined with a longitudinal database. Although political scientists have examined the state legislative process in adopting school choice policy, there is a gap in understanding the politics of delivering high-quality services over a sustained period of time. What does it take to widen the use of school choice (i.e., increasing demands) without lowering the standards (i.e., expanding services)? In short, students of educational policy and reform can continue to broaden the research agenda on school choice.

Social scientists and policy analysts who are conducting research in educational governance and reform are likely to become increasingly aware of the trade-offs among the scientific criteria in their work. For analytical purposes, we may consider two such criteria in establishing the legitimacy of our knowledge claims. First, our work needs to address significant real-world problems, such as improving the effectiveness of governance reform. Second, our work must contribute to a body of social scientific knowledge, including the growing recognition of the need for experimental design in educational policy. These two criteria generate important implications for time investment and resource allocation. When the work addresses a highly significant public issue and when its scholarly contribution is clear, the research is likely to earn a high degree of confidence among policy stakeholders and academic peers. Research articles that address school funding reform or the implementation of No Child Left Behind Act (2001) that are accepted in top peer-refereed journals are example of such works. Findings on program effectiveness that are grounded in RFTs are likely to receive increasingly wide recognition. In contrast, when the work has a moderate level of real-world relevance and when its scholarly impact is unclear, the scientific value of the research is likely to be called into question by policy stakeholders. For example, a study that takes a practical approach to address a specific issue in a particular context without taking into consideration alternative explanations may not be viewed as making a contribution to theories of school reform and governance.

Finally, the current focus on experimental design to address accountability issues will shape the training agenda for the next generation of researchers. There is a need to reduce curriculum barriers on the university campus so that students can access cross-disciplinary learning opportunities. In light of the new landscape in school governance and management, the traditional curriculum in school administration programs will no longer be adequate. Instead, the next generation of leaders in public education needs more vigorous training in decision making (weighing trade-offs and assessing costs and benefits), policy analysis, student assessment, civic engagement, and public communication. These and other new skills need to be grounded in multiple discipline-based knowledge and tools. In short, as innovations spread in school governance and policy, so must innovations grow in educational policy and leadership training programs in higher education institutions.

REFERENCES

Amato's shooting from hip continues to backfire. (2000, July 23). *Hartford Courant*, p. C.3.

Barr, R., & Dreeben, R. (1983). *How schools work.* Chicago: University of Chicago Press.

Bierlein, L. (1997). The charter school movement. In D. Ravitch & J. Viteritti (Eds.), *New schools for a new century* (pp. 37–60). New Haven, CT: Yale University Press.

Center for Education Reform. (2003). *What the research reveals about charter schools: Summary and analyses of the studies.* Washington, DC: Author.

Cibulka, J. (1999). Moving toward an accountable system of K–12 education: Alternative approaches and challenges. In G. Cizek (Ed.), *Handbook of educational policy* (pp. 184–213). San Diego, CA: Academic Press.

Cibulka, J. G., & Boyd, W. L. (2003). *A race against time: The crisis in urban schooling.* Westport, CT: Praeger.

Cleveland case poses new test for vouchers. (2002, February 10). *New York Times*, p. 1.

Coleman, J. S. (1987). *Public and private high schools: The impact of communities.* New York: Basic Books.

Donahue, J. D. (1989). *The privatization decision.* New York: Basic Books.

Fiske, E., & Ladd, H. (2000). *When schools compete: A cautionary tale.* Washington, DC: Brookings Institution Press.

Godwin, R. K., & Kemerer, F. R. (2002). *School choice tradeoffs: Liberty, equity, and diversity.* Austin: University of Texas Press.

Greene, J. (2002). *2001 education freedom index.* New York: The Manhattan Institute.

Greene, J. P., Peterson, P. E., & Du, J. (1998). School choice in Milwaukee: A randomized experiment. In Peterson & Hassel (Eds.), *Learning from school choice.* Washington, DC: Brookings Press.

Greenhouse, L. (2002, June 28). Ruling in Ohio case: Majority says Cleveland program offers "true private choice." *The New York Times*, p. A1.

Hallinan, M. T., & Dreeben, R. (Eds.). (2003). *Stability and change in American education.* Clinton Corners, NY: Werner.

Hassel, B. (1999). *The charter school challenge: Avoiding the pitfalls, fulfilling the promise.* Washington, DC: Brookings Institution Press.

Hassel, B., & Batdorff, M. (2004). *High stakes: Findings from a national study of life-or-death decisions by charter school authorizers.* Retrieved November 30, 2005, from http://www.publicimpact.com/highstakes

Hernandez, A., & Mahoney, M. (2002, September 18). Is the private sector qualified to reform schools? *Education Week*, pp. 34, 38.

Herrington, C. (1998). Use it or lose it: Commentary on "Knowledge utilization in educational policy and politics." *Educational Administration Quarterly, 34*, 147–152.

Hill, P. (1997). Contracting in public education. In D. Ravitch & J. Viteritti (Eds.), *New schools for a new century* (pp. 61–85). New Haven, CT: Yale University Press.

Hirschman, A. (1971). *Exit, voice, and loyalty.* Cambridge, MA: Harvard University Press.

Howell, W., & Peterson, P. E. (2002). *The education gap: Vouchers and urban schools.* Washington, DC: Brookings Institution Press.

Ill will comes with territory in takeovers. (1996, June 12). *Education Week, 15*, 1–3.

King, G. (1989). *Unifying political methodology: The unlikelihood theory of statistical inference*. New York: Cambridge University Press.

King, G., Keohane, R., & Verba, S. (1994). *Designing social inquiry: Scientific inference in qualitative research*. Princeton, NJ: Princeton University Press.

Kirst, M., & Buckley, K. (2003). Mayoral takeover: The different directions taken in different cities. In J. Cibulka & W. Boyd (Eds.), *A race against time: The crisis in urban schooling* (pp. 63–81). Westport, CT: Praeger.

Lubienski, C. (2003). Innovation in education markets: Theory and evidence on the impact of competition and choice in charter schools. *American Educational Research Journal, 40,* 395–443.

Mitchell, D., & Boyd, W. (1998). Knowledge utilization in educational policy and politics: Conceptualizing and mapping the domain. *Educational Administration Quarterly, 34,* 126–140.

Moe, T. (2001a). Private vouchers: Politics and evidence. In M. Wang & H. Walberg (Eds.), *School choice or best systems* (pp. 67–126). Mahwah, NJ: Lawrence Erlbaum Associates.

Moe, T. (2001b). *Schools, vouchers, and the American public*. Washington, DC: Brookings Institution Press.

National Research Council. (2002). *Scientific research in education*. Washington, DC: National Academies Press.

N.Y. state eyes district takeover. (2001, March 28). *Education Week, 20,* 20.

Orr, M. (1999). *Black social capital: The politics of school reform in Baltimore, 1986–1998*. Lawrence: University Press of Kansas.

Peterson, P. E., Rabe, B. G., & Wong, K. K. (1986). *When federalism works*. Washington, DC: Brookings Institution.

Schneider, M., Teske, P., & Marschall, M. (2000). *Choosing schools: Consumer choice and the quality of American schools*. Princeton, NJ: Princeton University Press.

Sroufe, G. (2003). Legislative reform of federal education research programs. *Peabody Journal of Education, 78,* 220–229.

Stone, C. N., Henig, J. R., Jones, B. D., & Pierannunzi, C. (2001). *The politics of reforming urban schools*. Lawrence: University Press of Kansas.

Teske, P., Schneider, M., Buckley, J., & Clark, S. (2001). Can charter schools change traditional public schools? In P. Peterson & D. Campbell (Eds.), *Charters, vouchers and public education* (pp. 188–214). Washington, DC: Brookings Institution Press.

Tiebout, C. (1956). A pure theory of local expenditures. *Journal of Political Economy, 64,* 416–424.

U.S. Congress. (2001). No Child Left Behind Act of 2001. Public Law 107-110, 107th Congress. Washington, DC: Government Printing Office.

Walberg, H., & Bast, J. (2001). Understanding market-based school reform. In M. Wang & H. Walberg (Eds.), *School choice or best systems* (pp. 3–38). Mahwah, NJ: Lawrence Erlbaum Associates.

Wall Street blues. (2002, September 4). *Education Week, 22,* 8.

Weiss, C. (1983). Ideology, interests, and information: The basis of policy positions. In D. Callahan & B. Jennings (Eds.), *Ethics, the social sciences, and policy analysis* (pp. 213–245). New York: Plenum.

Wilson, J. Q. (1980). *The politics of regulation*. New York: Basic Books.

Witte, J. F. (1997). *Achievement effects of the Milwaukee voucher program*. American Economics Association Annual Meeting, New Orleans.

Witte, J. F., & Thorn, C. A. (1996). Who chooses? Voucher and interdistrict choice programs in Milwaukee. *American Journal of Education, 104,* 186–217.

Wong, K. K. (1998). Laying the groundwork for a new generation of policy research. *Educational Administration Quarterly, 34,* 141–146.

Wong, K. K. (1999). *Funding public schools: Politics and policy*. Lawrence: University Press of Kansas.

Wong, K. K. (2001). Integrated governance in Chicago and Birmingham (UK). In M. C. Wang & H. Walberg (Eds.), *School choice or best systems: What improves education* (pp. 161–212). Mahwah, NJ: Lawrence Erlbaum Associates.

Wong, K. K., Langevin, W. E., & Shen, F. X. (2004). *The political economy of state takeover of local schools and its withdrawals.* Presented at the 100th annual meeting of the American Political Science Association 2004, Chicago, IL.

Wong, K. K., & Shen, F. X. (2001). *Institutional effects of charter schools: Innovation and segregation.* Paper presented at the 2001 annual meeting of the American Educational Research Association, Seattle, WA.

Wong, K. K., & Shen, F. X. (2002, Spring). Do school districts takeover work? Assessing the effectiveness of city and state takeover as a school reform strategy. *The State Education Standard, 3*(2), 19–23.

Wong, K. K., & Shen, F. X. (2003). Big city mayors and school governance reform: The case of school district takeover. *Peabody Journal of Education, 78*, 5–32.

Wong, K. K., & Shen, F. X. (2005). When mayors lead urban schools: Toward developing a framework to assess the effects of mayoral takeover of urban districts. In W. Howell (Ed.), *Besieged: School boards and the future of education politics* (pp. 81–101). Washington, DC: The Brookings Institution.

Wong, K. K., Shen, F. X., & Novacek, G. (2000, August 31–September 4). *Institutional effects of charter schools: Competition, innovation and segregation.* Presented at the 2000 Annual Meeting of the American Political Science Association, Washington, DC.

Wong, K. K., Anagnostopoulos, D., Rutledge, S., Lynn, L., & Dreeben, R. (2003). Implementation of an accountability agenda in high schools: Integrated governance in the Chicago public schools. In J. Cibulka & W. Boyd (Eds.), *A race against time: The crisis in urban schooling* (pp. 55–76). Westport, CT: Praeger.

Yin, R. (1998). Rival explanations as an alternative to reforms as experiments. In L. Bickman (Ed.), *Validity and social experimentation: Donald Campbell's legacy* (pp. 229–259). Thousand Oaks, CA: Sage.

Zelman v. Simmons-Harris, 236 U.S. 639 (2002).

Chapter 8

The Science and Politics of Urban Education Leadership: Toward a Reorienting Narrative

Dorothy Shipps
Teachers College, Columbia University

The history of attempts to create a science of educational administration has been bound up in a century-long debate between two different central tendencies of schooling in urban America. One, a persistent and well-developed narrative, emphasizes the economic functions of schools. The other, a critique of this economic functionalism, stresses schooling's political purposes. The economic narrative focuses on efficiency as the backbone of prosperity, whereas the critique highlights democratic values and various notions of justice and opportunity.

Both the economic and political expectations for public schools are legitimate purposes of American education, embedded in its origins (Cuban & Shipps, 2000). Yet alone neither provides a complete depiction of urban school leaders' responsibilities nor offers straightforward ways that education decision makers can solve the manifest problems of urban schooling. This is partly because the science of educational administration has been pulled, as in a tug-of-war, between these two views, excessively dependent on abstract concepts about leaders' roles as managers on the one hand, and weakly reflecting the political responsibilities of leadership on the other. This polarity began with the application of Taylorism to early 20th-century urban schools and the almost immediate criticism it generated.[1]

---

[1] A Marxist alternative narrative held sway for much of the world, bolstered by the example of the Soviet Union. But Lenin too came under the sway of Taylorism. Thereafter, practical Marxism lost its ability to substantiate an alternative narrative about how work should be produced and what equality and collectivity meant (Merkle, 1980).

The economic narrative is deeply embedded in the fabric of American life, especially our dependency on organizations. But the political critique relies on the economic narrative for its meaning, assuring their century-long entanglement (Roe, 1994; D. Stone, 1998). The way out of this dismal embrace requires envisioning an alternative political account about public education and its leadership. Fortunately, this polarized, unequal discourse also carries within it the elements of this reorienting narration.

WHY FOCUS ON URBAN SCHOOLING?

In many ways, urban schooling is the crucible in which public education founders or succeeds. Cities are where the American national dilemmas of race and wealth disparity concentrate, and city schools are the places where these dilemmas are ameliorated, managed, and negotiated for the next generation. Urban school systems have provided the test sites for experiments in educational innovation, often through governance reform. Such reforms are frequently aimed at making school systems congenial habitats for preferred educational leaders. This suggests the third reason: Because urban school systems are both problematic and frequently undergoing change, they have generated many prominent studies, creating generalizations that are extended, appropriately or not, to suburban and rural school environments (Cuban, 2001). Much of what we think we know about public schooling and its leadership, we draw from cities.

CHAPTER ORGANIZATION

In this chapter, I trace the persistence of what I call the Taylorist narrative, also known as the scientific efficiency movement. From the late 19th century into our own time, it has mutated into a series of neo-Taylorist adaptations, continuously elevating management as the central administrative function, and creating some well-known distortions in research on educational administration. I also sketch a broad political criticism of the scientific efficiency movement that became more specific over time. This critique has punched holes in the Taylorist account, while adopting governance change (e.g., decentralization vs. centralization) as a recurring antidote to the central administrative problem scientific efficiency fostered: the growth of a resistant educational bureaucracy.

But the critique has also unintentionally and paradoxically strengthened educational neo-Taylorism, the adherents of which have responded by shoring up their core position and using the critique to patch the exposed flaws. Furthermore, among the critics of neo-Taylorism, the split between centralization and decentralization advocates—each claiming accountability, democratic, and representative benefits—has weakened its own governance arguments.[2] Thus, despite its continued failure to improve urban schools, neo-Taylorism remains dominant, apparently strengthened in its staying power.

Aspiring for a way out of this lopsided debate, I draw analytical distinctions between the Taylorist account and its political critique. These differences are then used to suggest some elements of a new account that aims to embrace the scientific methods to which Taylorism is committed, while putting them at the service of different goals, values, and tests. One goal is an approach to the science of education leadership that takes seriously the critics' objections by focusing on education leaders' responsibilities as negotiators, coalition builders, and public communicators. Another is a politics of education reoriented from a series of critiques to a wholly different narrative that accounts for the same history but rests on different values.

The new narrative would take for granted neither the neo-Taylorist categories of hierarchy, bureaucracy, and division of labor, nor the roles of management, worker, and government overseer. Instead it might begin with varieties of governance: combinations of governmental and nongovernmental actors, institutions, and authorities that guide decision making and constrain choices. This alternative would explain the persistence of neo-Taylorist managerialism as one among several governing regimes possible for urban schools, albeit one that has had many compelling advocates, if much less social success than they have predicted.

TAYLORISM AND ITS PERSISTENCE

Taylorism, or as it was called in the lifetime of the aristocratic Quaker Frederick Winslow Taylor (1856–1915), "the Taylor system," was intended to "confer prosperity on worker and boss alike, abolishing the ancient class hatreds" (Kanigel, 1997, p. 1). This was to be accomplished by carefully observing, measuring, and recording the activities of workers on the job so they would have scientific evidence of their contribution to the productive process and therefore the compensation they were due. Bosses would benefit because the same evidence was the basis for differentiating compensation as an incentive to increase overall productivity. Thus, the Taylor system recast class-based animosity as a technical problem amenable to research evidence. Its goals and methods became commonplace in

___
[2]As Doug Mitchell (personal communication, July 7, 2004) helpfully noted, the debate between centralization and decentralization is but one of several touchstone governance issues that could have been selected here.

American industrial practice by the 1930s and earned worldwide acceptance two decades later.

The Taylor system involved careful, precise measurements of the time it took the highest class of workers (i.e., the most productive) to complete a given industrial task. Within this standard, Taylor crafted job descriptions and quotas against which the performance of all workers was measured, a process known today as *benchmarking*. The next step was to redesign tools and the work environment to enable motivated workers to meet the standard. As they approached it, workers were to be rewarded with financial incentives, called *merit pay* today. Consistent failure to meet the standard was a sign of one of two kinds of problems: a lack of motivation on the part of the employee, or poor management decisions about whom to hire, which tools and environment to provide, or how compensation was differentiated. Taylor personally had no patience for an unmotivated worker—he famously moralized to a 1911 congressional committee investigating scientific management that "soldiering," like other forms of sloth, was a crime equivalent to "robbing the poor" (Kanigel, 1997, p. 471). This approach to productivity put great emphasis on management decisions. Managers were needed to save workers from themselves.

Taylor's methods were disciplined and analytical, if not always scientific. He measured the unit of time it took to produce a small but essential movement in some worker's part of the productive process, like shoveling coal or molding steel, and attempted to make it as unwasteful of energy and time as possible. By summing all these units he calculated the most efficient way to perform the task—pushing workers to the ends of their endurance, and then adding a portion of time "for rest and unavoidable delays" (Kanigel, 1997, p. 320).

Everything Taylor did to arrange others' work was codified and became, he believed, crucial to effective management. Apart from selecting the right employees and firing those who could not meet the work standard, managers were expected to determine instructions for each job, keep track of workers' time, routinely measure the quality and quantity of the work produced, motivate workers with rewards and pressure, and discipline those who lagged behind. In addition, managers set the parameters by which pay would be used as an incentive system: bonuses based on prior work, a share of increased production, or Taylor's favorite—piece work.

These oversight responsibilities were so numerous and critical that carrying them out required a hierarchy of managers. Thus, those who adapted scientific management over the next century would focus much of their research on understanding and refining managers' decision-making responsibilities, adding to those Taylor enumerated: planning, coordination, budgeting, and environmental negotiation (Gross, 1964; Gulick & Urwidk, 1937; Pfeffer & Salancik, 1978).

Herbert Simon was perhaps the most famous of the empirical management theorists studying the processes of decision making. He aimed for a more grounded, yet still normative, science of management. Initially a critic of Taylor's mechanistic system, he was interested in the irrationality in human behavior, and the transactions between workers and managers. He acknowledged limits to rationality in human beings, but this did not mean for him that decisions were value relative. Instead, he concluded that bureaucracies were naturally selected forms of organization, surviving because they directed individuals toward the same organizational goal by constraining their choices and preselecting the information used by decision makers. Recognizing this, good managers coordinated the activities of workers by convincing them to accept corporate goals or otherwise inducing them to accept management decisions. Simon's study of managerial decision making (later reconceived as problem solving) focused on mathematical or computer modeling and prediction. As such, his empiricism updated and strengthened management studies as an abstracted science even as it justified the widespread use of rules of thumb or heuristics to guide decision making. His use of computer simulations in management training became the ideal against which other methods were measured (Waring, 1991, pp. 49–77).

Few of the theories of management that flowed from Taylorism stood on such firm empirical ground, however. Their developers have been, for the most part, a group that Stephen Waring (1991, p. 7) referred to as the "management mandarinate," who codify and market management theory. Most of this management theory can be seen as an attempt to improve efficiency by perfecting managerial control, either through the adoption of new technologies or by ameliorating Taylorism's tendency to create labor-management conflict.[3]

Some liberal progressives bolstered Taylorism with their own brand of social engineering. Herbert Croly (1869–1930), for instance, was strongly in favor of government regulation of businesses and workers' unions as a counterweight to economic clout and management prerogatives, neither of which was typically supported by the laissez faire capitalists who strongly embraced Taylor's ideas. Yet his response to scientific management per se was ambiguous. Progressivism, Croly argued, was to be achieved by emulating the organization of the newest and most modern economic institutions: huge, often multinational, corporations and unions, in which workers' entrepreneurship and competitiveness were subsumed under the corporate

---

[3]Waring (1991) believed that the two means were fungible in that they were only different management strategies to the same goal. One suggests that administrative centralization is the better path and the other invokes organizational decentralization, but neither considers nonmanagement alternatives to organizational problems (see Shipps, 2000).

goal of increased industrial capacity, "organized by technological bureau-cracies," and encouraged by business paternalism (Stettner, 1993, p. 104). Such attempts to be balanced by reconciling opposed values provided a po-litical justification for Taylorism while "America's capitalists constructed its foundation" (Lazerson, 1973, p. 278).[4]

The reconciliation has been ongoing. For instance, Peter Drucker (1939/1995), an international figure whose first of 39 books professed to expose the spiritual and social origins of fascism, later acknowledged that management's power in a firm could be accurately criticized as irresponsi-ble and illegitimate, without an overriding moral justification (1942/1995). He proceeded to provide the missing justification by echoing Taylor's own morality in which the laudable ends justify the inequitable means: If the worker-manager bargain is properly struck—and workers engage in self-control—strong management has the potential to eliminate poverty, con-tinue the expansion of mass education, and create social mobility. Manage-ment is therefore indispensable to a smoothly functioning world: "It masters the economic circumstances and alters them by conscious directed action" and "creates [the forces of the market] by its own action" (Drucker, cited in Beatty, 1998, p. 104; see also Deming, 2000).

Modern neo-Taylorists also valorize "top" management (Khurana, 2002). Today, as in Taylor's own era, corporate leaders take on the social ills of the day as unelected leaders whose mettle has been proven by the conspicuous success they have had in making money for shareholders. A few even run for office assuming that their high status and self-confidence will transfer into political success. As one put it, "Companies realize that with their elevated status as the dominant social institution, comes elevated responsibility" (Alberthal, 1999, abstract).

Taylor's narrative has been shored up and burnished for a century, but remains tied to a rational conception of the modern individualistic and in-dustrial (now postindustrial) world with a straightforward justification just below the surface: Everybody gets something. Management mandarins have continued to assure business owners and corporate shareholders that they will receive a high profit margin, stock value, or both, whereas workers will benefit by being fitted for the roles where they can perform well, and therefore are happiest. By using the science of management to guide their decisions, managers and supervisors can shed the callous reputation they developed in the days when they were seen by union workers as the emissar-ies of capital with whom labor struggled over capricious hiring practices,

---

[4]Croly was so confident about the efficacy of management science that he tried to establish a single, national graduate school of public administration. He also disparaged legislators and political parties as excessively indulgent of special interests and debilitating to "administrative independence and efficiency" (Stettner, 1993, p. 100).

unsafe workplaces, and much else. Management science harmonizes labor relations, the mandarins say, because once the notion of standardized work processes is established, its particulars are a matter of mutual negotiation. The economy is also expected to benefit because firms produce more wealth, and it is reinvested rapidly, creating jobs in the process. Taylor's depiction of his system as a "mental revolution" (Kanigel, 1997, p. 472) did in fact become a worldwide narrative of compelling practicality and idealism, sufficient to be renamed the "best system."

BORROWING FROM THE CORPORATE CLOSET

Scientific management's hold on modern American life resulted from the almost immediate transfer of its ideas to all sorts of social endeavors, as Taylor himself predicted. It took root in urban schools partly because poor, largely immigrant children were destined, it was then believed, to be industrial workers. Like sprawling factories, urban schools had also grown to huge proportions by the heyday of Taylorism, with many hundreds of children to educate and the need to organize the process. There were less practical reasons as well: Low-status, albeit primarily White, male, Protestant, school leaders and the academics who trained them looked to higher status business executives and the management ethos to legitimate their work (Callahan, 1962). Moreover, the desire to smooth over social disruption caused by urbanization and industrialization was strong. Progressives of all sorts hoped that the schools could remake society to fit this modern world and saw the large corporation as the ideal model (Spring, 1972).

Just as Taylor attempted to find the most efficient way to organize work by breaking it down into its constituent parts, educators identified the essential units of education, provided formulas for their proper arrangement, and advised school managers on supportive structures. School managers were expected, in turn, to remake schools in the image of the most effective organization of the day: the industrial corporation. Not surprisingly, this Progressive Era movement was driven by urban elites: academics captivated by the modernist story about social progress, politicians seeking social peace, and practical corporate leaders encouraged by their growing wealth to tackle social problems using the same system. David Tyack (1981, p. 58) named this the "interlocking directorate" of the era.

Urban school leaders who followed Taylor's principles translated them to schools by identifying the ideal student for each of several employment categories and life roles. They named the small elements of knowledge each needed and added them together to create a differentiated curriculum. Supplemented with the proper supplies, the correct configuration of classroom furniture, reports on student performance, and the appropriate movement of students through the day, the system was expected to produce the greatest learning with the least effort. That is, it would do so if higher authorities coordinated the activities and enforced discipline through a division of labor topped by a managerial hierarchy. To the extent possible, every one of these elements of the system was to be quantified and related to one another in precise proportions. The reward was to be students—sometimes referred to as the "raw material" or "products"—prepared so well for their niche in the economy that they would contentedly sustain a cycle of increasing production, but also be well trained in the responsibilities of citizenship and family life (Cubberley, 1916).

Professors of education convinced the superintendents of one urban system after another to allow them to conduct school surveys that assessed school operations against this Taylorist standard. Their reports provided detailed remedial instructions on what to measure, how to define jobs, whom to hire, how to organize the work, and who should have decision-making responsibilities (Callahan, 1962).

One academic from the University of Chicago, Franklin Bobbitt, graphically explained his lengthy instructions for revising the Denver public schools by way of a 5-page chart comparing the principles of good management in business with those appropriate to schools. He asserted at the outset that both "are subject to the same laws of good management. What brings success to the one will bring success to the other. What brings failure to the one will bring failure to the other" (Bobbitt, 1916, p. 111). In side-by-side columns, Bobbitt spelled out similarities between the two governance structures (e.g., each has a lay board of directors selected by stockholders, or citizens respectively), including the classifications and roles of employees (e.g., managers and workers, superintendents and teachers), as well as the common need for a consultant to intercede if the board disagrees with its general manager or superintendent. Underscoring the importance of management to the entire system, he devoted 7 of 11 points to their responsibilities and concluded, "All kinds of large organizations, whether commercial, civic, industrial, governmental, educational, or other are all equally and irrevocably subject to the same general laws of good management" (Bobbitt, pp. 111, 116).[5]

By mid-century this highly generalized management science of educational administration had become associated with the neutral study of organizations (Griffiths, 1964a). It was linked to the language of role definition, traits, and training of school administrators. The researchers who held the highest hopes for a science of educational administration continued to borrow freely from the research and managerial advice on business manage-

---

[5]I thank Jeffrey Mirel (personal communication, October 12, 2003) for alerting me to this graphic parallel between schools and business firms.

ment, translating those studies to the public school setting. For instance, the general approach of conducting research in contrived or simulated settings—where an individual worker's behavior could be observed, categorized, and quantified in relation to some performance expectation—was applied to the study of school leaders' decision making (Hemphill, 1964). It was also hoped that future research would attend more to the relationship between schools and their environments, perhaps spurred by the educational upheaval of civil rights controversies, collective bargaining, and federal intervention, but also following new developments in organizational theorizing (see, e.g., Carlson, 1964; Lipham, 1964).

However, many education administration experts did not conduct research. Like their management mandarin counterparts, they argued instead by analogy from studies conducted in industrial or governmental organizations (Dill, 1964). And they continued to mix empirical and normative goals in their theories, despite the denials of those who, like Daniel Griffiths, claimed values should not play a role in theory building. Somewhat ironically, even he became enmeshed by his avowed need for useful "presumptions:" decisions made about the world that precede empirical findings (Griffiths, 1964b).

In a neat parallelism to Bobbitt's (1916) comparison, nearly three quarters of a century later the National Alliance for Business (NAB) drew up its own chart relating contemporary businesses to schools, and in the process highlighted the persistence of the Taylorist narrative. The NAB described the requirements of "successful businesses" in one column and matched it with the requirements of "effective schools" in the other, asserting that both institutions had managers providing all of the following: strong leadership and vision, clear goals and objectives, strong quality requirements for products or student performance and behavior, a setting conducive to working (learning), worker involvement in decision making, high expectations for the performance of employees, up-to-date equipment and worker skills, and managerial autonomy. The one best system approach, it seemed, had endured for nearly 100 years.

The comparison went on to detail differences between the roles of chief executives in the two sectors, comparisons informed by NAB's poor assessment of urban schools. Executives in education, the report claimed, were "operating under constraints" that limited school effectiveness. Schools were public institutions "unable to limit media or citizen access," required to "serve all students assigned," with "limited organizational flexibility" to alter their student mix or services, and they were delivering a product "difficult and complex to assess and measure." Each of these strictures, and several others, were conceived as drawbacks or problems in restructuring school systems to fit the corporate organizational model NAB believed would produce the best performance (NAB, 1989).

Twenty-first-century efforts to measure the productivity of schools using a small number of output indicators—"incentivize" the adults in them to meet higher performance standards, privilege management above the other tasks of school leadership, and legislate the scientific basis for research—remain modern-day versions of Taylorism, creating new heroes and villains within the basic plot. Efforts to privatize public schooling by requiring that each school compete with others for students and services externalizes (removes from the school) the transaction costs associated with these contractual relationships and takes professional educators increasingly out of the management picture (Williamson, 1985).[6] Despite its failure to meet its own goals of increased student performance efficiency among poor, immigrant, racial, and ethnic minority children in urban schools, Taylorism persists, in schooling as elsewhere in society. The story line remains compelling even though the final chapter never arrives.

THE POLITICAL CRITIQUE

Taylorism was no sooner promoted than its excesses came under sharp criticism. It was deemed to be demeaning to teachers, ignorant of the substantive demands of educational leadership in democracies, and more arbitrary than empirical in its technology. Critics typically used the language of political science to describe their concerns, arguing that democracy, community, and equality were abstract virtues at least as important as efficiency. Even though they hoped by undercutting its logic to expose Taylorism's elite bias, its hidden mechanisms of cultural diffusion, and the holes in its technology, much of their criticism nevertheless eventually helped to shape a contemporary form of neo-Taylorism in the schools.

Trade unionists delivered their most damaging blows in the early years of the 20th century. They saw in the Taylor system an attempt to take the dignity and satisfaction out of human labor, to keep workers striving but impoverished, and to dehumanize everyone not destined to be a manager. Taylor's crucial management class, they argued, was an effort to provide a

---

[6]Transaction costs are the costs of conducting economic exchanges (e.g., drafting, negotiating, concluding, monitoring, and resolving disputes) under the standard economic assumptions that managers are both boundedly rational (limited) and opportunistic. Transaction cost analysis presumes that such contractual exchanges are the basic unit of economic analysis and that variations in organizational governance structures are the result of economizing transaction costs. For example, districts use internal labor contracts with tenure to hire teachers because the associated costs include the acquisition of transaction-specific skills. If teaching required only general-purpose skills (most smart people could do it) then it would be more efficient to externalize those transaction costs (let the market bear them) by hiring teachers one at a time with performance contracts.

new source of wealth and prestige for the idle rich (Kanigel, 1997; Wrigley, 1982). But teachers unions eventually embraced the forms of school management that encouraged worker participation and collaboration. Doing so gave them legitimate, albeit limited, ways to influence their working conditions, and yet did not require teachers to take responsibility for creating an alternative vision of schooling (Kershner, Koppich, & Weeres, 1997; Lieberman, 1997).

A later generation of critics focused on the expectations and self-image of urban school leaders. Superintendents, presumed to be heavily influenced by Taylorism, were questioned for serving as conduits for the cultural diffusion of high-status corporate practices and values to low-status schools. The business executives and professionals who dominated urban boards of education were said to be school leaders' role models, encouraging their sense of functioning as managers entitled to unimpeachable decision-making authority. Reinforcing the emulation of business tycoons were the professors who introduced industrial procedures and terminology into their educational administration courses on finance, law, and organizations (Callahan, 1962, p. viii; Zeigler, Jennings, & Peak, 1974; Zeigler, Kehoe, & Reisman, 1985). Although there remains great disagreement about the mechanisms through which urban superintendents came to align themselves with economic and governmental elites, the results have done nothing to hinder the close supervision and autocratic decision making Taylorism avowed (Cartwright, 1963; Cuban, 1976; Smith, 1964).

Criticism has also come from a variety of sympathetic management and educational scholars who quarreled with Taylor's means more than his ends. Take the calculation by managers of the amount of slack to be built into the work standard for any job. Taylor argued that once an endurance standard was set, 40% more time should be added to allow for delays and rest times. This seemingly precise adjustment was exposed as simply arbitrary by those hoping to show that what looked rational and scientific was little more than a smoke screen for the maintenance of privilege and power (Kanigel, 1997). When they argued for more precision, however, they reinforced the underlying premise that a work standard was the appropriate yardstick against which to set wages, rather than, say, the requirements of decent living in the firm's surrounding community.

An educational parallel is the contemporary dispute about the appropriate way to establish uniform student performance standards for various kinds of tests. Critics have repeatedly claimed that standards-setting activity is political rather than scientific (Heubert & Hauser, 1998; Linn, Baker, & Betebenner, 2002). As researchers seek greater inclusiveness by enumerating, for instance, testing standards for art history, or specifying achievement goals for special education students, they implicitly accept the premise that test scores are the appropriate method of measuring student performance. Identifying more palatable ways to adjust the standards or otherwise tinker with the technology of scientific efficiency ends up strengthening the Taylorist arguments. By accepting the premise of a single scientific reasoning, many educational researchers who began as moderate critics of some aspect of Taylorism became, unwittingly, neo-Taylorists.

The emphasis on centralization, bureaucracy, and efficiency found in Taylorism also spurred a practical countermovement that sought democratic participation for teachers, students, and parents, with the primary effect of focusing attention on the governance structure of public schooling. The philosophical basis for this alternative view lay in social learning through group deliberation, and its adherents followed the evolutionary social philosophy of John Dewey. These progressive "social reconstructionists" emphasized that schools were instrumental in the development of citizenship in a democracy, whereas the Taylorist "administrative progressives," as David Tyack and Elisabeth Hansot (1982) labeled them, highlighted the school's role in preparing workers for the economy (pp. 119, 220). But Dewey's dense writing left no clear guidelines about how to implement his ideas in classrooms and school systems. Relatively few social scientists were prepared to investigate his ideas empirically. Thus, despite widespread adoption of a pedagogical progressivism in rhetoric and expectations, his alternative vision of schooling—both democratic and problem centered—has been rarely instituted, particularly for nonelite public school students (Cuban, 1993).

More radical political arguments against scientific efficiency were brought to the surface by the Depression, when Taylor's utopian promise seemed a cruel hoax. George Counts made the connection between economic failure and schooling, in the process igniting a broad debate about how American society might be reconstructed by progressive educators.[7] Counts proposed that education take its direction from social analysis rather than from the "fallacies" of an impartial science of learning or the middle-class individualism inherent in child-centeredness. Critical as well of "agnosticism, skepticism or even experimentalism," he called for teachers to adopt instructional techniques that fostered collectivism, and insisted on the open deliberation of economic alternatives, like government planning, regulation, and even socialism (Counts, 1932/1969, p. 38). Counts audaciously advised progressive educators to indoctrinate students in both "the moral equality of men" and government's responsibility to manage the economy on behalf of workers (p. 41). But his remedy called on teachers to

---

[7]After a speech at the Progressive Education Association in February of 1932, at which Counts first issued the call, the remaining program was abandoned in favor of discussing the implications for teachers. Daniel Perlstein (2000) found that both educators and intellectuals contributed to the debate.

become leaders in a new society that would substitute one group of managers for another. And despite the attention he engendered, most disagreed with Counts' call for indoctrination. Many embraced the individualism that he decried, saw the Depression as a mere dip in the business cycle, or remained skeptical that schools could lead the struggle for a new social order. Dewey himself noted the "important difference between education with respect to a new social order and indoctrination into settled convictions about that order," calling instead for teachers to set up democratic conditions for student learning (cited in Perlstein, 2000, p. 62; see also Ravitch, 2001).

Gunnar Myrdal (1944/1962) would join the political argument a decade later, predicting a wave of planned social change based on the application of social science to smoldering racial and economic resentment. He saw both public schooling and federal law as the mechanisms of change.[8] According to Myrdal, education was assimilation. Schooling simultaneously informed Blacks that they lived at the bottom of a caste system and encouraged resentment over their deprivation because their own experience belied the American creed of liberty, democracy, equality, and individual opportunity. He anticipated not only that Blacks (and other minorities) would become increasingly dissatisfied with their poor treatment, but also that they would grow increasingly dissatisfied with the quality of schooling itself. The result, Myrdal warned, could be protest and upheaval unless the American social structure opened up and the schools altered the way they functioned.

By mid-century, Myrdal's (1944/1962) arguments had been reinterpreted as resulting from the condition of cities: Their social geography caused inequity and inefficient, failed schools (Rury & Mirel, 1997). This reconception cut both ways. Organizational theorists argued that class- and race-based inequities were part of the institutional environment of schools and concluded that they presented dilemmas that could only be managed, perhaps ameliorated, but not solved. The potential for political conflict inherent in such inequities was interpreted by neo-Taylorists as "a breakdown in the standard mechanisms of decision-making and 'a threat' to cooperation," a pathological experience that represents an administrative failure (March & Simon, 1964, cited in Zeigler et al., 1985, p. 19). School leaders were encouraged by their training to deny, avoid, or internalize conflict. Hence the common prescription since the civil rights era remained in place: Urban schools should focus on retaining White middle-class children rather than resolving the social inequities faced by poor Black and other minority children (Cohen, 1968; Conant, 1961; Havinghurst, 1966; Kozol, 1967).

---

[8]Myrdal (1944/1962) also thought increased unionization would encourage change.

On the other hand, political critics could take succor in Myrdal's (1944/ 1962) prediction that preparation for democratic citizenship and efforts to relegitimize the nation's governing system might soon trump preparation for economic participation and efficiency as the goals and core values of schooling. Cast in democratic terms, political conflict is natural behavior and its institutionalization is a primary tool for keeping leaders responsive and accountable. Political approaches involve regulating its excesses and, most importantly, establishing channels of access (e.g., standing subcommittees, citizen review commissions, routine interest group intermediation) so that relatively minor public concerns do not become magnified into much larger ones. Unlike managers, politicians are expected to bargain, negotiate, compromise, manipulate symbols, and build coalitions of support (Firestone & Shipps, 2005; Peterson, 1985; Wirt & Kirst, 1992).

The political approach influenced scholars who focused on equity issues in urban schools. They have advocated a variety of structural changes to institutionalize the negotiation of conflict over racial inequities (e.g., districtwide open enrollment, metropolitan resource sharing), leaning toward governance solutions that are large in scale and more centralized (Orfield & Eaton, 1996; Wells & Crain, 1997). Yet, it is clear that local politics mediate large-scale mandates. The reactions to court orders and federal mandates within school bureaucracies on school boards and among local political and business elites determine whether they are implemented and accepted with success (Hochschild, 1984; Jencks et al., 1972).

Thus, by mid-century the critics of Taylorism had become primarily concerned with whether the local governance structures for schools were functioning to provide representation, voice, and an equitable distribution of resources. In practice, this turned into arguments about whether school systems should be centralized or decentralized. Brief experiments with decentralization as a reaction to failed desegregation encouraged other reformers who had been looking for more meaningful mechanisms of democratic control (Gittell & Hevesi, 1969). They voiced concern that management hierarchies constructed to make work more efficient had become inaccessible bureaucracies so powerful in many cities that elected (or appointed) school boards were often polarized and dependent on the superintendent for information and executive decision making. David Rogers (1967, p. 474) developed a sense of outrage that is echoed to this day about the "rigidity and incapacity" of urban school officials (functionary and elected alike), which underpinned his call for decentralization.

Subsequently, neo-Taylorists also concluded that some form of political decentralization (e.g., creation of subdistrict boards or citizen advisory groups) would improve efficiency as a by-product of lay participation by providing school leaders with the social support they need to perform as effective managers (Hess, 1991; Zimet, 1973). This reinforced the Taylorist goals with a new governance argument. A related literature on effective schools has done much to enhance this reliance on leaders' prerogatives, underscoring the primacy of management in school success (Purkey & Smith, 1983; Witte & Walsh, 1990).

One group of decentralizers promisingly recenters its critique on the political functions of public schools in line with Dewey's earlier criticism, emphasizing radical democratic governance in which every school is continually (re)building its own community (Bryk, Sebring, Kerbow, Rollow, & Easton, 1998; Kantor & Lowe, 2000). But it faces criticism because locally controlled governance has great potential to increase disparities in cities where racial, ethnic, and wealth inequities are mapped onto the local social geography (Lewis & Nakagawa, 1995; Shipps, 1997). And their alternative notions of top leadership roles are admittedly vague.

Political decentralization as a response to Taylorism places too much emphasis on the solution, and too little on an alternative narrative about what is wrong with urban society that schools, if differently configured, could remedy. For instance, some analysis of Chicago's school-based decentralization in the late 1980s is accompanied by a provocative argument that links parental governance of individual schools to higher test scores, but its logic is strained and counterintuitive. The exercise raises the question: Is democracy intended only to increase test scores so that children's life chances may be more efficiently sorted? Moreover, political decentralization as a remedy for the ills of a large system seldom reduces the prerogatives or credibility of management, but has served in most instances to legitimate them (Malen, 1994; Weiler, 1993).

Other social scientists have recently come to advocate the opposite solution, also attacking bureaucratic intransigence in order to bolster their arguments for greater public accountability through political recentralization (Wong, Dreeben, Lynn, & Sunderman, 1997). Because the long-term trends have all been toward centralization (Tyack, 1993), these scholars seem to make a virtue of what exists, rather than propose a new solution.

Still others acknowledged a tension between decentralization and centralization as governance strategies for urban school systems, but argued for a kind of functional specialization: centralized decision making over the allocation of resources and their equitable distribution, but local control at individual schools to counter bureaucratic bloat and intransigence. Usually this was accompanied by calls for greater parental choice of schools in order to overcome the resistance that can be expected when parents have their systemwide influence limited (Hill, Pierce, & Guthrie, 1997; McDermott, 1999). And often it was followed by detailed arguments for changing the reward structures for the chief executives of schools or state- (or national-) level standardization of the measurements of student performance (Hess, 1999). Thus, intentionally or not, critics who point to the locus of control, but not to the issue of *who* governs, reinforce the neo-Taylorist narrative rather than challenging it.

Most of the empirical studies advocating such changes implicitly assumed that urban residents have little opportunity to improve their schools except through existing formal, institutionalized choices (e.g., mayoral or school board elections, court suits, enrollment lotteries). For instance, Wirt and Kirst (1992) defined the politics of urban education as the essentially autocratic allocation of scare resources to insatiable citizen demands, notwithstanding occasional use of the referendum to punish decision makers whose "actions are too offensive" (p. 223). Often it is the ballot box that is expected to serve as the primary means of citizen oversight, and structural changes like those described earlier are recommended when voting does not appear effective (Iannaccone & Lutz, 1994; Lutz & Iannaconne, 1978).

This type of anti-Taylorist criticism has foundered because it has become embroiled in its own internecine battle over the relative merits of centralization and decentralization. Other critical arguments (e.g., exposing contradictions in the technology of scientific efficiency, disparaging the lack of agency educators have in management-oriented schemes, decrying the overblown authority of school bureaucrats) are weakened by their very empiricism, accepting as given the immediate experience forged years ago during the origins of Taylorism. But as I argue later, the critics' more fundamental flaw is that they merely question an existing system, rather than offer an alternative narrative that would spawn a different vision of a science of education leadership.

TOWARD A REORIENTING NARRATIVE

Douglas Mitchell seemed to ask the impossible when he challenged us to square Daniel E. Griffiths' 1960s-style epistemology of theory building with our postmodern and often nonpositivist sensibilities as a way to salvage the politics and policy of education (Griffiths, 1964b). Can there be, as Griffiths insisted, a science of education leadership that rests on useful presumptions: decisions made about the world that precede empirical findings, but that also do not include statements of value? Can assumptions be derived from these useful decisions in support of theories that are not self-serving or arbitrary? Surely not, especially when political decisions (e.g., how they are reached, by whom, and with what intentions and consequences) are at least partly the object of study. Those who develop theories to guide the quest for scientific knowledge begin with presumptions that all contain value statements, obscured or apparent. The ethical responsibility is to reveal them.

I have attempted to show that Taylorism and its progeny have constructed an applied management science precisely because it has been
formed as a coherent narrative: a story with a beginning that took account
of its original social, economic, and political contexts, a middle that described in great detail what kinds of knowledge would be most useful, and a
future that held up the goal of a prosperous society without class conflict.
Criticisms of this narrative have too frequently done little more than unwittingly reify its underlying values and assumptions, especially efficiency, objectivity, and hierarchy (Roe, 1994). The odd contemporary combination
of faith in modern management science as a means for improving urban
schools on the one hand, and failure to see the promised results on the
other, is strong, if uncomfortable, evidence of the narrative's remarkable
persistence (Shipps, 2006).

To revive an alternative applied science of education leadership, we
need an alternative narrative as compelling and complete as the Taylor system. It may then be possible to formulate new propositions and empirically
testable arguments (D. Stone, 1998).[9] As a start to that daunting task, I have
extracted in Table 8.1 some points of contrast between the neo-Taylorist
narrative and an alternative by extrapolating from the criticisms outlined
earlier. The first and second columns identify some of the core elements of
Taylorism and the critics' political arguments against it. Each of these
points was outlined in the previous discussion. The third column draws
from the debate some propositions that could become the core elements of
an alternative narrative about a science of educational leadership.

Differences in Goals and Values

The argument for an alternative narrative begins with an articulation of
core values. Herbert J. Storing argued that Simon's bounded rationality approach to human behavior and consequent defense of bureaucracy and hierarchy rested on "unarticulated value judgments" that reified techniques
of manipulation by calling them "science" and was therefore as mechanistic
as Taylorism (cited in Waring, 1991, p. 61). His critique identified the core
issue to be tackled in any compelling narrative: Which values and virtues
should lie at its center?

Sensible candidates for a political alternative begin with arguments made
by John Dewey and his social reconstructionist followers. Like Taylorists,

---

[9]This is not a postmodernist narrative. Postmodernists deny the valorization of great men
in history while exposing White privilege, paternalism, and other relations of social power. I
suspect that denying our history only makes us less capable of seeing the present with clarity.
Moreover, cultural and social institutions like schools are deeply rooted in the historical conditions that mark their founding and early development; they are not free-floating.

TABLE 8.1

Taylorist and Political Narratives Compared

	Taylorist Narrative	Political Critique of the Taylorist Narrative	Alternative Political Narrative
The goal of public schooling	Preparation for economic participation and social harmony	*Taylorism ignores preparation for democratic citizenship and children's self-determination*	Preparation for democratic citizenship and self-determined productivity
Core value of schooling	Efficiency of performance and social harmony	*Taylorism subordinates democracy, community, equality to efficiency, and social peace*	Justice, free and open inquiry, and community
Keys to success	Faithful implementation of management solutions	*Taylorism is sustained by class- (and caste-) based coalitions that support one another*	Broad support for improved democracy and transparency, and acceptance of principled limits on executive authority
Greatest risk	Bureaucratizing control	*Politicizing instruction*	Neutral morality
Core leadership activities	Close supervision of teachers that buffers them from direct external interference	*Preferences of class-based governing bodies reinforce distinctions between managers and workers*	Reconciling teachers' professional autonomy with control by democratic communities
Leaders' professional accountability	Accountable for teachers' use of efficient means of transmitting knowledge and skills to students	*Identification with managers leads to requirements that teachers adopt approved pedagogy and avoid collaboration with nonprofessional adults*	Accountable for teachers' use of pedagogy that encourages students' democratic deliberation and problem-oriented social research skills
Leaders' approach to conflict	Conflict is a symptom of breakdown in consensus to be avoided, internalized, or otherwise managed	*Leaders' conflict avoidance leads to social mistrust, poor implementation*	Conflict is essential to leaders' responsiveness when institutionalized and restrained from violence
Method of creating knowledge	Careful measurement of discrete behaviors in controlled educational situations	*Countering Taylorism requires experiments with governance to encourage social creativity and to counter bureaucratic syllogism*	Naturalistic comparative analysis driven by widely understood and thoroughly communicated social inquiry into public problems
Meaning of science	Universalized cause-effect knowledge of efficient governance and instructional practices that are reliably linked to measurable predetermined goals	*Scientific efficiency requires misplaced precision, outcomes that are too narrowly defined, and self-serving causal arguments*	Situated knowledge of school governance and instructional practices empirically linked to students' democratic values and social problem-solving abilities

they sought to design schools to change society, but challenged the dominant values of their time and the causal arguments underlying Taylor's social and economic vision. Dewey's empiricism disparaged Taylorist values because they led to a science that "maintained sordid slums, flurried and discontented careers, grinding poverty and luxurious wealth, brutal exploitation of nature and man in times of peace and high explosives and noxious gases in times of war" (Dewey, 1927/1954, p. 175). Social reconstructionists esteemed a different set of virtues: free and open inquiry through democratic deliberation in communities, justice based on strict equality, and a communitarianism that was broad enough to encompass dissidents.

These are also values that Counts (1932/1969) invoked in his audacious call for free inquiry about forbidden topics, and that Myrdal (1944/1962) drew on in his efforts to square America with its professed values. They are similar to those that Amy Gutmann (1999) referred to as *nonrepression* and *nondiscrimination* in our own time. Such values lead to a different version of science in the service of educational organizations. Social reconstructionists Dewey, Counts, Myrdal, and their successors would have us harness human creativity to solve public problems like those of education through socially embedded learning and community building rather than rational accounting by a cadre of management experts.

These values encompass more than the critique of the neo-Taylorist focus on social peace and efficiency. They also address the overemphasis that scientific efficiency places on individual productive activity and its economic rewards. In his discussions of the problem solving at the heart of his definition of science, Dewey (1927/1954) helps us see that early 20th-century critics had democratic goals for schools that did not conflict with economic productivity as long as the latter was self-determined (not coerced) and democratically acceptable. Centering pedagogy (and social science learning in general) on solving children's (and society's) real problems—sometimes referred to as child-centeredness—meant educating them to become what we call today "critical thinkers," prepared to face new issues and comprehend unfamiliar data using applied scientific reasoning. These are skills indispensable to becoming full participants in a democracy. In this formulation, pedagogy and content are not distinct, and learning by doing is guided by the puzzles of life rather than the artifice of testable information. Dewey himself called his view of philosophy "experimentalism," a term that describes an alternative view of schooling, knowledge creation, and science (Ryan, 1995).

The contrasts with Taylorism are stark. Scientific efficiency stresses a common economic and social goal, while providing an outlet for individual choice in cultural matters. In its schema, schools are expected to help students adjust their life expectations to the goals of social harmony and economic prosperity. The proposed alternative envisions the common political goal of an increasingly engaged public solving its problems democratically and provides for individuals to choose their own means of productively contributing to society and economy. In this alternative, schools would function as communities to inculcate democratic values while teaching the habits and skills of solving social problems collectively.

Neither the Taylorist narrative nor the proposed political counternarrative has an advantage in student achievement. This is because democratic deliberation assumes sophisticated abilities to produce language and analyze others' use of it, the critical thinking and logical argumentation skills needed to debate alternative visions of the good life, and the specialized knowledge required to attain a productive place in the society of one's choosing (Gutmann, 1999). And as Dewey taught us, identifying and naming problems; conjuring possible solutions in specific contexts, including their ethical implications and cultural meanings; and developing the skills (and courage) for experimentation and revision are all required for social problem solving (Ryan, 1995, pp. 142–149).

The economic function of educating individuals for jobs would not be curtailed (nor could it be). Rather, it would be reconceptualized as skill development in the context of self-determination and social justice. Vocational education that claims to prepare students for entry-level jobs can be rethought as pleasurable experience that encourages empathy for a variety of adult roles. This would improve on the Taylorist conception in two ways. First, current curricula do not actually fulfill their stated economic purpose, and in any case employers seek workers with social skills (Silverberg, Warner, Fong, & Goodwin, 2004).[10] Second, a political narrative valuing work for its own sake and for the mutual understanding and relationships it fosters may help us conceive a remedy to the high levels of disengagement and mistrust that characterize many workplaces.

As important is recasting the sophisticated craft knowledge now publicly esteemed for developing careers and increasing personal wealth. Reenvisioning this core schooling activity as the development of knowledge needed to advance a variety of professional and social agendas may have a similar social impact. It could honor, for instance, collaborative proficiency over competition, individual contributions to socially valued collective pur-

---

[10]The latest National Assessment of Vocational Education report (Silverberg, Warner, Fong, & Goodwin, 2004) concluded that part of the problem with vocational education is its lack of a clear focus "around which to rally the commitment and efforts," because the goal of workplace preparation was recently muddled. A second goal was added: to facilitate students' acquisition of basic skills. Even so, the only evident benefit has been a small and declining earnings advantage (2%) up to 7 years after graduation. This differential is not seen for the majority of students who only take a course or two. There is no effect found on academic achievement, little to none on high school completion, negative to none on postsecondary enrollment, and none on completion of a degree.

poses over earnings growth, and creative ways to share scarce resources over wealth accumulation and protection.

In schooling practice, these changes may mean that all students have access to a series of basic technical languages and learning processes that can be adapted to many situations, and that fairly advanced craft-specific skills would be made available regardless of a student's age. One goal would be to encourage the development of rigorous and divergent speculation about common problems (e.g., terrorism, global viral epidemics, water pollution) rather than the overreliance on mechanistic and convergent thinking about these issues that arises from the pursuit of scientific efficiency.

Success would be understood differently as well. Whereas management mandarins insist that faithful implementation of their codified solutions will calm conflicts and reap efficiency rewards, the proposed alternative requires expanded democracy, information transparency, and the widespread acceptance of limits on executive authority. However, this entails more than an educational system judged by these values. It also requires, for example, an interrogating media presenting issues from multiple perspectives while actively encouraging public participation in decision making (Dewey, 1927/1954; Rosen, 1996), as well as other sources of credible and specific information about public issues. Even so, schools would surely be expected to lay the groundwork for a citizenship that is both activist and skeptical of ill-founded expertise claims.

Although none of these attributes is inimical to the American creed, they do raise the specter of moral neutrality and its consequences (e.g., those with superior insight or knowledge not being socially recognized). Even though all forms of despotism and extreme privilege would fail to meet the criteria explicitly limiting executive authority, neither anarchism nor atheism would be excluded from experimentation. Absent the common standards implied by social efficiency, experienced and wise counselors might go unheeded, and the expert use of mass media could well deceive, perhaps no less than is the case today. The ease with which a society might create and sustain safeguards should not be overstated: Moral certainty arrived at through democratic processes of contention and debate may be unachievable.

Some will find this uncertainty more humane than the imposition of a small set of political values that close off options. For others, it might unleash the specter of well-organized and powerful interest groups that dominate debate no matter how democratically intended. But such problems—moral uncertainty and powerful interests (e.g., business associations, teachers unions, religious factions) that seek dominant advantage in schooling—exist today. The neo-Taylorist response pursues certainty at the expense of democratic processes and casts interest group domination as value-neutral management. One result is a polarizing debate between neo-Taylorists and their critics, undermining trust in government officials and educational leaders as well as their reform plans. We are more likely, I suspect, to manage the dilemmas of moral uncertainty and address the distortions of power if they are part and parcel of our political narrative about how schools function.

Differences in Leaders' Roles

These alternative goals, core values, and tensions necessarily involve a different vision of educational leadership: one that privileges leaders' responsibilities as community organizers, coalition builders, and resource negotiators over their bureaucratic accountabilities as functionaries and loyal advocates of their superiors' decisions (Firestone & Shipps, 2005). In their analyses of school managers' apparent subservience to class-based values of social reproduction, Callahan (1962) and Zeigler (1985) among others criticized the scientific efficiency model of formal managerial training and informal socialization. The alternative, they seemed to suggest, would stress school leaders' political accountability among their professional responsibilities.

The critics' theoretical arguments have echoes in modern studies of school leadership. In 1947, the Kellogg Foundation's famous study of school administration began by commenting that school leaders lacked "knowledge of community processes and the role of schooling in the improvement of day-to-day life" noting, if only briefly, school leaders' responsibilities as political actors and moral exemplars (Morre, 1964, p. 16). In contemporary terms, the point is made by school superintendents and principals themselves, who, when asked, overwhelmingly agree that the most difficult problems of their work are coping with political demands and bureaucratic constraints, not technical or managerial issues. At the very least, school leaders tell us that even though neo-Taylorism has advanced school efficiency, it has not resolved the conflicts that leaders routinely must address in schools, or clarified how educators' professional accountability can be reconciled with the demands of democratic governance. And they report being ill-prepared to tackle these responsibilities (MetLife Inc., 2003; Public Agenda, 2001).

The political alternative proposes that leaders spend much of their time working to reconcile teachers' professional autonomy in classrooms with the legitimate demands for control by the communities who send their children to, and otherwise support, the public schools. Teacher autonomy is needed not only to enhance their own dignity, creativity, and participatory decision making, but also to ensure that students receive high-quality instruction to help them become inquiring learners and full participants in public life. This means leaders would worry less about supervising instruction and buffering teachers from outside interference than negotiating school goals, values, and pedagogies with parents, citizens, and community

elites. They would also foster sustainable coalitions of support for the resulting aims and encourage social inquiry into the implementation problems
that arise.

In their capacity as professional educators, leaders would be accountable
for providing teachers with opportunities to use pedagogical practices that
encourage democratic deliberation and community-oriented problem solving. This could mean designing methods of assessing students' abilities to
empathize with others' perceptions, communicate clearly, and apply scientific methods of inquiry to social problems. School leaders would not be accountable for teachers' use of efficient means of transmitting skills and
knowledge to students. Leaders' approaches to conflict would also change.
Instead of identifying conflict as a symptom of a breakdown in communication, a pathology to be avoided or contained, the counternarrative would embrace conflict as a natural and even stimulative engagement that is crucial to
leaders' responsiveness and to their moral and intellectual authority.
Leaders' responsibilities would be to institutionalize channels of access to decision making that permit as many voices as possible to be heard, bringing as
much "intelligence," to borrow Charles Lindblom's terminology, as possible
to the decision-making processes (Lindblom & Woodhouse, 1993).

Differences in the Creation of Knowledge and Meaning
of Science

In their version of applied management science, Taylorism and its progeny
valorize careful quantification of human behavior in small increments, and
aspire as much as technologically possible to eliminate the influence of factors that might alter individual reactions apart from those being measured.
This analysis attains the methodological standard of science when data are
examined in a disciplined manner and when results are calculated in statistical probability terms said to be causal. It reaches the educational gold
standard when such indicators of causality can be reliably linked to quantifiable student outcomes. These approaches to knowledge creation follow
from the Taylorist narrative, not the other way around.

In the political alternative, the method of creating new knowledge about
schools and their leadership would rest less on precise measurement of in-
puts and their statistical connection to outputs, and more on carefully recorded observations of relationships between governance decisions and results in naturalistic settings. Analysis would be drawn from social inquiry
that involved everyone in the community of interest. Causality would be inferred from intentionality and consequent human agency. Knowledge
about scientific methodology and data would necessarily be thoroughly
communicated, so that expert and layperson alike would be expected to critique the conclusions of scientific research, albeit at different levels of so-

phistication. This method of creating social knowledge would depend heavily on high-quality education, but also require an inquisitive press and many routine forums for public debate.

Yet, science itself is not about ends; it is a question of methods. This new political narrative about a science of educational leadership could not credibly claim the term while proposing radically altered methods of inquiry. It does, however, underscore that, like management science, the proposed new leadership science would be an applied methodology, adhering to expectations of careful observation and record keeping, testing, and retesting. Also like management science, the application would be to problems in the public realm. One major difference is that an elite cadre of mandarins acting alone could not conduct the proposed leadership science. If not widely understood, this knowledge-creation process would fail to make a difference.

The neo-Taylorist narrative also makes universality a research objective, a stance that has encouraged controlled statistical analysis, drastic limits on individual agency, and the intentional homogenization of naturally disparate educational environments. In the alternative narrative, universal generalization would not be the primary objective of knowledge creation. Instead, universal knowledge would be a rarely viable research claim, based on accumulated results from disparate settings, and in defiance of different guiding theoretical approaches. Moreover, it would only be sensible in political terms where the evidence was apparent to a broad range of individuals in the democratic polity. Rather, the first objective would be to create situated knowledge that withstands time.

The counternarrative of scientific research would expect to explain the links between a school's (or community's) governance and instructional practices and its students' demonstrations of democratic values and deliberative decision making. Students' choices of productive activity and the associated rewards (e.g., test scores, income) would be less important indications of achievement than their demonstrated ability to think critically about pressing social issues (e.g., evaluate political arguments for their underlying assumptions, determine relevant sources of information, test for trends and differences, envision perspectives unlike their own).

Two leadership examples may clarify. Today, volumes of educational research reinforce our understanding that nearly any planned change performs as expected somewhere, but not in most schools or communities. Neo-Taylorists respond to this demonstrable lack of generalizability by settling for (often small) statistical advantages. They further assume that a larger statistical advantage can be engineered by actively managing the environment through incentive and goal manipulation. The political narrative would have a different research response to the empirical diversity: It would attend to a community's social (e.g., intergroup trust, geographic dispersion, professional autonomy) and political (e.g., stable leadership, forums for debate, public-oriented media) resources that have encouraged mobilization for change in the past. Developing measurement instruments (perhaps promoting new indicators) that reflect these characteristics would be a central research task.

Strategic intervention would also be different. Rather than ranking a city's schools on a single continuum of test score performance, and rewarding movement along this yardstick while providing higher levels of coercion and supplemental resources to those at low rankings, schools could be grouped based on empirical estimates of local fiscal, social, and political resources. Research to guide improvements and reduce inequalities would involve civic actors in social inquiry; its success would be measured against local standards of democratic citizenship (e.g., empathic neighborliness, social entrepreneurship, community development, redistributive justice). The state would be accountable for supporting each city's standards and creatively compensating for its resource deficits.

Nor would research be constrained by distinctions between inside and outside forces (e.g., organizations and their environments). In political terms this means studying cross-sector coalitions. Until recently, there have been only a few theory-building studies examining school governance as a coalitional process. This implies a need to develop concepts about human associations that cross organizational boundaries, and classifications linking these associations to their intentionality. C. N. Stone (1998) and Stone, Henig, Jones, and Pierannuzi (2002) provided one such set of constructs in urban education, which Stone called governing regimes. Using their general approach, neo-Taylorist school systems and reform strategies can be considered one governing regime type among several possibilities, a distortion reflecting a particular distribution of power, unbalanced political skills, and the sense that economic rationales can be separated from political ones. The empowerment and equity concerns of the centralization and decentralization critics can be captured as a different governing regime responding to different distributions of power, political skill, and explanations of schooling (Shipps, 2003). By conceptualizing these types as separate regimes, we highlight a divergent range of possibilities for the reorganization of schooling. At the same time, a typology of school-governing regimes provides a framework for the empirical, comparative study of different school systems and the roles of leaders within them.

CONCLUSION

This chapter began by acknowledging that neither the economic nor the political purposes of education provide a complete depiction of leaders' responsibilities, nor does either alone lead to reliable ways to solve the problems of our urban schools. Despite the importance of both, I argued that our pursuit of school improvement is skewed toward the economic purposes, sustained by a century-old narrative that undergirds modern notions of progress and improvement. The political critique of that narrative, although trenchant and enduring, has not been able to rebalance the scales because it is only a critique, and therefore dependent on the economic narrative for its meaning. Creating an alternative political narrative puts the two kinds of purposes on more equal footing. These two ways of seeing schools, and the conceptions each has of leadership, accountability, conflict, knowledge creation, and science, can be contrasted and debated, even comparatively researched. In this light, the political narrative sketched earlier is intended to spur thinking about what a more balanced debate might include.

A less lopsided debate, at a minimum, encourages different kinds of questions and a more divergent set of answers. Rather than repeatedly refining the management training of principals, for instance, we might first ask what kinds of leadership behavior are needed in this situation—managerial, political or something else? Instead of researching and perfecting new methods to increase the certainty of preset outcomes, we could ask: What kinds of results are most desirable here, those that are quantifiable and universal or those that fit a small set of special circumstances at this moment? The answers would require examining the goals but also the values and related indicators of success we wish to foster. Of course, such questions are not new, but I take it as a premise of this volume that they are too seldom asked today.

However, even when the economic and political narratives are in full dialogue with one another, they fail to encompass all useful ways of seeing urban schools or their leaders. Nor do they contain all approaches to accountability, conflict, knowledge creation, or science in urban schooling. Other narratives, some found in this volume and some as yet unformed, begin with different goals, values, and keys to success, suggesting alternative notions of school leadership and the scientific pursuit of its improvement. Rejecting the comfortable certainty of even the modern and improved version of the best system requires an expansive stance that elicits other ways of conceptualizing urban schools and their leaders (e.g., as moral exemplars, master pedagogues, entrepreneurs). Developing a language for this intellectual diversity may be another necessary step toward loosening the bonds of neo-Taylorism. In this regard I have pointed to the historical and political analysis of regime theory.

But some readers will remain unconvinced that this is even necessary, an intellectual exercise perhaps, but not very practical. For those, I conclude with an admittedly partisan plea: Much of what today is called radical restructuring or reengineering is merely the latest application of the management science that Frederick Taylor initiated more than 100 years ago. The 20th century has repeatedly demonstrated that management science cannot resolve the problems it identifies. If business leaders and politicians of the last two decades can be believed, neo-Taylorism has not made the schools an engine of economic prosperity either. Nor by most measures of schooling or economic equity can the nation be said to be entering a society without class resentments. Allowing ourselves to remain constrained by the limits of a time-worn narrative not only ensures incrementalist responses to fundamental problems, but more importantly threatens to bind us even closer to elitist, undemocratic, and inequitable assumptions of the past. It is both crucial and plausible that we construct an alternative to neo-Taylorist management science as a guide to school improvement. This chapter has sketched one possibility; this volume points to others. Clearly, the time has come to invigorate the tired debates of the past by adapting them to new purpose.

REFERENCES

Alberthal, L. (1999). Corporate policy on community outreach and philanthropy. *Executive Speeches, 13*(5), 1–5.

Beatty, J. (1998). *The world according to Peter Drucker*. New York: Free Press.

Bobbitt, F. (1916). *Report of the school survey of school district number 1 in the city and county of Denver, Part 1*. Denver, CO: The School Survey Committee.

Bryk, A. S., Sebring, P. B., Kerbow, D., Rollow, S., & Easton, J. Q. (1998). *Charting school reform: Democratic localism as a lever for change*. Boulder, CO: Westview Press.

Callahan, R. E. (1962). *Education and the cult of efficiency: A study of the social forces that have shaped the administration of the public schools*. Chicago: University of Chicago Press.

Carlson, R. O. (1964). Environmental constraints and organizational consequences: The public school and its clients. In D. E. Griffiths (Ed.), *Behavioral science and educational administration* (pp. 272–276). Chicago: University of Chicago.

Cartwright, W. H. (1963). Review of Education and the cult of efficiency. *The Mississippi Valley Historical Society, 49*, 722–723.

Cohen, D. K. (1968). Policy for the public schools: Compensation and integration. *Harvard Education Review, 38*, 114–137.

Conant, J. B. (1961). *Slums and suburbs: A commentary on schools in metropolitan areas*. New York: McGraw-Hill.

Counts, G. (1969). *Dare the schools build a new social order?* New York: Arno Press. (Original work published in 1932)

Cuban, L. (1976). *Urban school chiefs under fire*. Chicago: University of Chicago Press.

Cuban, L. (1993). *How teachers taught: Constancy and change in American classrooms, 1880–1990* (2nd ed.). New York: Teachers College Press.

Cuban, L. (2001). *Leadership for student learning: Urban school leadership—Different in kind and degree (Essay)*. Washington, DC: Institute for Educational Leadership.

Cuban, L., & Shipps, D. (Eds.). (2000). *Reconstructing the common good: Coping with intractable dilemmas*. Stanford, CA: Stanford University Press.

Cubberley, E. P. (1916). *Public school administration*. Boston: Houghton Mifflin.

Deming, W. E. (2000). *The new economics* (Rev. ed.). Cambridge, MA: MIT Press.

Dewey, J. (1954). *The public and its problems.* Athens, OH: Swallow Press, Ohio University Press. (Original work published in 1927)

Dill, W. R. (1964). Decision-making. In D. E. Griffiths (Ed.), *Behavioral science and educational administration* (pp. 199–220). Chicago: University of Chicago Press.

Drucker, P. F. (1995). *The end of economic man: The origins of totalitarianism.* New Brunswick, NJ: Transaction Publishers. (Original work published in 1939)

Drucker, P. F. (1995). *The future of industrial man.* New Brunswick, NJ: Transaction Books. (Original work published in 1942)

Firestone, W. A., & Shipps, D. (2005). How do leaders interpret conflicting accountabilities to improve student learning? In W. A. Firestone & C. Rhiel (Eds.), *A new agenda for research in educational leadership* (pp. 81–100). New York: Teachers College Press.

Gittell, M., & Hevesi, A. (1969). *The politics of urban education.* New York: Praeger.

Griffiths, D. E. (1964a). *Behavioral science and educational administration.* Chicago: University of Chicago Press.

Griffiths, D. E. (1964b). The nature and meaning of theory. In D. E. Griffiths (Ed.), *Behavioral science and educational administration* (pp. 95–118). Chicago: University of Chicago Press.

Gross, B. M. (1964). The scientific approach to administration. In D. E. Griffiths (Ed.), *Behavioral science and educational administration* (pp. 33–72). Chicago: University of Chicago Press.

Gulick, L., & Urwidk, L. (Eds.). (1937). *Papers on the science of administration.* New York: Institute of Public Administration.

Gutmann, A. (1999). *Democratic education* (Rev. ed.). Princeton, NJ: Princeton University Press.

Havinghurst, R. J. (1966). *Education in metropolitan areas.* Boston: Allyn & Bacon.

Hemphill, J. K. (1964). Personal variables and administrative styles. In D. E. Griffiths (Ed.), *Behavioral science and educational administration* (pp. 178–196). Chicago: University of Chicago Press.

Hess, F. (1999). *Spinning wheels: The politics of urban school reform.* Washington, DC: Brookings Institution Press.

Hess, G. A. J. (1991). *School restructuring, Chicago style.* Newbury Park, CA: Corwin Press.

Heubert, J. P., & Hauser, R. M. (1998). *High stakes: Testing for tracking, promotion and graduation.* Washington, DC: National Academy Press.

Hill, P. T., Pierce, L. C., & Guthrie, J. W. (1997). *Reinventing public education.* Chicago: University of Chicago Press.

Hochchild, J. L. (1984). *The new American dilemma: Liberal democracy and school desegregation.* New Haven, CT: Yale University Press.

Iannaccone, L., & Lutz, F. W. (1994). The crucible of democracy: The local arena. In J. D. Scribner & D. H. Layton (Eds.), *The study of educational politics* (pp. 39–52). Washington, DC: Falmer Press.

Jencks, C. S., Smith, M., Acland, H., Bane, J. M., Cohen, D., Gintis, H., et al. (1972). *Inequality: A reassessment of the effect of family and schooling in America.* New York: Basic Books.

Kanigel, R. (1997). *The one best way: Frederick Winslow Taylor and the enigma of efficiency.* New York: Viking.

Kantor, H., & Lowe, R. (2000). Bureaucracy left and right: Thinking about the one best system. In L. Cuban & D. Shipps (Eds.), *Reconstructing the common good in education: Coping with intractable American dilemmas* (pp. 130–147). Stanford, CA: Stanford University Press.

Kershner, C. T., Koppich, J. E., & Weeres, J. G. (1997). *United mind workers: Unions and teaching in the knowledge society.* San Francisco: Jossey-Bass.

Khurana, R. (2002). *The search for the corporate savior: The irrational quest for charismatic CEOs.* Princeton, NJ: Princeton University Press.

Kozol, J. (1967). *Death at an early age.* New York: Bantam Books.

Lazerson, M. (1973). Revisionism and American educational history. *Harvard Educational Review, 43,* 278.

Lewis, D. A., & Nakagawa, K. (1995). *Race and educational reform in the American metropolis: A study of decentralization.* Albany: State University of New York Press.

Lieberman, M. (1997). *The teachers unions: How the NEA and the AFT sabotage reform and hold students, parents, and teachers hostage to the bureaucracy.* New York: Free Press.

Lindblom, C. E., & Woodhouse, E. J. (1993). *The policy making process* (3rd ed.). Englewood Cliffs, NJ: Prentice Hall.

Linn, R. L., Baker, E. L., & Betebenner, D. W. (2002). Accountability systems: Implications of requirements of the No Child Left Behind Act of 2001. *Educational Researcher, 31*(6), 3–16.

Lipham, J. M. (1964). Leadership and administration. In D. E. Griffiths (Ed.), *Behavior science and educational administration* (pp. 119–139). Chicago: University of Chicago Press.

Lutz, F. W., & Iannaconne, L. (1978). *Public participation in local school districts: The dissatisfaction theory of American democracy.* Lexington, MA: Heath.

Malen, B. (1994). Enacting site based management: A political utilities analysis. *Educational Evaluation and Policy Analysis, 16,* 246–267.

March, J. G., & Simon, H. A. (1964). *Organizations.* New York: Wiley.

McDermott, K. A. (1999). *Controlling public education: Localism vs. equity.* Lawrence: University Press of Kansas.

Merkle, J. (1980). *Management and ideology: The legacy of the international scientific management movement.* Berkeley: University of California Press.

MetLife Inc. (2003). *The MetLife survey of the American teacher: An examination of school leadership (Annual Survey).* New York: Author.

Morre, H. A., Jr. (1964). Ferment in school administration. In D. E. Griffiths (Ed.), *Behavior science and educational administration* (pp. 11–32). Chicago: University of Chicago Press.

Myrdal, G. (1962). *An American dilemma.* New York: Harper & Row. (Original work published in 1944)

National Alliance for Business. (1989). *A blueprint for business on restructuring education.* Washington, DC: Author.

Orfield, G., & Eaton, S. (1996). *Dismantling desegregation.* New York: New Press.

Perlstein, D. (2000). "There is no escape . . . from the ogre of indoctrination": George Counts and the civic dilemmas of democratic educators. In L. Cuban & D. Shipps (Eds.), *Reconstructing the common good in education: Coping with intractable American dilemmas* (pp. 51–67). Stanford, CA: Stanford University Press.

Peterson, P. E. (1985). *The politics of school reform 1870–1940.* Chicago: University of Chicago Press.

Pfeffer, J., & Salancik, G. R. (1978). *The external control of organizations: A resource dependence perspective.* San Francisco: Harper & Row.

Public Agenda. (2001). *Trying to stay ahead of the game: Superintendents and principals talk about school leadership.* New York: Author.

Purkey, S., & Smith, M. S. (1983). Effective schools: A review. *Elementary School Journal, 83*(4), 247–252.

Ravitch, D. (2001). *Left back: A century of battles over school reform.* New York: Simon & Schuster.

Roe, E. (1994). *Narrative policy analysis: Theory and practice.* Durham, NC: Duke University Press.

Rogers, D. (1967). *110 Livingston Street: Politics and bureaucracy in the New York City school system.* Lexington, MA: Lexington Books.

Rosen, J. (1996). *Getting the connections right: Public journalism and the troubles in the press.* New York: Twentieth Century Fund.

Rury, J. L., & Mirel, J. E. (1997). The political economy of urban education. In M. W. Apple (Ed.), *Review of research in education* (Vol. 22, pp. 49–110). Washington, DC: American Educational Research Association.

Ryan, A. (1995). *John Dewey: The high tide of American liberalism.* New York: Norton.

Shipps, D. (1997). The invisible hand: Big business and Chicago school reform. *Teachers College Record, 99*(1), 73–116.

Shipps, D. (2000). Echoes of corporate influence: Managing away urban school troubles. In L. Cuban & D. Shipps (Eds.), *Reconstructing the common good: Coping with intractable dilemmas* (pp. 82–105). Stanford, CA: Stanford University Press.

Shipps, D. (2003). Pulling together: Civic capacity and urban school reform. *American Educational Research Journal, 40,* 841–878.

Shipps, D. (2006). *School reform, corporate style: Chicago, 1880–2000.* Lawrence: University Press of Kansas.

Silverberg, M., Warner, E., Fong, M., & Goodwin, D. (2004). *National assessment of vocational education: Final report to Congress.* Washington, DC: U.S. Department of Education.

Smith, T. L. (1964). Review of education and the cult of efficiency. *History of Education Quarterly, 4,* 76–77.

Spring, J. H. (1972). *Education and the rise of the corporate state.* Boston: Beacon Press.

Stettner, E. A. (1993). *Shaping modern liberalism: Herbert Croly and progressive thought.* Lawrence: University Press of Kansas.

Stone, C. N. (Ed.). (1998). *Changing urban education.* Lawrence: University Press of Kansas.

Stone, C. N., Henig, J., Jones, B. F., & Pierannuzi, C. (2001). *Building civic capacity: The politics of reforming urban schools.* Lawrence: University Press of Kansas.

Stone, D. (1998). *Policy paradox: The art of political decision making* (2nd ed.). New York: Norton.

Tyack, D. B. (1981). City schools: Centralization and control at the turn of the century. In J. Israel (Ed.), *Building the organizational society* (pp. 57–72). New York: Free Press.

Tyack, D. B. (1993). School governance in the United States: Historical puzzles and anomalies. In J. Hannaway & M. Carnoy (Eds.), *Decentralization and school improvement: Can we fulfill the promise?* (pp. 1–32). San Francisco: Jossey-Bass.

Tyack, D. B., & Hansot, E. (1982). *Managers of virtue: Public school leadership in America 1920–1980.* New York: Basic Books.

Waring, S. P. (1991). *Taylorism transformed: Scientific management theory since 1945.* Chapel Hill: University of North Carolina Press.

Weiler, H. (1993). Control versus legitimation: The politics of ambivalence. In J. Hannaway & M. Carnoy (Eds.), *Decentralization and school improvement: Can we fulfill the promise?* (pp. 55–83). San Francisco: Jossey-Bass.

Wells, A. S., & Crain, R. L. (1997). *Stepping over the color line.* New Haven, CT: Yale University Press.

Williamson, O. E. (1985). *The economic institutions of capitalism: Firms, markets and relational contracting.* New York: Free Press.

Wirt, F., & Kirst, M. W. (1992). *Schools in conflict* (3rd ed.). Berkeley, CA: McCutchen.

Witte, J., & Walsh, D. (1990). A systemic test of the effective schools model. *Educational Evaluation and Policy Analysis, 12,* 188–212.

Wong, K. K., Dreeben, R., Lynn, L. E., & Sunderman, G. L. (1997). *Integrated governance as a reform strategy in Chicago public schools (Research Report).* Philadelphia: National Center on Education in the Inner Cities.

Wrigley, J. (1982). *Class politics and public schools: Chicago 1900–1950.* New Brunswick, NJ: Rutgers University Press.

Zeigler, L. H., Jennings, M. K., & Peak, G. W. (1974). *Governing American schools: Political interaction in local school districts.* North Scituate, MA: Duxbury Press.

Zeigler, L. H., Kehoe, E., & Reisman, J. (1985). *City managers and school superintendents.* New York: Praeger.

Zimet, M. (1973). *Decentralization and school effectiveness: A case study of the 1969 decentralization law in New York City.* New York: Teachers College Press.

Part **IV**

SCIENCE AND SENSATIONALISM: RENEWING THE FOUNDATIONS

The two chapters of Part IV provide a constructive reinterpretation of the scientific foundations of educational policy, politics, and school administration. They distinguish between the sensational experiences that form the building blocks of scientific knowledge and the sensationalism that has driven the use of social science theory and methods in recent education policy debates.

Chapter 9 argues that the crisis of confidence facing scientific research in education has been created by contradictions between Aristotelian and Platonic epistemologies that are responsible for the unbridgeable gulf between the defenders and the critics of 20th-century social science theories and methods. When modern science separated itself from its intellectual roots in alchemy and astrology, Platonic philosophy became the province of religious thought whereas Aristotelian thought framed science and its methods. Twentieth-century phenomenology is shown to have a different framework for scholarly inquiry and research, and is advanced as a needed reconstruction of knowledge verification.

Chapter 10 draws together insights presented throughout the book into an integrated framework for the study of educational policy, politics, and administration. It shows how the phenomenological epistemology described in chapter 9 provides the schema needed to link moral and factual questions into a common inquiry methodology. At the center of the argument presented here is the proposition that reliable knowledge and confident professional practice are properly understood from the perspective of vocation. Scientific knowledge can be vouchsafed only by a cadre of scholars who take science to be their vocation. Vocation, it is argued, is the personal side of a collective cultural enterprise. Hence, vocations are sustained by embedding them within cultural institutions—the university being the primary institutional form for clarifying and sustaining vocational science.

Chapter 9

Sensational Science: Generating Valid and Reliable Knowledge of Educational Administration, Policy, and Politics

Douglas E. Mitchell
University of California, Riverside

In the small Czech town of Kutna Hora there is an alchemy museum recalling modes of inquiry and scholarly discipline that predated the modern era. Among the captions for the many displays is one that reads:

> Alchemy resembles a physical science, but it is also, above all, a mystical experiment. Its nature is simultaneously materialistic and spiritual, and it contemplates primarily the relation between the life of metals and the universal spirit. It desires to free matter through spirit, and to free spirit through matter. In many respects it imitates Art, in its highest form: the traditional "Art of Love." It encourages Man to defeat Time—it is a quest for the Absolute. (Alleau, n.d.)

Another of the captions reminds us that alchemy was motivated by a powerful agenda of practical actions; it was neither idle curiosity nor a search for abstract "knowledge for its own sake." As Alleau summarized:

> Alchemy is concerned with three main activities. First is the search for the Philosopher's Stone, which makes possible the transmutation of base metals into gold. Second is the preparation of the Elixir of Life which prevents aging and perhaps offers eternal life. Third is the creation of harmony through the integration of opposites.

Important lessons relevant to the theme of this book are underscored by these cryptic reflections on our collective history. First, they remind us that

213

what we have come to regard as science had its origins in an intensely political and highly spiritual search for power—the power of wealth, the power to hold back the inevitable debilitations of finitude and death, and the power to control psychic anxiety. Moreover, contrary to some popular interpretations of their work, these prescientific inquirers into the mysteries of the universe were certain that success or failure hinged on discipline—on a willingness to organize their inquiries in ways that accepted presuppositions and precisely followed appropriate methods. Taking a perspective generally eschewed by modern scientists, these prescientific inquirers recognized that facts and values are inextricably bound together in such a way that the truths they were seeking could never be known through objectification and disengagement from social loyalties and transcendental commitments. They conducted their work with a deeply held sense that spiritual and intellectual orientation is as much a part of inquiry as is objectivity.

Eighteenth-century Enlightenment philosophy and science departed radically from this premodern worldview. Enlightenment science set objectivity as the standard for scientific inquiry, suppressing attention to values. For more than two centuries an Enlightenment rejection of subjectivity and any intellectual link between facts and values served to create science professions and practices synonymous with modernity and widely believed to be the most reliable way of attaining the alchemists' goals. This Enlightenment view of science and of knowledge has come under intense scrutiny in recent years, however, as social constructivists, postmodernists, critical theorists, radical feminists, and even biblical fundamentalists have challenged its privileged political position and sought to articulate theories of knowledge that challenge its intellectual dominance. The critics of the rationalist, scientific, and Enlightenment views of knowledge have asserted that scientific claims to knowledge are unjustified and misleading.

AN EPISTEMOLOGICAL PERSPECTIVE

To interpret modern science and its passionate critics, it is necessary to review the foundations of epistemological philosophy—that branch of philosophy dealing with questions of how reliable and valid knowledge is possible. I undertake this task with some trepidation as I am far from a professional philosopher, but it is unavoidable if progress is to be made. I start by noting that recorded human history began quite a bit before the emergence of philosophical thought. As reviewed by Frankfort and Groenewegen-Frankfort (1951), an era of mythological interpretations of the relationships between mankind and the social and natural world in which we live went through a long and meaningful history well before the advent of formal philosophy. Moreover, as the late Joseph Campbell (1949) reminded this generation so forcefully, mythological interpretations of the place of mankind in the universe continue to provide a rich source of insight and meaningful responses to some of the most profound and perennial questions of personal and social meaning.

The crucial element in the transition from mythological to philosophical thought, Frankfort and Groenewegen-Frankfort (1951) persuasively argued, was the emergence of self-consciousness. Before access to knowledge can become problematic, it is first necessary to become aware that, in some important respect, we are objects—albeit sentient, subjective objects—of our own experience. We have to become aware that the mystery and unpredictability of our experience is, in part at least, the consequence of our separation from it. Our knowledge of the physical and social world is, of course, sharply bounded by our limited experience of it, but it is also, in principle, obscured by the fact that our sentient consciousness, our mind, is only partially processing and understanding the experiences we do have. Once self-consciousness becomes manifest we become aware of separation and limitation in our ability to attend to all we experience and, even more, to meaningfully interpret all the experiences to which we have attended. In short, self-consciousness makes epistemological philosophy both possible and necessary. There is always a temptation to retreat from self-consciousness—to lose ourselves in the ecstasy of experience itself and to avoid the painful intellectual alienation that accompanies self-consciousness. Historically, religious and cultural rituals have served this goal of negating self-consciousness and revitalizing the mythological experience of immediate engagement in the lived moment. But the price of this ritualized annihilation of self-consciousness has been abandonment of the concept of historic direction and human purpose beyond immediate experiencing.

From its earliest moments, Western philosophy has tried to deal with the most dramatic consequence of human self-consciousness—an unavoidable, confusing, and sometimes terrifying awareness of a deep separation between appearance and reality. Before philosophy it was not necessary to wrestle with this distinction because the engaged participants in the prephilosophical world un-self-consciously met the world as immediately there, experiencing it as being just what it appeared to be—a world alive with spirits and rendered mystifying by the actions of gods rather than merely unpredictable because of an ignorance of natural laws. For prephilosophic antiquity, the paramount intellectual problem was resolving the anxiety of human finitude and powerlessness in the face of mortal dangers arising from the unpredictable spirits inhabiting every aspect of personal and social life. The result was narration—telling stories of transcendental agents at work offering guidance about how to navigate the dangers posed by everyday living and insights into its meanings and ultimate purposes.

The primary problem, and the prerequisite condition, of Greek philosophy was resolving the first question of the self-conscious mind: How can we penetrate the constantly changing appearance of things in order to come to know our world as it truly is? The world of the self-conscious philosopher is now seen as out there, beyond the horizons of our perceptions of it. Periodically, our illusions of contact with the really real world are shattered and we experience anew the fundamental alienation of self and world that is intrinsic to self-consciousness. But then there are also moments of reunification with our world—moments in which we reach confidence that we know our world and can successfully follow its rules in the practical conduct of everyday affairs. These moments of reunification are transient, however, as understanding breaks down and we find the world once more to be, surprisingly, not what it appears to be. The self-conscious philosopher asks again and again how in our hall-of-mirrors world we can distinguish false images and harmless errors of misapprehension from reliable knowledge of the world as it is in itself. How is reliable knowledge to be separated from erroneous presumption? How, in short, can we really come to know anything?

The ancient Greek philosophers developed two alternative solutions to the appearance–reality problem. The first, set forth by Plato (1972), is idealism, an epistemological view asserting that appearances cannot be actively penetrated through any human effort and thus cannot be forced to yield contact with reality itself. Instead, the appearances that arise in our sense experiences trigger from our minds a recognition experience, an awareness that our knowledge of reality is pregiven as categories of perception in the mind. That is, the experiences mediated through our senses have the effect of stimulating our minds to conceptualize the realities that are responsible for them, but that are not directly accessible to our senses. The phenomenal world of sense experience serves as a stimulus to conscious recognition and awareness of realities that are, in principle, already inarticulately known to us.

Idealistic knowledge of this sort is widely recognized in religion and the arts, where people become convinced of the transcendent meaning and significance of their experiences arising through exposure and reflection rather than through systematic, aggressive inquiry. Much of the modern world tends to reject this epistemology, but it is easily recognized in the conversation of parents with their adolescent children who ask something like, "How will I know that I have met Mr. or Ms. Right and am ready for marriage?" When parental answers take the form of, "Don't rush it, you'll know it when it happens," they are embracing a Platonic epistemology, asserting that experience will trigger a recognition moment in which the mind recalls essential meaning. This epistemology is also confirmed in the experience of religious conversion when, as John Wesley (1988) reported, one is "strangely warmed" by an encounter with an unavoidable transcendent reality. This same type of experience was confirmed in a more secular way by a powder metallurgist who participated in developing the first British atomic bomb. He reported that he and other members of the development team were awestruck and profoundly moved to a deepened sense of personal and social responsibility by the awareness of what they had achieved that fateful day in the Sahara desert. Though more secular than John Wesley's experience, this reaction is no less confirming of the Platonic notion that experience triggers something already deeply embedded within the person.

In sharp contrast with Platonic idealism, Aristotle (1984) developed an epistemology asserting that the gap between appearance and reality is bridged through systematic analysis of experienced phenomena and rational interpretation of the underlying realities that must be responsible for the experienced appearances. This view, usually called essentialism or empiricism, is central to the development of modern sciences. It asserts that, although our senses never present to us the entirety of any real object or event, they do present authentic and essential aspects of an ultimate reality that is responsible for stimulating the senses. Reality, not mental activities, is asserted to be the true source of sense experience, leaving us only with the knotty problem of inferring from our sense perceptions what realities could be responsible for them. Thus, the true distance between two points (say, the earth and the sun) can be discerned through triangulation of multiple observations from different vantage points. And the nature and dynamics of the physical, biological, and social universe can be inferred from triangulated close scrutiny of our experiences—particularly as we systematically synthesize inferences drawn from multiple experiences of the same noumenal reality. For the essentialist, knowledge is garnered through an aggressive process—experimental manipulation and close observation in ways that create more and more adequate perspectives from which inferences can become more and more reliable and valid.

THE EVOLUTION OF EPISTEMOLOGICAL PHILOSOPHY

As suggested by the graphic presented in Fig. 9.1, epistemological philosophy has undergone a number of important developments since the grand divide between idealism and essentialism launched by Plato and Aristotle. As suggested in the top part of the figure, the Greeks initiated the idea, later reaffirmed and elaborated in the seminal works of Immanuel Kant, that the phenomenal appearances of things are wholly separate from their noumenal essences, that our senses record and present to our minds only appearances, never the thing in itself. Because things in themselves remain

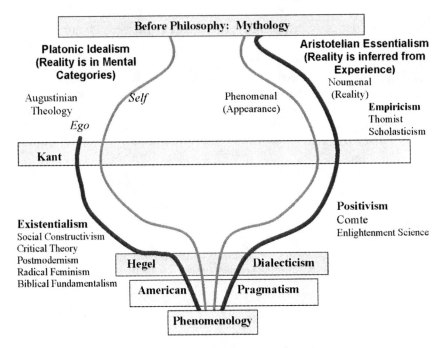

FIG. 9.1.   A graphic history of philosophy.

mysteriously beyond human contact, it is fairly easy for religious theologies to equate contact with the really real to contact with the transcendental being of God. Saint Augustine (1993) is credited with adapting Platonic idealism as the underlying epistemology for Christian theology. Theological idealism asserts that the categories of mind with which we recognize noumenal realities are given by God in an act of revelation that empowers the mind to a true understanding of the universe and our proper place within it. This theological embrace of idealism effectively secularized the Aristotelian view, making the knowledge derived from rational interpretations of empirical data suspect, with regard to both its moral virtue and its ultimate validity—a situation that made it easy to see Galileo and the heliocentric cosmologists as heretics. Nevertheless, the Aristotelian epistemology acquired a strong following and eventually became the cornerstone of the natural sciences—particularly astronomy, physics, and chemistry.

Scholastic legal theory adopted an Aristotelian epistemology, developing rules of evidence that assumed truth is determined by triangulation across multiple evidentiary sources. This encouraged theologians to consider the possibility that inferences about God's presence and actions could also be discerned through accumulated sensory data rather than dramatic revelation. As the modern era emerged from the Dark Ages, the scholastic theologian Thomas Aquinas undertook to reconstruct Christian theology on such an Aristotelian foundation.

Immanuel Kant (2003) owns a special place in the history of epistemology. It was he who recognized that the problematic gap between appearance and reality applied just as profoundly to human consciousness as to our experience of the world. That is, human beings not only appear to themselves as objects of inquiry and knowledge, but are also plagued by problems of illusion and false consciousness that obscure just as thoroughly consciousness of self as consciousness of the world. Hence, Platonic idealism faces a profound challenge within the mind itself: Not only are we limited in our capacity to attend to and categorize ordinary experience of the world, we cannot be confident that our mental categories are not themselves mere appearances or phenomenal objects rather than the purported noumenal realities embodied in the transcendental categories of the really real world. Since Kant, anxiety and uncertainty about our understanding of the world within which we live has been radically compounded by a parallel anxiety and uncertainty about whether we know ourselves. If transcendental experience (of God or merely of the ultimate nature of reality) mediates the categories with which we recognize and interpret our experience, how do we know what those categories are? Can the categories that appear to be useful be only illusory, grounded in our phenomenological selves rather than in our transcendental egos?

For this reason, Kant's name is associated with the widest separation between Platonic and Aristotelian epistemologies in Fig. 9.1. The primary epistemological effect of his shocking recognition of the potentially illusory appearance of the mind to itself was a deepened awareness of the radical difference in viewpoint between Aristotelian empiricism, with its emphasis on methodically exposing experience to experimental investigation and rational analysis, and a widely endorsed and predominantly religious Platonism that emphasized the importance of purity of mind and acceptance by faith of the transcendental authority of God, as well as the transcendent importance of church and state authority systems.

Both the Platonic and the Aristotelian traditions began to evolve in new directions. On the Aristotelian side, logical positivism (pioneered by Comte, 1970) emerged in the form of a belief that honoring inquiry methods codified as the scientific method—objectivity, simplicity, experimentalism, rationalism—would surely and confidently enable us to penetrate the veil of ignorance that allowed illusory appearances to be mistaken for noumenal realities. To some degree, this was merely a matter of giving up on the social agendas of the alchemists and astrologers (creating wealth, assuring eternal life, controlling anxiety, and predicting the future) to concentrate on the production of knowledge for its own sake. Though the pre-scientific enterprises of alchemy and astrology had failed in their social purposes, the records of those failures gradually opened up interpretations of the natural and eventually the social world that could be relied on to facilitate creation of technical control over natural and social processes, and to enable the human community to create wealth, maintain health, and control personal anxiety with social and chemical engineering rather than transcendental intervention. Although the arrogant belief that complete knowledge of the natural and social world would evolve from rigorous application of Comte's logical positivist methodology has been abandoned, modern science remains the crowning achievement of the Aristotelian epistemological viewpoint.

On the Platonic side, recognition of the gap between appearance and reality applied to self-consciousness (i.e., the distinction between subjective ego and the objectified self) raised serious questions about whether it would ever be possible to know when our minds were in contact with the transcendental source of authentic knowledge and when they were being deceived by appearances and were only attributing transcendental significance to the fulminations of an unbounded imagination. This uncertainty gave birth to existentialism, which in both its religious and its secular forms asserted that we could not, in principle, be confident of the authenticity of our mind's interpretations of experience and thus needed to shift our attention away from the search for reliable knowledge and toward a search for personal and social responsibility. That is, the existentialists—Soren Kierkegaard's (1960) works are typical of the religious variant; Jean Paul Sartre (1948) was among the leading representatives of a more secular strain—accepted the intellectual absurdity of the human condition, asserting that we are hurled into a world of which we can have no certain knowledge and must live out an existence without certain purpose or structure. The result was to focus attention on the possibility that meaning is given through an exercise of responsible commitment to a more or less freely chosen purpose rather than through the discovery of life's meanings that are initially hidden from our consciousness.

EXISTENTIAL CRITIQUES OF MODERN SCIENCE

By the late 20th century, the existentialist viewpoint had captured the imagination of a broad array of scholars who began to assert its superiority over the Aristotelian model. Social constructivists, postmodernists, critical theorists, radical feminists, and biblical fundamentalists are, each in their own way (or perhaps I should say ways, because none of these groups presents a unified approach to the task), challenging the reliability and validity of Enlightenment science. They are challenging the objectivity (or objectification) of its inquiry methods, the essentialist Aristotelian epistemology undergirding its truth claims, and, above all, its privileged political position as the preeminent liberator of the human spirit from the scourges of poverty, finitude, and ontological anxiety that defined the work agenda of their precursor alchemists and astrologers a millennium ago. The social constructivists are most concerned with the inquiry methods and their undergirding epistemology. The biblical fundamentalists are most concerned to preserve specific truth claims, including the validity of direct access to transcendental experience of the divine (through prayer and revelation), recognition of specific interventions of God in the otherwise regular order of human and natural events (seen in creation and miracles), and the inspired truth claims of specific sacred texts. Postmodernists, critical theorists, and radical feminists all devote substantial effort to challenging the political dominance of Aristotelian Enlightenment science, charging that this dominance has been achieved by degrading crucial functions of the human intellect, including the capacity to discern moral and artistic truths and the capacity to imagine and evaluate alternative futures that never come into view using the realist methods of Enlightenment science. Though they are critical of the Aristotelian epistemology and its implied objectivist methods, these movements are most intensely committed to challenging what they see as the politically privileged position of modernist science, which they believe to be responsible for the alienation of the human spirit from questions of justice, community life, cultural sensitivity, personal responsibility, authentic experience, and the ultimate nature and purposes of human life.

Arising initially in the humanities and social sciences, these challenging movements turned their attention in the 1990s to the heartland of modern science—physics, chemistry, and biology—creating what has come to be known as the "science wars" (Parsons, 2003; Segerstrêale, 2000).

DIALECTICISM, PRAGMATISM, AND PHENOMENOLOGY

In the early 19th century, Georg Hegel (1931), anticipating the futility of trying to resolve contradictions between the Aristotelian and Platonic epistemologies, radically recast the whole problem of epistemology. Hegel showed that the problem of knowledge is utterly transformed once we recognize that our experience of the world, and of ourselves, has a dialectical character. That is, human experience oscillates between un-self-conscious subjective moments of engagement when we are truly experiencing our experiences, and moments of reflective disengagement from that experience as we struggle to interpret it and make sense of it. Reflecting the ancient alchemists' urge to find a harmony among opposites, Hegel saw that in our engaged moments our experience is filled with tensions and contradictions—tensions and contradictions that we seek to resolve through reflective thought and synthesis of these tensions into new comprehensive holistic meaning structures. Through this dialectical process, Hegel thought, the human community is working its way toward a comprehensive understanding of the universe and of our place within it.

The American pragmatists (Dewey, 1948; James, 1963; Mead, 1934; Pierce, 1958) developed a similar, but less sophisticated, epistemological breakthrough. They postulated that knowledge is not an abstract mapping of human experience (of either the self or the universe), but is a set of practical guidelines for acting successfully within that universe to realize human purposes. Thus, knowledge is developed in something like the Hegelian dialectical process as human beings oscillate between attempts to act on their personal and social purposes and attempts to analyze and interpret the strategies needed to act successfully. The typifications of objects, persons, events, and processes that result from the analysis process are vouchsafed as reliable and valid knowledge by their adequacy in orienting people toward successful actions in the future. Here again, the classical separation between appearance and reality is not found at the center of the pragmatists' epistemology. Rather, it is the dialectical relationship between thought and action that is the central problem.

Although the pragmatists joined Hegel (1931) in recognizing the inappropriateness of basing an epistemology on an assertion that knowledge of reality could be either methodologically distilled from experiences (because they are typically confounded by uncertain and illusory appearances), or transcendentally triggered in the human mind by exposure to these appearances (because illusions are triggered at least as often as authentic insights), they tended to be more interested in describing and interpreting practical knowledge than in defining its epistemological status. James (1963) and Mead (1934) were interested in interpreting the psychology of action; Dewey (1948) more in the handling of public policy problems, particularly educational design; and Pierce (1958) in the sociology of action in communities. It was not until European phenomenological epistemologies were developed in the 20th century that a thorough and elegant advance beyond the Greek traditional starting points was fully articulated.

The European phenomenologists, most notably Heidegger (1962), Husserl (1962), and my personal favorite Merleau-Ponty (1962), traced the epistemological problem to its roots and offered a fundamentally new epistemological framework. The central philosophical proposition in phenomenology is as simple as it is profound. They asserted, simply, that trying to bridge the easily recognized gap between appearance and reality is the wrong way to construct the problem of knowledge. Instead, they argued that in moments of engaged experience, human beings are in direct contact with reality as it is—that there is no noumenal reality lying behind experienced phenomena (or ensconced in the human mind to be remembered and recognized as we contemplate experienced sensations). In this assertion, they do not mean to argue that we always understand our experiences or are able to produce infallibly accurate descriptions of the phenomena we are experiencing. They are quite aware of the fallibility of knowledge and of the perpetual problems of confusion and illusion that plague our experiencing.

For the phenomenologists, the problem with the Greek epistemologies is that they failed to recognize that experiencing and reflecting on experience do not go on simultaneously and that it is this lack of simultaneity between experiencing and reflecting that creates the fundamental epistemological problem. For the Greeks, epistemological analysis assumed that experiencing and reflecting were integrated in the sense that our experiences (phenomena) are available for reflection even as they are being experienced and thus must not be providing us with access to reality itself because we are constantly plagued by confusion and illusion. The phenomenologists observed that this problem does not arise at the moment of experience, but only when we are reflecting on that experience in order to make sense of it. So the problem, as the phenomenologists saw it, is how we "mind" our experience, not how we have it. They saw the Platonists as mistakenly thinking that the experiences were only "re-minders" of transcendentally given knowledge that can be directly accessed by the mind. In this way, the Platonic epistemology separates true knowledge from concrete experience, trivializing experience as merely the occasion of contacting transcendental reality rather than as the actual source of contact with authentic reality. At the same time, they saw the Aristotelians as mistakenly thinking that there is a layer of reality lying beyond our sense experiences, a noumenal layer that must be inferred because it cannot be directly experienced. The Aristotelian epistemology makes experience central to the development of knowledge, but then asserts that the experiences themselves are never sources of authentic contact with reality, once again displacing attention from the experiences themselves in order to concentrate attention on the rules of inference that might lead from our awareness of the phenomenal appearances that are found in our consciousness to the actual objects toward which these experiences point when properly understood.

Of course, the problems of confusion and illusion central to the Greek epistemologies and associated with our human alienation from the ground of authentic knowledge are very real, and we must ask how the phenomenologists addressed these issues if we are to understand how authentic knowledge can be both embodied in everyday experience and remain misunderstood and misinterpreted in the process of reflecting on that experience. Here phenomenological epistemologies become complex and are often hard to follow. Moreover, somewhat differing solutions are provided by each of the major phenomenologists. Even if I were fully capable of it, space here does not allow for a complete treatment of the differences between Husserl (1962), Heidegger (1962), and Merleau-Ponty (1962), so I must confine myself to the presentation of how the phenomenological perspective, as I have found it represented in the works of Merleau-Ponty, resolves the problems of illusion and confusion while insisting on the authenticity of experience itself.

The linchpin of the phenomenological epistemology lies in distinguishing sensation from perception in the chain of events that constitute our experiences of reality. Sensation is the result of the work done by our sense organs—shape, color, tone, texture, flavor, odor, pattern, and so on. Perception involves attributing to these sensations a meaningful place in our understanding of the material, social, and transcendental world. In the Platonic sense, perception consists of recognizing the sensations as emanating from a meaningful world. But in the Aristotelian sense, perceptions also characterize and preserve for reflection sensations that have been generated by a really real world from which they emanate. If there were no discontinuity between engagement in the moment of experience and reflection on the meaning of those experiences, the phenomenologists would have nothing to add to the Greek epistemological debate. What is important for the phenomenologists is that experiential sensations are not remembered as such, but are remembered as perceptions, and perceptions arise as we integrate sensations into the meaning system with which we anticipate and organize experience.

Perhaps a simple illustration will make this point clearer. A number of years ago I was driving along a darkened California road when a very large tumbleweed rolled out onto the road directly in front of me. When I saw the shape rolling onto the road I was sure it was a huge boulder, not a harmless tumbleweed, and immediately slammed on the brakes, nearly losing control of the car before harmlessly hitting the rolling tumbleweed. On reflection, I was able to remember the aspects of the moving tumbleweed that should have indicated to me that it was not the boulder I had imagined. But in the heat of the moment, my commonsense orientation led me to perceive unexpected nighttime driving events as potentially dangerous with the result that I interpreted the visual sensation of the tumbleweed as a dangerous boulder. My illusory experience grew directly out of the way in which orientations and predispositions toward immediate action led me to perceptually organize the sensory data provided by my night vision. The phenomenologists are observing, in short, that sensations are turned into perceptions through an intellectual process that relies on the framework of sense making we are routinely using to orient ourselves toward the social and natural world presenting itself to us through our senses.

Phenomenology departs from Platonic idealism by asserting that reliable knowledge is the result of proper understanding of our sensory exposure to reality, not the remembering of some truth stored away in the mind and merely stimulated to consciousness by our experiences. At the same time, phenomenology departs from the Aristotelian view by asserting that any interpretation of our sense data requires an active minding of it—a minding process that includes locating sensational experience within a schema of interpretation used to focus attention on some sensations while suppressing our awareness of others. The minding or framing process interprets sense data in terms of historical sequences of action, social definitions of status and value, and physical typifications of objects and events within a more or less coherent conceptualization of the physical universe.

Michael Polanyi (1967) captured the essence of this epistemology in *The Tacit Dimension*. Polyani began by noting that human beings are uniquely characterized by "knowing things we cannot tell." That which we know consists of the sensations registered by our senses, but that lie below our consciousness of them because they are the "details" from that we attend to the holistic conceptions formed by their integration.

SENSATIONAL SCIENCE: PURSUING
PHENOMENOLOGICAL KNOWLEDGE

Embracing a phenomenological epistemology requires redefining scientific inquiry to fit its reconceptualization of knowledge. Phenomenological inquiry begins with the recognition that a claim to knowledge involves a claim to have abstracted from the lived moment of active engagement a concept or proposition that points to and interprets the lived experiences to which it refers, but that is itself contained entirely within our reflective moments and is therefore, in principle, beyond validation through direct experience. Where Aristotelian empiricism asserts that scientific methods are capable of objectifying experience and validating knowledge by distancing observers from the objects of their inquiry and triangulating sense perceptions to test the reliability of the inferred nature of the world as it is in itself, phenomenologists recognize that such distancing destroys the very experiencing it is trying to validate. Where idealist and existentialist researchers seek to discern authentic interpretations of personal and social meaning systems embedded in shared cultures by exploring the ordinary opaqueness of taken-for-granted meaning systems and penetrating illusory false consciousnesses that obscure the ultimate nature of the human condition, phenomenologists assume that these symbol systems are rendered authentic or illusory on the basis of how adequately they serve to map a really real world that exists both logically and historically prior to its interpretative symbolization in cultural systems.

Phenomenologists agree with the idealists and existentialists that knowledge can only be claimed to be really known as it is embodied in the symbol systems and narratives used by human communities to establish identities, communicate meanings, and interpret ongoing relationships within the natural and social worlds where human life is enacted. They also agree with the Aristotelian empiricists that knowledge is knowledge about patterns of experience within a real world that, though it is reflectively constructed, is not socially or psychologically constructed independent of the givenness of the world itself. Phenomenological research will arise only when methods are devised, understood, and applied in ways that keep these two aspects of knowledge in mind.

Phenomenological methods establish the connection between authentic sensational realities and their interpretation as knowledge claims within the reflective process. Phenomenology as a method of inquiry insists that knowledge, though captured and articulated only in symbolic forms within reflective minds, is nevertheless fully grounded on sensations generated by our sense organs. Sensational experiences, phenomenologists insist, are authentic, but not yet symbolized, contacts with reality. They are transformed into reflective and intellectually meaningful knowledge as we reflect on them and fit them into a more or less comprehensive worldview, or what Thomas Kuhn (1962) called a "paradigm." The reason perception, conceptualization, and meaning assignment are problematic is that sensations can only undergo these processes when persons bring to their experiences a taken-for-granted worldview or interpretative framework that directs attention to salient sensations, deflects attention from irrelevant ones, and simultaneously offers to preinterpret all of them.

The most widely read phenomenologists use slightly different terms for characterizing the way in which our taken-for-granted interpretive scheme interacts with sensory data to generate knowledge. Husserl's (1962) key term was *judgment*, Heidegger (1962) used the concept of *appropriation*, and Merleau-Ponty (1962) used the term *intentionality*. All three asserted that perception and sense making are purposeful in that we reflect on sense data in ways that fit them into preexisting interpretive schemas. The preexisting interpretive schemas are essential for orienting ourselves to our experience and acting meaningfully in relation to the world as we understand it. Without this taken-for-granted interpretive framework, perception itself becomes impossible.

Merleau-Ponty (1962) explored this idea at some length in his extended discussion of the phenomenon of a phantom limb—an ordinary experience people have when they lose a limb due to an injury or surgery. For varying lengths of time (from a few days to many weeks) after a limb has been lost, most people continue to feel it and believe it still to be present. They often report that the limb itches or pains them or otherwise makes its presence known. Oddly, however, people who have lost a leg, when asked to stand during this period when they are still experiencing the presence of both legs, are able to balance on the one remaining leg without being aware that they are unconsciously compensating for the missing limb. So the phantom limb is an illusion, but an illusion that, at some level, is recognized as such by the person having it. Merleau-Ponty, based on his extensive hospital experience with such cases, interpreted this situation to mean that our bodies are part of our self-image and life project, that they "count in our scheme of things" and are thus resistant to being reconceptualized as substantially changed in form or ability. He concluded, in short, that in order to fully experience the sensations generated by our reconfigured body we must reconstruct our life project to take account of this new condition. This reconstruction process takes time, time during which we overlook or suppress reflective awareness of important bodily sensations and continue to rely on the earlier schema for interpretation of life experiences that previously fit our bodily capabilities. The process of reorganizing our life project is ordinarily relentless, however, and the phantom limb experience fades away as we come to incorporate our new bodily configuration into expected future experiences.

This creation of a relatively stable framework for registering and interpreting sensations is one crucial aspect of the fact that human beings are time-binding animals: We live constantly in the tension between a remembered past and an imagined future. We bind time by thematizing our experiences, telling ourselves "what is going on here" in the form of a story line that leads us to expect future events to be meaningfully linked to past activities. We become invested in the story line, relying on our assumed understanding of it to mobilize our energies, plan our actions, and interpret our present situation. The story line is built up over time by taking the sensations generated in our bodies as points of authentic contact with a real world, but points of contact that are merely sensational, leaving for the reflective mind the task of discerning and characterizing their thematic structure. The more confident we become in knowing what is going on, the harder it becomes to subject ephemeral and changing sensations to renewed reflective scrutiny and reinterpretation. Because we have learned to stand on our own two feet, as it were, we find it an awesome task to reconceptualize what our futures will be like if we are forced to rely on a single leg—we supply the second, phantom limb, until we can reorganize our life project to accommodate its loss.

The phenomenologists insist, however, that this interpretative framework is no hoax, and no mere social construction, but is grounded in truly sensational contact with the world (the social as well as the natural world) as it really exists. Importantly, this time-binding framework includes purposefulness as well as thematic structure. That is, our orientations toward time are utilized not simply to tell us what is happening in ways that keep us from being disoriented by daily events, but they also are used to formulate judgments about what courses of action are more appropriate for realizing our life projects, telling us when we are endangered and when we might be fulfilled.

Time binding is not the only phenomenologically structured element in our taken-for-granted interpretive schemas of action. We are also phenomenologically oriented to space and to social relationships. Just by living through space and time, we accumulate a taken-for-granted schema for characterizing elements in the spatial world. Our world becomes populated with objects, locations, and persons whose meanings integrate them into patterns that have the qualities of permanence (and variability) but also properties of aesthetic beauty (and ugliness), and properties of utility or threat to the successful execution of our life enterprises. Our physical life space is not neutrally out there to be perceived and analyzed, it is powerfully arrayed as a stage or playing field within which we enact purposeful lives—lives in which significance and triviality, actualization and nothingness, dignity and ignominy are constantly at stake.

When it comes to interpreting the phenomenology of social relationships, the work of Alfred Schutz (1972) stands out as a seminally clear and illuminating discussion of how taken-for-granted schemas interact with sensational contacts among associates and strangers to create the dynamics of a meaningful social world. Social relationships are not just perceived in terms of persistence and change; they are elaborately structured by affective bonds into communities. They are also inevitably moralized and evaluated so as to form systems of obligation and opportunity, systems of intrinsically meaningful authority and objectified systems of power relations.

SENSATIONAL SCIENCE METHODS

I want to conclude this chapter with a brief discussion of how sensations can be made the focus of a new conception of scientific inquiry—a framework for research that we might call sensational science. Sensational science redirects our understanding of inquiry methods by exploring the specific processes used to explore and reexamine sense data in the process of updating our store of reflective knowledge. Before doing so, it may be helpful to comment briefly on some of the ways in which contemporary empiricist, idealist, and existentialist methods are already evolving in this direction, but are still inadequate to the task of interpreting educational administration, policy, and politics.

I have already noted that social constructivists, postmodernists, critical theorists, radical feminists, and biblical fundamentalists have introduced idealist and existentialist epistemologies into contemporary scientific methods. Although the shift away from Aristotelian empiricism properly emphasizes the "mindedness" of scientific knowledge, and revitalizes our awareness of how cultural values and political power relations are inextricably bound up with the development and interpretation of knowledge claims, this shift also has the effect of undercutting the ability to establish whether resulting knowledge claims are validly linked to reality rather than being expressions of the ideological interests of the scholars who make them.

For some scholars, especially a prominent group of those who consider themselves to be postmodernists, this is exactly what is intended. For these scholars, cultural knowledge symbols are intellectually linked into a self-referential network. All symbols are seen as only referencing other symbols in a circular pattern that can never assert meaningful links with any reality beyond the social and political interests of specific groups that endorse them and use them to define social relationships and stabilize hierarchical social structures. From my perspective, this epistemological position is not only intellectually inadequate, it is having a profoundly negative impact on the historically crucial role of the university as the one social intuition assigned the responsibility of arbitrating competing claims to legitimate knowledge. If the existentialist conviction that all knowledge claims are valid only within the self-interested framework of a given cultural or political group—and the corollary assertion that situated consciousness can never be reliably penetrated to make contact with universal realities—are accepted, knowledge is reduced to the status of a tool or weapon, reinforcing particular systems of political and cultural control. Once that is accepted as the epistemological bedrock, no institution can claim to be, or be recognized as, the arbiter of competing claims. Universities are reduced to the status of political and cultural battlegrounds whose primary cultural virtue is that most of their occupants lack training in the use of lethal weapons.

My fervent hope is that the existentialist epistemology of constructivist, postmodern, and critical theory scholarship represents a passing phase in these traditions and that they will be able move on to a phenomenological epistemology that redirects attention to the realistic adequacy of knowledge claims as well as to their cultural and political potency. Otherwise, I fear social scientists will simply become the script writers for "Wag the Dog" politicians whose truth claims are assumed to be arbitrated only by their success or failure in political power struggles. Certainly the effort to legislate standards for scientific investigation found in the No Child Left Behind (NCLB, 2002) reauthorization of the 1965 federal Elementary and Secondary Education Act represents a profound politicization of the task of arbitrating knowledge claims that has for more than a century been assigned by democratic societies to their universities. The standards articulated in NCLB are based squarely on an Aristotelian rather than a phenomenological epistemology, which means that they are either confirming the politicization of knowledge claims asserted by the existentialist critics of enlightenment science or they represent a halting and inadequate political response to the breakdown of confidence in universities as the proper places for specifying the appropriate standards for accepting or rejecting knowledge claims.

Within the Aristotelian empiricist tradition there have also been a number of confusing and to some extent disturbing advances in methodology. Beginning about the time Thomas Kuhn's *The Structure of Scientific Revolutions* (1962) was becoming required reading among social scientists, education scholars gave up on the notion that our work could, or even should, be driven by an effort to produce a broad comprehensive theory of school organization, administration, policy, or politics. Whereas the period covered by David Tyack's *The One Best System* (1974) history was dominated by the notion that schools are public bureaucracies whose control and improvement rested on refining and elaborating our knowledge of just how such bureaucracies work to achieve their purposes, virtually all recent empirical scholarship seems to have abandoned the notion that we will ever have a comprehensive theory of schools and schooling and that we should, instead, let a thousand theories bloom, letting competing claims to knowledge coexist without insisting that contradictory findings produced by divergent but theoretically guided research studies must mean that at least one of the theories is wrong. We seem to have taken to resolving disputes with box score and meta-analysis syntheses of divergent and contradictory findings as if truth naturally emerges as the average among theoretically incommensurate analyses.

Mainstream Aristotelian research in education has yet to take seriously two other important developments that bear directly on how we might sift competing truth claims in the field. The first is the dramatic emergence of nonlinear dynamics or chaos theory in the natural sciences. Chaos research has drawn attention to two crucial features of many natural phenomena with dramatic implications for the study of schooling. First, chaos theory demonstrates that there are radical discontinuities in many causal relationships. In other words, relationships that may appear quite linear and dependable over a limited range of experience can suddenly and dramatically change and cease to fit our conceptual or mathematical models entirely. We simply have not learned how to incorporate this new way of thinking about chemical and mechanical processes into our studies of school operations and impacts.

The second crucial idea documented by research on complex and chaotic phenomena is that there are emergent realities that are produced within nonlinear systems as the relationships among key variables change. These emergent realities are produced by the configuration of elements within a complex system, not by the addition or removal of subcomponents. The importance of this fact was highlighted by Feynman, Leighton, and Sands (1989) when they noted that once chemists had completely deciphered the composition of hemoglobin (in the 1960s), the surprising conclusion was that nothing really new had been learned about the behavior and significance of hemoglobin itself. To learn about hemoglobin, Feynman et al. concluded, one must study it holistically because this vital compound is ultimately defined by the pattern into which its constituent parts are arranged, not by the parts themselves. And the significance of the pattern can only be discerned by studying the whole, not by taking it apart. This insight is being confirmed in studies of the self-organizing capabilities of systems characterized by having many individual elements programmed with a few simple rules. So far as I can tell, we have, as yet, no convincing evidence that schools are (or are not) chaotic systems and that there are (or are not) emergent realities that must be taken into account to understand them. For example, we do not have any way of knowing what new realities are present when schools develop unique histories or when they grow in physical size.

Another development in contemporary research studies utilizing the Aristotelian empiricist paradigm is recognition that our most sophisticated statistical data analysis techniques—hierarchical linear modeling and structural equation modeling—rather than leading us toward better contact with reality, are helping us to see more clearly that theories are mental constructs produced as guesses about what patterns might be found in our encounters with reality. Our data analysis techniques, contrary to what many of our graduate students believe, do not isolate the truths in the data; they only allow us to determine whether preformed judgments about reality are sufficiently close to the patterns found in our data sets to keep us from having to reject them as inadequate explanations. That is, as data analysis technologies have moved us farther away from naive confidence that the data display reality for our examination, they have deepened our realization that knowledge of the really real can never cross the epistemological gap between appearance and reality. This is not philosophically new, of course. Ever since the work of David Hume (1965) we have been philosophically aware of the fact that correlations among events, no matter how large the sample or how reliable the correlation, do not confirm specific causality. The explosive growth in statistical methods during the middle years of the 20th century, and their incorporation into readily managed computer programs during the last quarter of a century, have misled many professionals and policymakers into a belief that the correlation coefficients are more real than their sense experiences and have led to a willingness to impose requirements on professional practice that assume that the correlations are unequivocal reports of causality.

Rapid emergence of the so-called "new institutionalism" following the seminal essay by Meyer and Rowan (1977) represents another startling and intriguing development within the Aristotelian empiricist paradigm. This essay, in combination with a very broad array of other scholarly works, made it scholarly commonplace to talk about organizational cultures, and to recognize that symbolism and affectivity are as intimate a part of organizational behavior as are realism and rationality. This awareness is drawing empiricist Aristotelian research closer to the insights of the Platonic idealists by underscoring role of moralization, norm setting, symbolization of meaning, and expressions of commitment in defining organizations themselves, not just the individuals that inhabit them. Despite this progress, however, the Aristotelians and the Platonists remain poles apart on the question of how values, beliefs, and symbols are integrated into social systems. For the Platonists, the social systems are themselves symbolic creations made real through commitment to a metanarrative that interprets the social system's values and meanings. For the Aristotelians, however, values and norms remain properties of sentient individuals. To link these two perspectives we need an epistemology capable of clearly specifying where social and individual values are experienced and how those experiences can be nurtured into knowledge statements.

Applied phenomenology, as delineated by Schutz (1972), consists most fundamentally in learning how to undertake a "phenomenological reduction" or to "bracket off" the taken-for-granted presuppositions used routinely to preinterpret and render perceptually meaningful the sensory data being registered by our sense organs. Interpreting this process is complicated because, at first glance, it might be taken to be a denial of the phenomenological insight that sense data cannot be perceived without relying on a pre-existing interpretive framework that focuses attention and anticipates the probable meanings of the data. But the phenomenological reduction does not mean causing reflective consciousness to abandon its interpretive function altogether and simply register the incoming sense data—that is not humanly possible. Rather, what is meant is that the reflective mind is to become conscious of the routine preconceptions that are used in the course of ordinary commonsense daily living and to set those taken-for-granted schemas aside in order to test the possibility that some other interpretive presuppositions will change perception and interpretation of the sensory data in meaningful ways.[1]

---

[1] I am indebted to Aimee Howley (personal communication, March 27, 2005) for calling to my attention the provocative work of James Heap and Phillip Roth (1973), who painstakingly detailed some of the many misunderstandings of phenomenology to be found in the social sciences. They delineated four distinctive types of phenomenological sociology. Although the position developed here does not fit neatly into any of their types, they recognized in their Type IV the critical elements being examined here—recognition that knowledge is "constituted

Gibson Winter (1966) developed the concept of doubt in a helpful interpretation of Schutz's (1972) work. Winter pointed out that we go about our ordinary affairs utilizing a commonsense orientation to our sensory data—an orientation that is accompanied by "suspended doubt." For example, we jump in the car and head off to the grocery store without really thinking about whether the car will start, how the engine propels it, and so on. Moreover, we can drive along familiar streets barely noticing their sights and sounds as we concentrate on our destination and suspend all concern about what meaning these sights and sounds might have—meanings that were quite important to us when we were first learning how to get from the house to the store. As Winter noted, this taken-for-granted system breaks down when there are surprising or disappointing consequences, when events do not unfold as expected. This breakdown calls into question whether we can successfully pursue our interests using the taken-for-granted interpretive schema and invokes what Winter called "ideological reflection" and "relative doubt." Our interpretation of the sense data is then of the order of, "Why won't the car start?" or "What is blocking traffic up ahead?" This sort of doubting of the adequacy of an interpretive schema does not rise to the level of a phenomenological reduction because it continues to be governed by our interests and purposes. Rather, as Winter carried forward his analysis, the kind of reflective process Schutz was after in the performance of a phenomenological reduction consists of imposing what Winter called "radical doubt" by undertaking what he referred to as "scientific reflection" on the sensory data. This radical doubt is diagnostic in character; it utilizes the flexibility and power of the reflective mind to try on alternative interpretive schemas. It is of the order of, "I wonder why grocery stores are all located in big shopping malls," "How can burning gasoline inside an automobile engine actually generate useable power for driving?," or perhaps "Why do so many drivers use cell phones when they are fully aware that it is a dangerous practice?"

The point here is that the phenomenological reduction does not involve trying to recall and reexperience the sensory data in itself without any interpretive framework. Rather, it involves trying on alternative frameworks to determine if the data become reconceptualized and acquire new meanings.

---

in and through intentional acts of consciousness" (p. 363) and that the most difficult aspect of social theory for the phenomenologist is the proper grounding of intersubjectivity. Space does not allow for a full development of the concept here, but I follow Gibson Winter (1966) in seeing that the only viable account of intersubjectivity is recognition that individuality is abstracted from social collectivity. That is, individuals are born in and through communities and discover their individuality only after having experienced themselves within a prior community. As a result, with Winter, I hold that intersubjectivity is directly accessible to consciousness—individual consciousness, not social consciousness, is the experience that needs to be explained.

Above all, the phenomenological approach insists that the sensory data, not the interpretive schema, establish the point of contact with reality. The objective of phenomenological inquiry is to find that interpretive schema that takes account of all of the sensory data. This is where phenomenological research parts ways with the multiple theory or multiple framing conceptions popularized by scholars such as Bolman and Deal (2003) in their *Reframing Organizations* text for administrators. Where Bolman and Deal proposed interpreting organizational behavior using multiple interpretive frames, they placed their confidence in the practical significance of the resulting guidelines for administrative action rather than insisting that a reliable and valid claim to knowledge rests on the ability of an interpretive frame to take into account all of the available sensory data.

The phenomenological reduction idea has been more often embraced by researchers utilizing anthropological and ethnographic approaches to data collection, because they are intimately aware of the extent to which their ability to notice sensations stirred by exposure to field research settings are guided by the presuppositions and biases they bring with them into the setting. Additionally, researchers in this tradition conduct their work in ways that encourage them to collect new data (expand their repertoire of sensory experiences) whenever a new interpretive schema seems to be recasting their interpretation of the field setting. Thus they can more easily determine if a revised schema has the power to expand, rather than redirect, their research conclusions.

Recent advances in statistical data storage and analysis are making it possible for researchers seeking patterns in quantitative data to adopt a phenomenological inquiry approach to their data analysis. The search for alternative patterns in even the most complex quantitative data sets is becoming easier and easier. The problem with much of the data mining that is taking place, however, is that the search for patterns is not directed toward the reconstruction of commonsense meaning systems that can then serve as the basis for new and more effective patterns of practical action. Moreover, the traditions of quantitative data analysis research do not encourage the testing of new patterns against additional data sets in order to verify their reliability.

CONCLUSION

Epistemological philosophy has made scientific investigation of the nature of reality both possible and necessary. In the long history of human efforts to understand the character and human meanings of the natural and social worlds in which we find ourselves, epistemological convictions have directed the work and framed our interpretation of its results. University scholars are in the midst of an epistemological crisis—a breakdown in the privileged status of our institutions as the arbiters of claims to have rightly conducted searches for appropriate data, properly analyzed the data we have collected, and made the results of our research available to the larger community in ways that strengthen rather than threaten their opportunities for peaceful and prosperous existence. Too often those of us who are privileged to work in the university have settled for righteousness rather than rightness in our conclusions and have sought political rather than intellectual leverage over the interpretation of social institutions and their problems. It is time, as the foregoing review has sought to demonstrate, for us to insist that granting Doctoral degrees means that the recipients are philosophically competent and prepared to accept responsibility for the intellectual adequacy as well as the political significance of every aspect of their work.

REFERENCES

Alleau, R. (n.d.). *Notes on exhibits in the Kutna Hora Alchemy Museum.* Kutna Hora, Czech Republic.

Aristotle. (1984). *The complete works of Aristotle: The revised Oxford translation* (J. Barnes, Ed.). Princeton, NJ: Princeton University Press.

Bolman, L. G., & Deal, T. E. (2003). *Reframing organizations: Artistry, choice, and leadership* (3rd ed.). San Francisco: Jossey-Bass.

Campbell, J. (1949). *The hero with a thousand faces.* New York: Pantheon Books.

Comte, A. (1970). *Introduction to positive philosophy* (F. Ferrâe, Trans.). Indianapolis, IN: Bobbs-Merrill.

Dewey, J. (1948). *Reconstruction in philosophy* (Rev. ed.). Boston: Beacon Press.

Elementary and Secondary Education Act, U.S. Congress (PL 89-10, 1965).

Feynman, R. P., Leighton, R. B., & Sands, M. L. (1989). *The Feynman lectures on physics.* Redwood City, CA: Addison-Wesley.

Frankfort, H., & Groenewegen-Frankfort, H. A. (1951). *Before philosophy, the intellectual adventure of ancient man: An essay on speculative thought in the ancient Near East.* Harmondsworth, England: Penguin Books.

Heap, J. L., & Roth, P. A. (1973). On phenomenological sociology. *American Sociological Review, 38*(June), 354–367.

Hegel, G. W. F. (1931). *The phenomenology of mind* (J. B. Baillie, Trans., 2nd ed.). London: Allen & Unwin.

Heidegger, M. (1962). *Being and time.* New York: Harper.

Hume, D. (1965). *Essential works* (R. Cohen, Ed.). New York: Bantam Books.

Husserl, E. (1962). *Ideas: General introduction to pure phenomenology* (W. R. B. Gibson, Trans.). London: Collier-Macmillan. (Original work published 1928)

James, W. (1963). *Pragmatism, and other essays.* New York: Washington Square Press.

Kant, I. (2003). *Critique of pure reason* (N. K. Smith, Trans., Rev. ed.). Houndmills, England: Palgrave Macmillan.

Kierkegaard, S. R. (1960). *Selections from the writings of Kierkegaard* (Rev. ed.). Garden City, NY: Doubleday.

Kuhn, T. S. (1962). *The structure of scientific revolutions.* Chicago: University of Chicago Press.

Mead, G. H. (1934). *Mind, self and society from the standpoint of a social behaviorist* (C. W. Morris, Ed.). Chicago: University of Chicago Press.

Merleau-Ponty, M. (1962). *Phenomenology of perception.* New York: Humanities Press.

Meyer, J., & Rowan, B. (1977). Institutionalized organizations: Formal structure as myth and ceremony. *American Journal of Sociology, 83,* 340–363.

National Defense Education Act, U.S. Congress (PL 85-864, 1958).

No Child Left Behind Act, U.S. Congress (PL 107-110, 2002).

Parsons, K. M. (2003). *The science wars: Debating scientific knowledge and technology.* Amherst, NY: Prometheus Books.

Pierce, C. S. (1958). *Values in a universe of chance: Selected writings of Charles S. Pierce* (P. P. Wiener, Ed.). Stanford, CA: Stanford University Press.

Plato. (1972). *The republic of Plato* (F. M. Comford, Trans.). New York: Oxford University Press.

Polanyi, M. (1967). *The tacit dimension.* London: Routledge & K. Paul.

Sartre, J. P. (1948). *Existentialism and humanism* (P. Mairet, Trans.). London: Methuen.

Schutz, A. (1972). *The phenomenology of the social world.* London: Heinemann.

Segerstrêale, U. C. O. (2000). *Beyond the science wars: The missing discourse about science and society.* Albany: State University of New York Press.

St. Augustine. (1993). *Prolegomena; Life and works; Confessions; Letters* (P. Schaff, Ed.). Grand Rapids, MI: Eerdemans.

Tyack, D. B. (1974). *The one best system: A history of American urban education.* Cambridge, MA: Harvard University Press.

Wesley, J. (1988). *Journal and diaries* (W. R. Ward & R. P. Heitzenrater, Eds.). Nashville, TN: Abingdon Press.

Winter, G. (1966). *Elements for a social ethic: Scientific and ethical perspectives on social process.* New York: Macmillan.

Chapter 10

Coherent Knowledge and Confident Professional Practice

Douglas E. Mitchell
University of California, Riverside

In this concluding chapter I want to summarize the central arguments advanced throughout this volume and to reflect on how they point toward the development of coherent knowledge and the constitution of confident professional practice in education. We have been wading in pretty deep waters, however, so my summary is a bit tentative and the new directions urged on the field are more an invitation to dialogue than an unequivocal declaration of new principles. As tentative as the conclusions are, however, I dare not delay in advancing them. Intellectual turmoil in the field is severe; dysfunctional frustration and impatience threaten the integrity of scholarship and invite both hasty policies and unproductive programs and practices. Indeed, though professional, political, and scholarly desires for knowledge regarding educational administration, policy, and politics grow stronger with each review of the public schools, confidence in the moral value, coherent meaning, and practical utility of most claims to a true understanding by both political and scholarly leaders has declined precipitously over the last four decades. Like the faithful flock of the country preacher who writes at various points in the margins of her sermon text, "This is a very weak point, shout like h---!," educators, policymakers, and participants at scholarly conferences are routinely treated to shrill, dramatic, and sensationalist claims to knowledge—claims typically followed by calmer, more rational, but invariably less clear and more skeptical discussions of whether the dramatic claims can be sustained. Though the theory movement was celebrated in the 1950s and 1960s as promising a reliable scientific foundation for educational policy and practice, it faces serious challenges today. The political system has come to rely on Congress and federal executive agencies to legislate the norms of scientific practice. Meanwhile, academe is dominated by complex and arcane discussions of how to establish political and intellectual integrity in the field. Taken separately, and even more when taken together, the chapters in this volume demonstrate why pessimism, frustration, and political anger are so widespread and so difficult to keep at bay.

The chapters in Part I make it clear that the knowledge problem has dramatically altered institutional relationships among the schools, the universities, and the government. As Margaret Nash documents in detail in chapter 1, the status of the nation's research universities ebbs and flows with confidence in the political neutrality and practical significance of the knowledge claims made by the scholars who work within them. And, she notes, their status is in jeopardy today because knowledge has come to be seen as a tool or weapon of politics, something to be vetted for its incipient political influence even before it can be declared reliable. There are few university scholars who are prepared to join Socrates in drinking the hemlock of political rejection—they are much more likely to seek elevated social and political status by following research agendas dictated by funding agencies, pursuing lucrative consulting contracts, or evangelically representing particular interest groups or pet policy solutions.[1] One major result is the proliferation of self-consciously partisan think tanks dedicated to developing and dispersing knowledge claims aimed at furthering the purposes of key social and political groups.

Another important contributor to the contemporary decline in confidence is disappointment over the collapse of the grandiose promises of progress held out for public schools by the original promoters of the theory movement. The founders of this school of research and scholarship thought they could build on what they saw as a promising start made by their scientific management predecessors by developing a politically and socially neutral knowledge base, capable of guiding complex policy and practice decisions. Whereas the founders emphasized development of ex-

---

[1]This point was made eloquently in a recent article in *The Los Angeles Times* (Cart, 2005) headlined "Land Study on Grazing Denounced." The article began, "The Bush administration altered critical portions of a scientific analysis of the environmental impact of cattle grazing on public lands before announcing Thursday that it would relax regulations limiting grazing on those lands, according to scientists involved in the study" (p. A30). The article went on to report that the only scientists who complained, or would even respond to requests for interviews, were two who had recently retired from the Bureau of Land Management. Active scientists would not take calls or discuss the report. What is clear, however, is that the report was adjusted so that it supported the political decision, rather than the decision modified in light of the report. Although the practice of administrative rewriting of reports remains relatively rare, voluntary adjustment of scientific findings to fit politics has become an all too familiar scenario in the dialogue between researchers and politicians.

planatory theories, implicitly leaving application to education professionals, some recent scholars and much of current federal education policy have shifted back to the earlier notion that "what works" research findings should contribute directly to the improvement of educational practice, and are not in danger of being distorted or misused in ways that exacerbate biases and inequalities. Mitchell and Ortiz in chapter 2 document the promises of the theory movement's founding gurus and explain why these promises are not being realized. Brian Rowan's spirited defense of the continued viability of the theory movement in chapter 3 begins with a refreshing recognition of the differences between the pursuit of truth and a search for consequences. His defense of the theory movement's formulation of the knowledge problem retreats significantly from the high-blown promises of scientifically guided educational systems. He defends the theory movement as being right in its orientation to how knowledge claims can be appropriately evaluated, however, while acknowledging that the kind of knowledge thus generated must be politically, morally, and culturally vetted before it can provide the policy and practice guidance the founders of this movement thought would flow rather more automatically from their conceptions and methods.

Focusing on the role of the judiciary in shaping key public policy and practice decisions, Paul Green (chap. 4) highlights another important dimension of the relationship between knowledge and institutional influence. He shows that judicial knowledge is deeply concerned with precisely formulated concepts. For the judiciary, adjudication of the correspondence between facts and legal concepts is a matter for juries to decide, but knitting the concepts themselves into a seamless cloak of legal principles for the juries to use in adjudicating rights and responsibilities lies at the core of legal knowledge building and is the domain of judges, lawyers, and legal scholars. Legal knowledge consists, in the first instance, of an understanding of the contradictions that are created when concepts are misunderstood or misapplied. What makes this knowledge reliable is the confidence with which it traces core concepts to legal first principles, such as liberty, equality, democracy, or the pursuit of happiness. Viewed in this way, legal knowledge creates a framework for testing the meaning and significance of specific facts—a framework that is just as fundamental to the human community as are the scientific frameworks of the natural and social sciences. Moreover, well-developed legal frameworks can be neither undermined nor confirmed by the methodologies utilized to vouchsafe scientific theories and conclusions.

In Part II, the contributions by Ronald Heck and Gail Furman reproduce in agonizing detail the nature of the knowledge problem as it affects educational administration and administrative policy. In chapter 5, Ron Heck documents the explosive proliferation of methods and theoretical concepts utilized by researchers to examine administration and policy questions. He reports that this proliferation has virtually obliterated the progressive idea that knowledge will naturally become more comprehensive and more coherent over time, and has sharply reduced rather than strengthened our confidence in resulting knowledge claims. Divergent methods are producing inconsistent and contradictory conclusions, or at least producing a widespread sense that it is impossible to evaluate knowledge claims on the basis of methodological adequacy, leaving researchers to struggle for political support and access to high-status outlets for their research, aiming to become influential in knowledge debates rather than having a basis for distinguishing reliable from unreliable inferences from their data.

Meanwhile, Gail Furman (chap. 6) insists that scholars following the traditional canons of social science methods have systematically missed, ignored, or perhaps actively repressed appropriate understandings of the moral dimensions of schooling. Moreover, if we do not know what good is being pursued (or thwarted) by any given administrative policy or action, she argues, we have no real knowledge with which to guide school programs and practices. In short, Gail Furman argues that the definition of what works is properly limited to those processes and policies that move schools toward the realization of their fundamental moral purposes. Hence, we cannot know what works until we have linked our understanding of school operations to an equally deep understanding of educational purposes. Her analysis reminds one of the oft-repeated observation that Nazi planners seeking to exterminate the Jewish population sometimes studied what works to determine, for example, whether their labor camps produced enough economic value to offset their slowness in pursuing the genocidal goal, or whether they should proceed with lethal gassing as a more efficient mechanism than shooting or hanging their victims. Such studies make sense only if there is absolutely no moral compass to place efficiency and effectiveness in the context of a choice between good and evil ends. By arguing that facts and values belong to different domains of knowledge and analysis, traditional scientific methods have made it almost impossible to confidently know whether what works is working for the betterment of public education or for its destruction.

The two chapters of Part III reproduce a similar tension among competing knowledge claims purporting to describe reliable patterns of action in the world of educational politics. Kenneth Wong's careful review in chapter 7 captures a central theme in scholarly work on school governance and politics—categorization and documentation of the origins, trajectories, and impacts of specific political strategies and events. Such documentation distills clearly identifiable points of reference out of the helter-skelter actions of daily life, identifying patterns that empower administrators and policymakers to get in front of the curve in order to act strategically by making at least some successful predictions of the consequences of their behavior.

In chapter 8, Dorothy Shipps offers a contrasting view. Rather than conceptualizing explanatory schemas derived from detailed categorization of actions and events, she would have us focus on the ways in which an overarching narrative of action tells individuals and social groups what they should expect to see unfold within their bureaucratic and civic institutional systems. Competing narratives, she argues, are providing alternative rationales for interpretation and differing tactics for strategic action. The diverging narratives are drawn from more or less adequate interpretations of the specifics of observed patterns and trajectories of action. But by offering an overall story line, the narratives serve to mobilize awareness and stimulate abiding orientations toward action. All too often, however, the actions implicit in each narrative, like those urged on us by neurotic fixations, are repeated over and over again without producing any discernable progress toward their intended goal. These metanarratives create social stability and make actions understandable, but they also obscure important linkages between actions taken and the results produced. Thus, Shipps argues, the scientific management narrative inspires us to strive again and again to manage an unmanageable educational system rather than govern it with appropriate sensitivity to the political contexts within which it is embedded.

By the time we reach the end of chapter 9, I hope it has become painfully obvious that real progress in the search for coherent knowledge and confident professional practice begins with a thorough understanding of epistemology—a convincing analysis of how knowledge can orient and empower human actions within the world as it really is (or perhaps to demonstrate that real knowledge is impossible and thus that the human community is condemned to live in a dream world of arbitrarily embraced ideologies and solipsistic confusion). Chapter 9 argues for a phenomenological epistemology, built on the twin propositions that authentic experience of the world as it is arises through bodily sensations generated as we are engaged in a lived moment, and that these sensations can only be turned into stable perceptual and conceptual knowledge as we withdraw from engagement into a reflective moment of existence. The world is mediated to us through our bodily senses, bringing to consciousness the phenomenal experiences recognized by the ancient Greeks as constituting the appearance of things. However, just as the Greeks recognized, these appearances are ephemeral and transitory until captured in an act of reflective interpretation. Thus, the prepared mind that has formed a taken-for-granted orientation schema is ready to recognize, in the sensations that are encountered, a world that either confirms this taken-for-granted orienting schema or is surprised, delighted, shocked, or disappointed by a mismatch between the phenomenal sensations and the anticipatory set with which the reflective mind automatically and un-self-consciously tries to incorporate them into themes of action and typifications of objects, persons, and events.

In the remainder of this chapter I explore in some depth the nature of this reflective processing of phenomenological experience and examine how the process of reflection can develop both coherent knowledge frameworks and the personal confidence needed to engage in effective professional practice. In doing so, I show how the resulting coherent knowledge frameworks and confident pursuit of professional practice bring together two core ideas: civic culture and personal vocation. In his widely read essays on "Politics as a Vocation" and "Science as a Vocation," Max Weber (1946) laid the foundation stones for the analysis being developed here. These two essays underscored the fact that authentic professional vocations require both passionate engagement and a deep sense of responsibility for the future of the societal system within which the profession is embedded. Within his historical period, Weber's exploration of professional vocations was primarily concerned with problems of personal and civic responsibility. He did not live long enough to face the troublesome issue of how professionals in a society arbitrate competing claims to knowledge, which has become the defining intellectual problem for the first decades of the 21st century. Hence, we need to explore the linkage between civic culture and professional vocation in a rather different way than he did.

My argument is developed in three steps. First, I examine three divergent strategies for arbitrating claims to scientific knowledge, showing that a phenomenological approach to this vitally important task emphasizes coherence and comprehensibility, even more than the notions of reliability and correspondence with reality that have dominated traditional scientific truth tests. Thus, a phenomenological epistemology makes professional responsibility both possible and necessary—possible because it defines the nature of responsible action, and necessary because it demonstrates that knowledge without responsibility is not possible. Second, I explore the phenomenology of confident action, revealing that it involves moral commitment as well as an appreciation of cause–effect relationships and a capacity for clearly conceptualizing social structures and dynamics. Finally, I argue that when joined together, coherent knowledge and confident professional practice define the cultural mission of public education and the nature of the personal vocational commitments required to work effectively within this mission.

ARBITRATING SCIENTIFIC KNOWLEDGE CLAIMS

Three basic strategies for arbitrating claims to knowledge have been developed over the last century. Each is aligned with one of the three epistemological traditions described in chapter 9. They include: (a) the *method-*

ological strategy, where claims are evaluated on the basis of how well those who make them have adhered to accepted rules for encountering, recording, analyzing, and interpreting the experiences that are purported to prove that the knowledge claims are reliable; (b) the *theoretical strategy,* where claims are evaluated on the basis of whether they are coherent, comprehensive, and comprehensible enough to appropriately orient one to a meaningful world of participation and action; and (c) the *phenomenological strategy,* where knowledge claims are evaluated on the basis of whether they have been merely projected onto experience by naive acceptance of the taken-for-granted presuppositions and schemas used to orient attention and preinterpret sensational experience, or have been garnered through acts of reflective reinterpretation that remain faithful to the originally experienced sensations.

Method as the Producer of Truth

Perhaps the most important accomplishment of modernity, shared by science and jurisprudence, was the elevation of method to a central role in the determination of truth. Where there are established rules of evidence—agreed-on methods for recording, analyzing, interpreting, and sharing experiences—knowledge claims can be reviewed for the extent to which they have been developed using these agreed-on methods rigorously and thoroughly. Franklin (2001) provided a detailed history of how scholastic scholarship and jurisprudence developed elaborate and detailed methodologies for establishing confidence in both factual and epistemological claims to truth long before the mathematics of probability had been developed. As he put it, his book was:

> a history of rational methods of dealing with uncertainty. It treats, therefore, methods devised in law, science, commerce, philosophy, and logic to get at the truth in all cases in which certainty is not attainable. It includes evaluation of evidence by judges and juries, legal presumptions, balancing of reasons for and against scientific theories. . . . (p. ix)

As Franklin pointed out in great detail, devotion to method as the sole criterion of truth has routinely tempted civic communities to rationalize differential respect for various social classes and even physical torture in order to force certitude into situations where conjecture and uncertainty are all that can be reasonably achieved.

Nevertheless, methodological validation of truth claims remains the most widely recognized strategy for distinguishing between wishful thinking, naiveté, or unjustified biases on the one hand, and valid and reliable claims to substantial knowledge on the other. Virtually all programs of advanced study in education require substantial coursework in research methods, and the blind reviewers of research journal manuscripts are invariably urged to review the adequacy of the research methods described by the authors. Moreover, methodological fault finding is by far the most frequent type of criticism heaped on published knowledge claims.

For a brief period in the first half of the 20th century it looked as if the canons of a universal scientific method could be fleshed out in ways that would lead to near universal acceptance of the rules for conducting analysis and, therefore, for accepting the knowledge claims of scientific research. Experiments utilizing randomized interventions and suitable control groups were expected to yield authentic, positive-definite identification of important variables and to lead to the development of accurate and reliable interventions into the dynamics of social as well as natural processes. But, even as these methodological ground rules were being clearly articulated and organized into systems of inquiry, questions were being raised on two fronts about the whole enterprise of methodologically driven studies of human social and organizational behavior. One line of questioning challenged the claims of objectivity and value neutrality held to be essential to the rigorous application of the emerging scientific method. These critics saw the emerging scientific studies of society as being given privileged social and political status and influence although their conclusions were colored by un-self-conscious (possibly even pernicious) biases generated by value positions that, in principle, could not be abandoned. The other line of questioning arose from those who saw the scientific agenda as producing fragmentary, incoherent interpretations that overvalued isolated variables and denied access to integrated and holistic interpretations of social actions and processes.

Over the last half-century, discussions of the methodological underpinnings of social science knowledge claims have become convoluted and arcane. Quantitative methodologists have argued that the assessment of mathematical probability within data sets drawn from multiple cases is the very essence of generalization, whereas qualitative methodologists make interpretations of meaning the touchstone of truth and insist that statistically generalized knowledge is invalid and probably unreliable. Experimentalism with randomization of treatments is touted by federal policymakers as the gold standard for research reliability whereas critics proclaim that experimentalism is incapable of authentically reproducing the conditions under which educational programs and practices are actually implemented and thus cannot help but lead to unsupportable conclusions. Critical and postmodern theorists eschew an interest in generalized knowledge, opting instead for local knowledge that is neither permanently true nor applicable in other settings.

When we ask what is wrong with this picture, we are gradually led to realize that the idea that method alone could assure reliable knowledge claims is simply not adequate to the problem before us. This is not because method is not important, but because method is framed within a set of epistemological commitments, and divergent epistemological convictions bring with them divergent beliefs about what methodologies can be trusted to interpret experience.

Theory as the Delineator of Truth

For those who adopt the theoretical strategy for assessing knowledge claims, a truth claim is judged not by the method of its production, but by whether the knowledge claim is sufficiently coherent, comprehensible, and comprehensive to effectively orient knowing persons to the world of action that it purports to explain. That is, theoretical knowledge elicits our confidence by explaining how things really work in ways that enable us to use that explanation to anticipate events and guide strategic action toward goals we choose to pursue. As noted earlier, Paul Green's review of judicial knowledge development in chapter 4 shows how that field of scholarship tests truth claims by their theoretical elegance more than by any kind of methodological rigor in assessment of factual data. Recognition of the importance of theory building in the development of legitimate knowledge claims is by no means confined to legal analysis, however. Formal separation between methodological and theoretical strategies for evaluating knowledge claims are at this point fully institutionalized in university departments as diverse as physics and sociology. Moreover, higher status is generally accorded to the theoretical physicists and the theoretical sociologists whose work consists of theoretically broadening and deepening interpretations of research to produce the most general knowledge claims possible. Nowhere is this clearer than in Brian Greene's recently popularized book, *The Elegant Universe* (1999). In this work, he reported methodologically tested truth claims in a purely illustrative way while seeking to build and present to his readers a comprehensive theory of the physical universe. He utilized string theory to link Einstein's general relativity theory with quantum mechanics, not because methodological rigor leads to this knowledge claim, but because the theory is more comprehensive and more elegant than its predecessors. In social theory building, the names of Max Weber, George Herbert Mead, Talcott Parsons, Jonathan Turner, and Randall Collins are all associated with efforts to produce theoretically elegant and conceptually meaningful explanations of complex social behavior. They all saw the development of theory as central to their scholarly work and evolved theory to capture and display core propositions that are seen to be true because they are part of an integrated network of explanation, not because each element of that explanation has been subjected to methodological review. These theorists became leading figures in sociological knowledge construction by demonstrating theoretical ingenuity rather than methodological sophistication.

At least since the work of Thomas Kuhn (1962), theoretical truth claims have run into the same kind of internecine conflicts that have beset scholars working on clarifying the methodological strategy. Competing, divergent, and contradictory social theories have proliferated and efforts to organize and synthesize them do not seem to be able to do more than catalogue the divergent types and document the ways in which their incompatible claims to truth are necessitated by divergent assumptions about the fundamental nature of social and physical reality. We are being forced to recognize, as the theologian Paul Tillich (1963, p. 71) noted, that "every epistemological assertion is implicitly ontological" and that "therefore it is more adequate to begin an analysis [of] existence with the question of being rather than with the problem of knowledge."

In short, neither the theoretical nor the methodological strategy has been able to adequately frame an answer to the question: How can we distinguish authentic knowledge from fantasy, wishful thinking, or intellectual error?

Phenomenological Consciousness as the Producer of Truth

Sharply contrasting with the methodological strategy (with its devotion to grounding truth claims in agreed-on procedures for recording, analyzing, and interpreting data) and the theoretical strategy (devoted to testing how well truth claims are reflected in comprehensive and coherent networks of explanatory concepts) is a third alternative—a strategy resting on the human capacity for phenomenological consciousness of social and natural experience. This phenomenological strategy for assessing knowledge claims was developed and refined during the 20th century. It relies on testing the ability of any given claim to represent real-time sensational experience in ways that enhance the capacity of the reflective mind to comprehend and act strategically within the natural and social world. What the phenomenological philosophers have demonstrated is that a prior intellectual and emotional commitment is required in order for human beings to perceptually recognize and reflectively contemplate the sensory data generated during lived-moment experiencing. As noted in chapter 9, Merleau-Ponty (1962) saw the starting point for all perception as lying in the human capacity for intention. He insisted that human perception does not arise by merely existing in bodily contact with the sights, sounds, tastes, odors, and textures encountered in the course of daily existence. Rather, we employ a preprocessing orientation toward those sensations—an orientation that directs our attention toward some sensations and away from others. Moreover, this directing of attention is systematic, presenting our senses with a taken-for-granted schema for assessing the meaning and significance of sensational experience. Our lives are projects that we are in the midst of pursuing, and the sensations that catch our attention are those that bear on the fulfillment or frustration of this life project. When, for example, we are engaged in a conversation, we concentrate our attention on grasping the meaning of the messages received from our conversational partner and on transmitting our own messages in response. For this reason, we become quite unconscious of the grammar or the mechanisms of pronunciation being used, except when a discord is struck confusing us about the meaning of the message content. Hence, in the natural attitude of engagement in our life projects, we process sensational experiences efficiently by directing our attention away from the sensations themselves and onto the significance that they are seen to have for the success or failure of our life project and for our own actualization or nothingness.

It is not always recognized that this personally important process of utilizing purposeful intentionality to prestructure our attention to, and interpretation of, life experiences has a social counterpart in the form of shared cultures. Cultures, from this point of view, represent the collective life project of cultural group members. Cultures intend for their members a social and historical actualization that confirms their collective existence and validates the personal life projects of the individuals within them. This means, as Gibson Winter (1966) carefully argued, that collectivity precedes individuality, both logically and historically. Individual identities arise through a dialectic of incorporation into, and differentiation from, the cultural collectivities into which we are born. That is why cultural aliens are confused about how to act in relation to the members of any given culture and why building a workable self-identity requires knowing the taken-for-granted perceptions and norms of the cultures in which our individual identities are embedded.

The dialectic construction of identity through alternating periods of collective incorporation and individual differentiation can be described in many different ways. The world's great religions all recognize that individuals are essentially estranged from their true identities and from their fellow human beings until they discover themselves grounded and incorporated into the divine—a process that also involves reconciliation with nature and with fellow human beings. A similar dialectic, one closer to our quest for knowledge in matters of educational administration, policy, and politics, is captured in the idea of a scientific paradigm delineated in Thomas Kuhn's (1962) description of *The Structure of Scientific Revolutions.* Kuhn's notion that every substantial scientific enterprise is grounded in the tentative acceptance of an overarching, taken-for-granted framework for recognizing, analyzing, and interpreting sense data embraces an essentially phenomenological epistemology. Kuhn's view that a pregiven orientation toward a puzzle-solving process that constitutes normal science corresponds in all of its critical elements to the phenomenologists' argument that orientation toward purposeful action is the prerequisite to perception and thus a prerequisite to conceptualization, analysis, and interpretation of our sensory experiences.

Despite the fact that the core ideas of phenomenology were developed more than half a century ago, this strategy for assessing claims to knowledge is not very well understood. The phenomenological strategy is not often confused with the Aristotelian orientation toward the use of methodological rules for recording, analyzing, and interpreting sensory data. However, the empiricist Aristotelians often cannot see what the problem is, and thus feel that the phenomenologists are needlessly complicating a straightforward matter of winnowing the data to find the true interpretations that have timeless reliability and predictive power. For the thoroughgoing Aristotelian empiricist (whether positivist or behaviorist), presuppositions are not intrinsic to the investigatory process. They are merely the source of hypotheses to be tested and possibly a threat to the reliability and validity of their conclusions. The belief in a world that is out there to be probed and pummeled by experimental action and recorded with scientific instruments makes it appear that objectivity can rid the scientist of bias and lead to an authentic representation of the true nature of the experienced world. The Aristotelians see the world as truly out there—not directly experienced, but waiting for researchers to collect indicator data that point to the really real truths that can be inferred from them. Aristotelians, like the authors of the Education Sciences Reform Act (2002), see breakdowns in the reliability of knowledge claims as the result of either failure to apply the rules of the scientific method or the intrusion of impermissible ideological bias into the process.

By contrast, the phenomenological strategy for assessing truth claims is easily and often confused with Platonic idealism. Both agree that knowledge resides in the mind, that experiencing is transitory, and that knowledge of our experiences becomes substantial and stable by interpreting it using schemas for anticipating and remembering. Both support a constructivist epistemology asserting that meaning is either personally and psychologically or socially and culturally constructed by human minds asserting meaning and attributing significance to ephemeral sensations. The difference between them is as profound as it is subtle, however. Where Platonism asserts that knowledge is transcendentally given (either as an inborn mental capacity to properly categorize experience or through divine revelation that instills proper categories of thought), phenomenology insists that the construction of proper categories of thought arises through a dialectical process, a dynamic interaction between minding and experiencing as we move back and forth between lived moments and reflective moments. That is, phenomenologists assert that we construe our experience, but we do not construct it. We construe experience by recognizing its relevance to both our personal life project and the cultural enterprise that confirms our significance and gives our personal life project its meaning and purpose. For the phenomenologist, as for the Aristotelian, the categories of under-standing are embedded in and mediated through our experiences—they are authentic to the extent they properly represent the experienced world. The difference is that, for the phenomenologist, the method for garnering the truth is inextricably bound up with the ways in which human percep-tion is dependent on prior commitments of intentionality and purpose. These prior commitments are, in turn, bound to the ways in which experi-ence confirms or disappoints the intentions we bring to them.

In summary, from a phenomenological perspective the ultimate crite-rion for arbitration of a knowledge claim lies in its ability to provide a co-herent interpretation of our experience—coherent in the sense of provid-ing both meaningful typifications of key objects, persons, and events and giving an intelligible thematic structure to the various sequences of action in which we are involved. This coherence, like a Kuhnian paradigm, orients us to our life enterprises and empowers us to act effectively in their pursuit. Coherent knowledge is necessary, but is not a fully sufficient basis for practi-cal action, however. Practical success requires confident as well as informed engagement in action. I turn, then, to a phenomenological view of the character and origins of professional confidence.

THE PHENOMENOLOGY OF CONFIDENT PROFESSIONAL ACTION

The starting point for understanding how professional confidence is possi-ble is to ask why such confidence is problematic. Confidence is a variable, of course, present sometimes and absent at others; some people have more, others less. Is this because confidence is the natural state of human exis-tence and we need to understand how it comes to be weakened, or because anxiety, uncertainty, and hesitancy are the natural state of affairs and confi-dence is a positive accomplishment? Theologians from virtually all of the world's great religions have asserted that human self-consciousness begins with the experience of ontological anxiety, alienation, or estrangement. They assert that human self-consciousness is brought about by an awareness that we are transcended by the natural and social world on which we are deeply dependent but cannot fully control. This experience of alienation, born of our awareness of human finitude, robs consciousness of any immediate sense of the meaning and purpose for existence and leaves the human spirit yearning for an understanding of the purpose of life and the meaning of natural and human actions. This view is largely confirmed by contemporary psychologists, and is taken, without further elaboration, as the appropriate point of departure for an exploration of the phenomenology of confidence presented here.

If ontological *angst* is the natural human condition, how can it be overcome sufficiently to allow for purposeful and rational action? The answer to this question lies in the moral evaluation of human experience. Moral judgment differentiates experience, distinguishing the significant from the trivial as well as the good from the reprehensible. Through moral evaluation, some experiences are rendered serious, significant, and worthwhile, whereas others are recognized as superficial, mundane, and worthless (or worse). Ontological alienation and anxiety are overcome through the attachment of systematic moral meaning systems—interpreting the positive experiences specifying human purpose and interpreting social relationships and the place of individuals and social groups in the natural and social world. Thus interpreted, the potential for participating in these morally evaluated experiences releases emotional energy—defining risks and specifying how life becomes fulfilling or frustrating, actualizing or destroying the self.

Max Weber (1946) raised this aspect of human experiencing to a principle of sociological analysis. He framed the interpretive school of sociology by asserting that the meaning of any action can only be fully understood by understanding its subjective meanings for the actors and their relevant audiences. Although both private and social behaviors have observable structures, their ultimate meanings are given by how those structures are construed by the participants.

This understanding of the role of subjective meaning in interpreting the structure of social action led Weber (1946) to recognize the important role played by Protestant sectarian religion in creating and sustaining modern capitalist economies and in establishing appreciation and support for the bureaucratic forms of social organization needed to make these capitalist economies work. Protestantism, in his view, made rational action and moral commitment virtues, essential elements of a righteous life. In so doing, Weber concluded, Protestantism created the social foundations of a capitalist economy—imbuing organizations with purpose and defining their positive meanings for both the organizational members and the larger society.

Morality of this sort is a unifying concept in both religion and politics. In both spheres of action, the ordering principle for action is the moral assessment of alternative actions. The theologian Paul Tillich (1963, p. 136) put morality at the core of the relationship between religion and culture. He followed Kant (1955) in asserting that the bedrock of social relationships is

TABLE 10.1
The Symbolic Forms of Religious and Political Morality

Symbolic Forms	Religious Morality	Political Morality
Intellectual reflection	Moral philosophy	Ideological utopianism
Personal experience	Confessional witness	Democratic preference
Communal membership	Church membership	Foundational roots
Textual authority	Scriptural exegesis	Constitutionalism

a "moral imperative"—an unconditional demand for responsible action in relation to others. Tillich summarized:

> The reason for the unconditional character of the moral imperative is that it puts our essential being as a demand against us. The moral imperative is not a strange law, imposed on us, but it is the law of our own being. . . . The moral command is unconditional because it is we ourselves commanding ourselves. (p. 136)

In order to respond to the moral imperative, to make moral decisions and take moral actions, action alternatives have to be understood symbolically. That is, concrete circumstances must be seen as pointing beyond themselves to their transcendental meaning and significance.

There are at least four different ways, found in both the religious and political spheres, to grasp the symbolic moral significance of various action alternatives. The four approaches are not entirely parallel, but they are presented for comparison in Table 10.1. Forms of symbolic interpretation are described in the first column, the religious forms of morality in the second column, and political morality forms in the third column.

Intellectual Approaches to Morality

Intellectual analysis leads to a moral consciousness only if the thought processes reach the limits of human understanding and point beyond ordinary experience to define the moral imperatives that stand over against the ontological isolation and alienation of empirical observation and ordinary human understanding. In the religious sphere, there is a long tradition of moral philosophy that presents as its primary conclusion the need for the meaning of events in this world to be seen and understood from the perspective of some transcendental reality. All of the great religions of the world have found strong philosophers to formulate the core propositions of their moral philosophy. Protestant and Roman Catholic theologies are well represented in the works of St. Thomas Aquinas and Paul Tillich. For these moral philosophers, reflection on the human condition leads directly to an awareness of a transcendental reality that, though not directly experienced, is made necessary in order to render ordinary experience meaningful. The key concepts in this religious imagination are alienation and finitude. Theologians assert that human imagination is capable of what Michael Polanyi (1967) called "tacit knowing"—the ability to recognize problems and circumstances as real and important without being able to know explicitly what they are. Being alienated from the natural and social world, with a finite capacity for understanding, the human intellect nevertheless tacitly grasps the larger truth that transcendental reality holds a moral imperative before all humanity.

In the political sphere, the equivalent intellectual approach to discovering symbolic meaning comes from the tradition of ideological utopianism. John Stuart Mill (2002), Jean Jacques Rousseau (1954), Karl Marx (Marx & Bender, 1972), and the American Federalists, to mention only a few of the more widely read utopians, all held a view of the political action guided by moral principles of liberty, equality, and community. The moral dimensions of these utopian ideologies were held, in the language of the American Declaration of Independence, to be "self-evident." By self-evident, the utopians did not mean that the morality is easily or universally recognized, but only that when fully articulated it would have a compelling effect on readers and listeners, calling them to action that would be known to be moral by the clarity with which the political case is presented.

Morality Rooted in Personal Experience

Whereas the philosophical and utopian traditions expected everyone to be able to recognize the moral imperatives implicit in the human condition, a more individualistic and personal morality has also been formulated in both the religious and political spheres. In religion, personal morality is seen as springing from encounters with revelatory experience and communicated through confessional witness. The Biblical stories of Isaiah's temple vision and of Paul's conversion on the road to Damascus, and the personal stories of St. Augustine, the Prophet Muhammad, and Martin Luther all illustrate the central core of this religious tradition. These men all reported themselves to have been gripped by a special experience that transformed their self-understanding and their sense of responsibility in the world. The important point of their experience for the analysis being presented here is that their symbolic reinterpretation of their own situation, and the situation of all mankind, was transmitted to large numbers of followers through a personal confessional witness in which they asserted the validity and significance of their personal experience and used that experience to provide symbolic interpretation of the experience of others. Martin Luther's confessional witness to the Diet of Worms—"Here I stand, I can do no else" (Atkinson, 1971)—captures the way in which this religious experience reverses the normal process of symbolic communication, making the confessor the origin of moral principle rather than the follower of others' moral imperatives.

In the political sphere, personal, experience-based, morality leads to an embrace of democratic preference, rather than leadership through confessional witnessing. That is, acceptance of the proposition that individuals uniquely symbolize their own moral imperatives leads to a political environment characterized by either repressive totalitarianism or liberal democratic tolerance. The first case arises when one person or group arrogates to themselves the right to set the moral preferences for the whole of society, the latter when respect for individual differences in moral consciousness is retained. It was the combination of liberal utopianism with belief in the inevitable individualism of moral conscience that led to the formation of the American political system.

The Communal Foundations of Moral Conviction

Basing personal identity on membership in a religious or civic community is accompanied by the acceptance of the moral framework of that community. Incorporation into membership in either a religious or a political community is never a simple matter of registration or certification. In each case, rites of passage from alien or sojourner to communicant or citizen involve identification of fundamental moral principles and avowals of loyalty to those principles. The transformation of aliens into members involves a combination of complex processes. The history of the group is seen as demonstrating the significance and efficacy of its central values. Explicit identification and interpretation of moral axioms is often undertaken. Additionally, symbolic rituals are required and are designed to be embarrassing or intimidating to individuals who do not accept their moral meanings. And, of course, rites of excommunication (or shunning), deportation, or criminalization of immoral behavior are created to sharpen the lines of demarcation between the core community and those not within its membership.

In most religious communities, the transition from heathen to believer is presumed to be governed primarily by embrace of the doctrinal beliefs, overarching mythology, and sacred rituals of the religious group. Confession of faith, following an admission of prior status as outsider (and possibly transgressor of sacred law), is the critical event. It is followed by baptism or some other ritual of incorporation.

In political communities, the origin of community identity lies in what Simone Weil (Weil & Panichas, 1977) and Hannah Arendt (1968) called "foundation experiences"—a morality myth that articulates the origins and destiny of the political community. In this context, political communities are not always nation-states. The Holocaust formed a foundation experience not only for the modern state of Israel, but for Jewish identity in the entire world. Similarly, interpretations like Alex Haley's *Roots* (1976) have provided political identities for a variety of ethnic subcultures in this country.

Moral Authority Born of Sacred Texts

The fourth common approach to the development of moral consciousness in both religious and political communities is the interpretation of core documents that acquire the status of sacred texts. The belief that core moral principles are to be found through proper exegesis of the sacred text is characteristic of Protestant fundamentalism, just as it is of the strict constructionist approach to constitutional law. Strictly speaking, the sacred text approach only displaces the problem of the phenomenology of moral symbolic consciousness. Declarations like the one appearing on a recent California bumper sticker reading, "God said it, I believe it, that settles it," do not, of course, settle how the sacred text being proclaimed came to be imbued with the authority ascribed to it. Some combination of the other three routes to moral consciousness must be responsible for the imbuing of a sacred text with the authority to define the content of a specific moral code.

To summarize, confidence overcomes ontological anxiety and alienation through the development of moral consciousness that orients individuals and groups to the meaning and purposes of their individual and collective existence. Phenomenological analysis of the origins of moral consciousness reveals that it has its roots in political and religious experience, provided with value-laden and symbolic meaning by ontological philosophical reflection, revelatory personal experience, acceptance of membership in a purposeful community, or a combination of these. Sometimes the vehicle used to define the concrete content of the moral imperative is found in the form of a sacred text, but text-based morality only displaces the phenomenological problem onto the question of how the text acquired its symbolic status. What remains is to see how the morality that produces confidence is embedded in personal vocations and cultural enterprises.

COHERENT KNOWLEDGE AND PROFESSIONAL CONFIDENCE ARE JOINED IN PERSONAL VOCATION AND CULTURAL MISSION

Personal vocation and cultural mission are created when moral consciousness is linked to phenomenological knowledge. Vocations merge the three dimensions of phenomenological consciousness, giving our lives intentional purpose and strategies for action. The three central dimensions of vocational commitment are: (a) recognition of the thematic structures or motifs that link past, present, and future into historical sequence so that the fulfillment or frustration of our life purposes can be discerned; (b) an active typification of objects, persons, and events in ways that orient us to action opportunities and possibilities; and (c) a confirming virtue, a moral specification of why our vocational calling is worthy of committed engagement. Each of these elements can break down, of course, disorganizing our lives, distracting us from vocational commitments, and rendering our lived moments confusing and nonsensical. They can also present themselves to our consciousness as terrifying or mystifying dimensions of experience that drag us through life on trajectories we would rather avoid or ignore. Most importantly, however, these three aspects of every vocational calling provide the basis for evaluating professional action alternatives. Let us explore each briefly.

Vocational commitments provide thematic structure to our historical existence, enabling us to remember and plan our actions. As noted briefly in chapter 9, one of the central insights of the phenomenologists is that time binding—linking past, present, and future events into a coherent stream—is a profound accomplishment. Sensory data come instantaneously and fleetingly, making it necessary for us to mind our experience, to register and interpret the sensations encountered in our daily existence, bringing them into reflective consciousness and linking them to memories of past sensations and anticipations of future experience. This time binding is accomplished by interpreting our experiences thematically in reference to a purpose or project. That is, we do not and cannot track all of our sensational experiences and we do not arrange our memories of them in a simple chronological order. Experiences are necessarily arranged in terms of significance or relevance to some overarching purpose or imagined future. In this respect, John Dewey (1948) and the American pragmatists were right in asserting that what vouchsafes a conceptual scheme as constituting knowledge is whether it orients our interpretations of ongoing events and guides our actions within that event stream. The arrangement is not possible without an organizing framework of intentions, a remembrance of progress toward and an anticipation of fulfillment (or frustration) of projected goals.

Vocational commitments situate our lives by locating us within a social and natural world of meaningful objects, persons, and events, enabling us to distinguish resources for action from threats to our well-being. In addition to their orientation to historical time, vocations are oriented to space and to the social and physical elements toward which action is directed. The objects, persons, and events that we experience in the here and now are never simply there, populating our field of perception and action as inert, undifferentiated matter. To the contrary, we differentiate and typify them according to how they count in our scheme of things, how they threaten or support our ongoing life purposes and goals. There are, of course, many objects, events, and persons that are neutral with regard to our specific life purposes, but our experience of those elements in our potential perceptual field is shadowy and fleeting while our attention is fixed on those infused with energies that contribute to our own actualization or nothingness. Strangers pass through our lives barely noticed whereas loved ones inspire us to ecstasy or grief, fulfillment or despair. Events are trivial or significant, not by their physical size or energy, but by their relevance to our life purposes, to our vocational calling to action.

Vocations encapsulate our definitions of virtue, enabling us to distinguish among competing moral purposes and engage in practical actions aimed at their realization. Vocational activities are not simply biological or physical sequences of action, they are infused with moral significance. It is this moral significance that calls us to adopt them as purposeful enterprises because moral seriousness is what defines our lives as having worth and dignity, motivates or depresses our energies, and fuels our commitment to purposeful action. This moral dimension makes life a rendezvous with destiny—a vocational calling to be a person of worth by accepting the mandate of virtue and becoming a boon to our fellow citizens.

These three dimensions of our personal vocations have exact parallels in the larger cultural systems in which our vocational lives are embedded. Cultures have heritages or traditions with future as well as past significance. Cultures typify persons, objects, and events, providing systems of status, role, rank, class, formal and informal memberships, and so on—imbuing some with potency, significance, and purpose and others with insignificance or irrelevance. And cultures articulate collective moral purposes: the cultural destiny of members and nonmembers.

Americans have embraced progressivism as a central element in their cultural time binding. This progressivism has provided the central theme to our understanding of the character of science and to our politics and social policy deliberations. Other cultures are less committed to progressivism; some see life as cyclic or even as static in its historical themes. Cultures also have powerful symbol systems and rituals for separating objects, persons, and events into classes that are loaded with significant meanings. Status and prestige differences among persons and groups, for example, result from collectively typifying differences in their place within, and value to, the cultural project. Similarly, physical objects are typified according to their role in the economic system or their significance as objects of art, or both. All of these typifications are encapsulated in language systems and ritualized behaviors that both express and reinforce the typifications that exist. The whole set of thematic traditions and typification patterns are incorporated into an overarching cultural morality that distinguishes civic virtue from civic vice. Virtuous civic actions accept and follow the thematic and typification norms that are ritually reinforced in daily life. Questioning and rejecting these norms create threats to the cultural project and bring those who do so under suspicion and close scrutiny.

Most civic cultures remain open, however, to leadership aimed at challenging and reconstructing the taken-for-granted character of existing cultural patterns. American progressivism has provided a specific place for such leadership challenges. Historically, our culture has been particularly open to technology and science as cultural transformation mechanisms. We have been much less tolerant of political and religious challenges to the cultural status quo, but even here some challenges have broken through and reoriented significant elements in the culture. Slavery, originally ratified in our Constitution, was successfully challenged. Some rights (e.g., suffrage) were extended to women. But the status quo has shown enormous power to resist most challenges to its established norms and social relations.

PUTTING IT ALL TOGETHER

The foregoing discussion sought to link science and morality as the twin foundations of collective culture and personal vocation. Scientific knowledge provides culture and vocation with their rational components, providing intellectual structure and strategic direction to a cultural enterprise and meaningful purpose to vocational engagement within the culture. Science is also the tool for critical reevaluation of cultural norms and personal beliefs regarding effective action. Moral commitment provides the affective dimension, focusing and energizing action. Moralizing action is essential to motivation, but also endangers scientific reflection by giving action a taken-for-granted frame of reference that focuses attention on some experiences while inviting neglect or outright repression of attention to others. Thus, science must, itself, become a vocation in order to survive. The scientific attitude is one that questions the taken-for-granted, asking that it become more fully rational by attending to and interpreting an increasingly broad range of our lived moments. Moreover, in order to develop this scientific attitude it is essential that scientists bracket off the taken-for-granted moral purposes and intellectual presuppositions of the culture.

It was for this reason that anthropology developed the tradition of conducting research in cultural contexts where the researcher is an alien rather than a cultural native. Equally important, the sociologist or political scientist gains perspective by making the familiar strange, by questioning how the culture's taken-for-granted framework makes sense, and where it does not make sense. This can only be achieved if scientific inquiry becomes, itself, a morally serious vocation. The scientist does not become a more effective inquirer by adopting a particular version of the competing moral commitments that are motivating action in the culture, researching in order to assist one political faction or social status group rather than another. The effective scientist is the consummate cultural outsider—holding up a mirror that reflects back to the cultural actors both the moral and the intellectual presuppositions that are guiding action, and exploring the alternative reflective reconstructions of experience that reconstitute accepted norms of practical action.

The theory movement was right to emphasize the explicit theoretical modeling of practical action, but it was wrong in thinking that this modeling would become more potent by being disengaged from moral commitment. The postmodernists, critical theorists, radical feminists, and even the Biblical fundamentalists are right in asserting that knowledge is always grounded in moral seriousness and that scientific rationality is a source of political power. They are wrong, however, in believing that all moral seriousness is intrinsically political. Professional vocation is the essence of a moral seriousness that simultaneously recognizes that all practical action is directed to moral ends and makes the primary aim of professional action the illumination of cultural meaning systems and the building of support systems enabling other members of the culture to acquire and pursue meaningful life projects.

REFERENCES

Arendt, H. (1968). *Between past and future: Eight exercises in political thought* (Enl. ed.). New York: Viking Press.

Atkinson, J. (1971). *The trial of Luther.* London: Batsford.

Cart, J. (2005, June 18). Land study on grazing denounced. *The Los Angeles Times*, pp. A1, A30, A31.

Dewey, J. (1948). *Reconstruction in philosophy* (Enl. ed.). Boston: Beacon Press.

Education Sciences Reform Act, U.S. Congress (PL 108-279, 2002).

Franklin, J. (2001). *The science of conjecture: Evidence and probability before Pascal.* Baltimore: Johns Hopkins University Press.

Greene, B. (1999). *The elegant universe: Superstrings, hidden dimensions, and the quest for the ultimate theory* (1st ed.). New York: W. W. Norton.

Haley, A. (1976). *Roots* (1st ed.). Garden City, NY: Doubleday.

Kant, I. (1955). *The critique of pure reason* (J. M. D. Meiklejohn, Trans.). Chicago: Encyclopaedia Britannica.

Kuhn, T. S. (1962). *The structure of scientific revolutions.* Chicago: University of Chicago Press.

Marx, K., & Bender, F. L. (1972). *Karl Marx: Essential writings.* New York: Harper & Row.

Merleau-Ponty, M. (1962). *Phenomenology of perception.* New York: Humanities Press.

Mill, J. S. (2002). *The basic writings of John Stuart Mill* (2002 Modern Library pbk. ed.). New York: Modern Library.

Polanyi, M. (1967). *The tacit dimension.* London: Routledge & K. Paul.

Rousseau, J.-J. (1954). *The social contract.* Chicago: H. Regnery Co.

Tillich, P. (1963). *Morality and beyond* (1st ed.). New York: Harper & Row.

Weber, M. (1946). *From Max Weber: Essays in sociology* (H. H. Gerth & C. W. Mills, Trans.). New York: Oxford University Press.

Weil, S., & Panichas, G. A. (1977). *The Simone Weil reader.* New York: McKay.

Winter, G. (1966). *Elements for a social ethic: Scientific and ethical perspectives on social process.* New York: Macmillan.

About the Authors

Gail C. Furman is Professor of Educational Leadership and Program Coordinator at Washington State University and served as President of UCEA from 2000 to 2001. In addition to her recent work on research perspectives in the field, her research interests include moral leadership, an ecological perspective on social justice, and the concept of community in schools. Recent publications include the book *School as Community: From Promise to Practice* (2002); a chapter on "Leadership for Democratic Community in Schools" (with Robert J. Starratt) in the NSSE yearbook (2002); and articles in the *Journal of Educational Administration* and *Educational Administration Quarterly* (*EAQ*). Her articles in *EAQ* were recognized with the Davis Award for outstanding article in 2004 (Honorable Mention) and 1998.

Paul Green is Associate Professor of Educational Politics, Social Policy, and the Law in the Graduate School of Education and the Political Science Department at the University of California, Riverside. He has served as a secondary school teacher in several urban school systems and held the position of principal in a secondary alternative high school. Professor Green's areas of research include the politics, policies, programs, and practices at the federal, state, and local levels in advancing or impeding equality in lower and postsecondary institutions for poor youth and children of color.

Ronald H. Heck is Professor of Educational Administration and Policy at the University of Hawaii at Manoa. His research interests include educational leadership, school effects on learning, and performance assessment. He is the author of *Studying Educational and Social Policymaking: Theoretical Concepts and Research Methods* (2004).

Douglas E. Mitchell is Professor of Education and Director of the School Improvement Research Group at the University of California, Riverside. He is past-president of both the Politics of Education Association and the Sociology of Education Association and recipient of the Stephen K. Bailey Award for research contributions to the politics of education. Education politics and policy have been the focus of his research and scholarly writing Published writings include more than 100 books, journal articles, and monographs covering topics in social science theory and utilization, school program and policy analysis, state legislative decision making, labor relations, teacher incentive systems, public support for public schools, and school board elections.

Margaret A. Nash is Assistant Professor of Curriculum and Instruction at the Graduate School of Education, University of California, Riverside. She is a historian of education and the author of *Women's Education in the United States, 1780–1840* (2005). Her work also has appeared in *History of Education Quarterly, Teachers College Record,* the *Journal of the Early Republic,* and the *History of Higher Education Annual.*

Flora Ida Ortiz is Professor Emerita, University of California, Riverside. She specializes in school careers, socialization processes, and planning and designing educational facilities. Some of her published works include: *Career Patterns in Educational Administration* (1982) and *Schoolhousing: Planning and Designing Educational Facilities* (1991). Representative recent journal articles are: "Using Social Capital in Interpreting the Careers of Three Latina Superintendents" (2001) and "Essential Learning Conditions for California Youth: Educational Facilities" (2004).

Brian Rowan is the Burke A. Hinsdale Collegiate Professor in Education at the University of Michigan. A sociologist by training (Stanford University), Rowan's scholarly interests lie at the intersection of organization theory and school effectiveness research. Over the years, he has written about schooling as an institution, paying special attention to the organization and management of instruction in schools, the nature of teachers' and school leaders' work, and how schooling affects students' academic achievement. He consults widely with research and development organizations in the United States, has served on the editorial boards of leading journals in education, and is the author, coauthor, or editor of four books, over 50 scholarly articles, and numerous technical reports and research monographs.

Prior to joining the faculty at the University of Michigan, Rowan was Associate Professor and Chairperson of the Department of Educational Administration at Michigan State University and a senior research director at the Far West Laboratory for Educational Research and Development in San Francisco, California.

Dorothy Shipps is Assistant Professor of Education at Teachers College, Columbia University. Research for her forthcoming book, *School Reform Corporate Style: Chicago 1880–2000* (University Press of Kansas) earned her the honor of being named a Carnegie Scholar for 2000 to 2001. She was coeditor with Larry Cuban of *Reconstructing the Common Good in Public Education* (2000) and the author of numerous articles and chapters on the civic capacity needed to sustain school reform, and the politics of mayoral control. Her research interests include business involvement in education and the historical and political analysis of urban schooling.

Kenneth K. Wong is the Walter and Leonore Annenberg Professor in Education Policy at Brown University, where he also directs the Urban Education Policy program. He was the founding director of the IES-funded National Center on School Choice when he was on the faculty at Vanderbilt University. He has published extensively in school governance, urban politics, and state finance.

Author Index

Subject Index